LUCY CALKINS ✦ TED KESLER

RAISING THE QUALITY OF NARRATIVE WRITING

This book is dedicated to Laurie Pessah.

FirstHand
An imprint of Heinemann
A division of Reed Elsevier Inc.
361 Hanover Street
Portsmouth, NH 03801-3912
www.heinemann.com

Offices and agents throughout the world

Photography: Peter Cunningham

Library of Congress Cataloging-in-Publication Data

CIP data on file with the Library of Congress.
ISBN 0-325-00864-7

Printed in the United States of America on acid-free paper
10 09 08 07 06 ML 2 3 4 5

Acknowledgements

This book is dedicated to Laurie Pessah who has, for several decades, joined me at the helm of the Teachers College Reading and Writing Project. Laurie is the organizational and interpersonal heart of the Project. She brings all the people, places, and projects together, matching eighty-five staff developers to hundreds and hundreds of schools across the nation. Laurie's unerringly astute instincts inform these decisions, and then she also keeps track of all the work and all the players. All of us at the Project regard Laurie as utterly indispensable to all that we do and all that we are.

I am grateful also to Ted Kesler, who has been a contributing author to this book. Ted contributed to some of the extensions in the book and especially, on the CD, and he read through the manuscript half-a-dozen times, filling in gaps, working on the charts, tracking down the drafts of children's work, and supplying model texts. His input was enriched by his knowledge of children's literature and of qualities of good writing. I thank him for his help.

The book stands on many shoulders, but there are a few classroom teachers have made especially strong contributions to it. The brilliant teaching of Mary Chiarella, Lis Shin and Kathy Doyle helped this book immeasurably. Their children's work fills the pages of this book, and for years, I have learned about teaching writing by teaching in their company. Mary Chiarella joined me in a think tank during the final months when I was revising this book, and her ideas about the relationship between elements of story and narrative craft made a difference. Natalie Louis, a spunky, creative, child-centered co-author from the primary series, helped me break new trails for this unit. Katherine Bomer, author of *Writing a Life* and a close friend of the Project, added her ebullient love of writing and her insights; I am grateful to her for her help on this manuscript and for her support in professional development. My ideas on narrative writing have been enriched by the wisdom of Ralph Fletcher, Barry Lane, and especially Mary Ehrenworth; Mary, along with Janet Angililo, also helped me think about teaching grammar and punctuation. If it takes a village to raise a child, it takes close to that many people to plan a unit of study! I am grateful to all these brilliant educators.

I want to especially acknowledge Katie Ray, whose brilliant work on reading-writing connections informs all I do. Katie was a staff developer at the Project years ago and continues to enrich our thinking, especially on the topic of reading-like-a-writer.

The photography in this book and in all of my books is the work of Peter Cunningham, an extraordinary artist. It has been a great joy to see the beauty in New York City schools through his eyes. I thank Peter MacFarlane and the teachers and children at P.S. 180 in Harlem, Carol Stock and the teachers and children at P.S. 199 in Manhattan, and Melanie Woods and the teachers at P.S. 29 for welcoming Peter and his camera into their midst.

Finally, the book grew out of a close partnership with my editor, Kate Montgomery. This book required extra-care because when I finished work on it, the manuscript was like the Secret Garden, overgrown with flowers, vines, fruit trees of all sorts, all needing to be trimmed and brought under control. I have written about Kate's contribution in detail elsewhere, but this book, like every book in the series, bears the special imprint of her brilliance.

Raising the Quality of Narrative Writing

Welcome to Unit 2

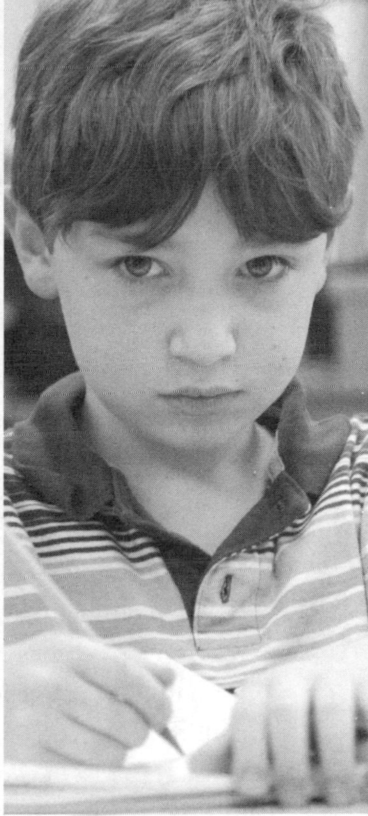

A Personal Narrative

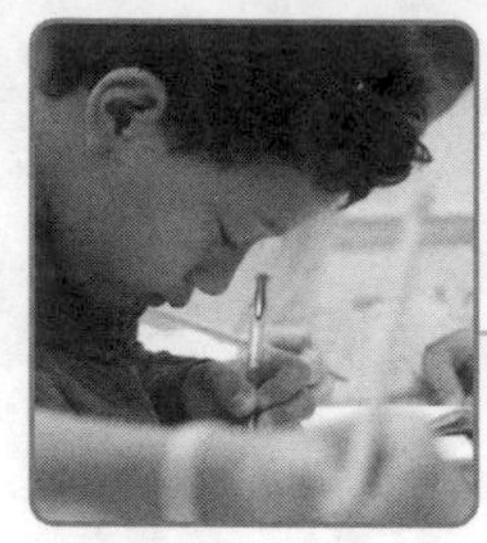

Welcome to the Unit

Raising the Quality of Narrative Writing

Although this unit is titled *Raising the Quality of Narrative Writing*, the real goal is to improve the quality of *writing*—and of the *writers*—in general. We invest another month of work in personal narrative writing (before shifting to a focus on expository writing) because we know that real progress comes not from constantly exposing children to yet another form of writing but from working long enough within one form to help children write longer, more significant, more conventional, and more graceful pieces in general.

We begin the unit by telling children they will be revisiting narrative writing and helping them understand this means they will need to draw on all they already know. This is a perfect opportunity to teach children that writers carry with them and draw on a cumulative repertoire of strategies. For example, we say, "You already have a whole repertoire of strategies for generating narrative writing," and briefly direct children's attention to the charts listing strategies they learned during the earlier unit. When children begin to draft new personal narrative entries, we can ask them to look back at the piece they published (after revision and editing) at the end of the previous unit. Since they learned to write focused, sequential stories that included direct quotations, details, paragraphs, and end punctuation, we suggest that their new entries should demonstrate all they have already learned as writers. This unit, then, emphasizes that learning to write is cumulative, and that any new work that writers do will always stand on the shoulders of previous work. Among other things, this unit, then, can definitely teach children that each day of writing is much more than a time to practice that day's minilesson!

Once the unit has gotten underway with this emphasis on writers' drawing on all they already know as they begin a new cycle of writing work, it will be important to find ways to lift the quality of students' work. Chances are good that the stories children wrote during the first unit of study were sequenced, detailed, and, sadly, a bit dull.

One important way to lift the level of writing in this unit is to help children bring forth more significance in their writing. For starters, we teach children strategies for generating narrative entries that stand a greater chance of having emotional weight and of following a story arc. Specifically, we teach children a few new strategies for generating narrative writing that, over time, have proved to evoke especially powerful, shapely stories. For example, we teach students that when a writer wants to write a powerful personal narrative, we sometimes write about the first (or last) time we did something, or about a time we learned something, or a time we felt a strong emotion—hope, worry, sadness. The resulting stories are often significant and shapely.

A second way to lift the level of student writing is to rally children to look really closely at the ways in which writers create texts that matter. We encourage children to read texts like those they will write, to let those texts affect them, and then to pause and ask, "What has this writer done that has affected me?" That is, this unit places a new importance of reading-writing connections.

Since we are guiding students to notice aspects of published texts that we believe will be especially important to them, this unit relies on assessment. Are children already writing focused, detailed, chronological pieces? If not, we'll want to teach the easiest way to focus personal narratives, which is to limit the time span of the story. Sometimes teachers refer to focused narratives as "small moment stories," although the technical word that writers use for this is scenes (as in scenes of a play, not scenery).

But once children grasp what it means to write effectively about a brief episode, we can show them that narratives need not stay within the confines of a half-hour episode! Narratives actually comprise several scenes glued together with bits of exposition (or narration) between them. For children who are ready to learn this, then, we can point out that in any short story, writers often put a few scenes (or small moments) one after another. This is what many people mean when they say that a story has a beginning, a middle, and an end. For example, the child who has written a Small Moment vignette about getting a bike for her birthday will construct a better story if she sets up the incident by first telling about an earlier time when she begged for the bike. Similarly, the child who writes about defending the goal in a soccer game will construct a more effective story if he first backs up to re-create the moment when he put on his goalie pads and worried they might not be thick enough.

Whether children are writing one episode or linking several together, we will definitely teach them that writers focus their pieces not only by narrowing the time-frame in which they write but also by deciding on the angle from which to tell a story. We teach children to ask, "What am I trying to show about myself through this story? What do I want readers to know about me? How can I bring that meaning out in this episode?" As part of this, we help children learn that the same story can be told differently, depending on the theme the writer wants to bring out. An episode about falling from the monkey bars could be written to show that the writer was afraid but conquered her fears or to show that peer pressure goaded the writer to take reckless risks.

In this unit, it is especially important to select a few touchstone texts for children to study. Ideally, they will be personal narratives—but sometimes teachers may choose instead a fictional story, explaining that although the text is really fiction, it is written as a narrative and can therefore demonstrate narrative craft. I recommend the narrative about a red sweater embedded in "Eleven," by Sandra Cisneros. I also recommend selected pages from Jean Little's memoir *Little by Little*, Patricia MacLachlan's *Journey*, Gary Soto's *A Summer Life*, Amy Ehrlich's *When I Was Your Age: Original Stories About Growing Up*, and the anthology, *Chicken Soup for Kids*. Some picture books can be useful in this unit including Crews' *Shortcut*, Yolen's *Owl Moon*, Keats' *Peter's Chair* or Willems' *Knuffle Bunny*.

Once students have drafted, it is important to teach them to revise. Of course, we'll encourage children to draw on all they already know about revision, and the lessons from the first unit are not inconsequential ones! In addition, in this unit we teach children that a writer's revisions are always informed by our sense of how stories tend to go. This, then, becomes our entrée into teaching students that stories are not, in fact, chains of equally-developed mini-stories (as illustrated by a timeline), but that instead, stories include problems and solutions, and are characterized by rising action, increasing tension. Of course, when children develop the heart of a story as they did in the previous unit, what they are really doing is turning a timeline into a story mountain . . . and this is the graphic organizer that we spotlight as a tool for revision in this unit. Once we've helped children realize that it can help to think of one's personal narrative as a story, then it is not hard to teach children that the beginnings and endings of their stories need to relate to their story mountains. That is, if a child writes about the day he gets a bike, he may want to set up this vignette by showing first that all his life he longed for a bike. Children learn, then, significant ways to craft effective stories, and all of this knowledge will be important as they continue to grow as writers.

The Plan for the Unit

The bends in the road for this unit are as follows:

- Children first look at texts that resemble the sort of thing they hope to write, raising their expectations for what it can mean to write powerful personal narratives.
- Children draw on all the strategies they already know for generating personal narratives and also learn new strategies including the idea that writers sometimes write about first

times, last times, turning points in our lives, or about times we felt strongly. Children gather entries in their writers' notebooks, and we aim for those entries to be focused narratives. Children are encouraged to remember all they learned during the preceding unit and to think, "Am I drawing on all that I know in order to write these entries?" That is, what children learned once through revision now, hopefully, becomes part of drafting.

- Children select a seed idea and rehearse for the draft they will soon write. They recall strategies they learned earlier in the year for developing a seed idea, and they learn to ask, "What is it I *really* want to show in my story?" and to realize that a narrative can be told differently depending on the meaning the writer wants to bring forth. Children study leads of published books and draft and revise their own leads.
- Children draft, writing fast and strong and trying to maintain a point of view.
- Children draw on a growing repertoire of strategies for revising writing, including bringing out the internal story, moving forwards and backwards in time, weaving actions, dialogue and thoughts together, and so forth.
- Children reconsider and revise their draft in the light of a story mountain, asking, 'How might my beginning and my end link to the main thing that I want to show in this story?"
- Children edit drafts, drawing on all they've learned.

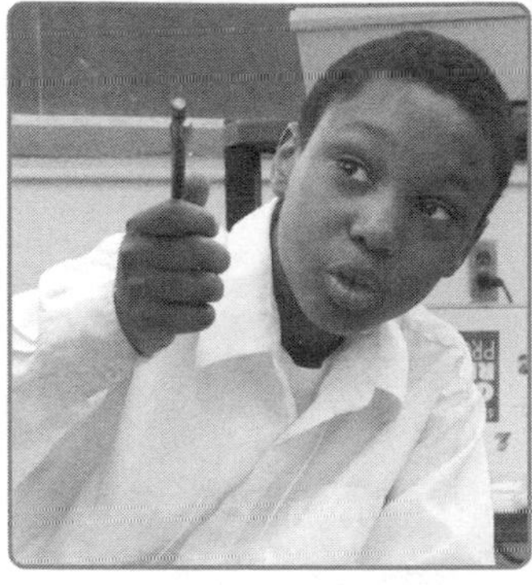

READING WITH A WRITER'S EYE

IN THIS SESSION, YOU'LL TEACH STUDENTS THAT ONE WAY WRITERS MAKE WRITING POWERFUL IS BY EMULATING NARRATIVE WRITING WE ADMIRE.

GETTING READY

- Copy of Cisneros' "Eleven" for each student
- Excerpt of red-sweater scene from "Eleven," on chart paper or overhead
- Lessons from Mentor Personal Narratives chart
- Copies of other published focused personal narratives (refer to Bibliography for choices), in folder on each table
- See CD-ROM for resources

When I first began teaching, *I was overwhelmed and disheartened. I even wondered if this profession was for me. I met with Don Graves, who has been a mentor of mine since I was an adolescent. "I'm not sure I'm cut out to be a teacher," I told him. "I can't seem to make it work for me."*

Don gave me the best advice of my life. "Lucy," he said, "you need to surround yourself with examples of good teaching, to spend time with teachers who are the kinds of teachers you want to become."

I was at that time reading Charles Silverman's Crisis in the Classroom, *a book that extolled the British Primary Schools. And so, even though I'd been teaching (or trying to teach) high school, I flew to England to spend a year apprenticing at the best school I could find, Bicester Primary School. That one year gave me an image of what schools can be like, and for the rest of my career, I've revised, adapted, and built upon that image. Now when I work with teachers across New York City and in other parts of the country, the first thing I suggest is this: Visit a school where the writing workshop is thriving. This will give you an image of what a writing workshop can be.*

Children, too, need images of what good work looks like, so when we teach writing, we need to immerse them in the sorts of texts we hope they will write. We launch this unit by inviting children to read several mentor texts, noticing not only the content but also the craft of those texts, learning from what the authors have done. Today's session aims to convey that writers study texts they admire and ask, "What did this author do that I could try?"

In this unit, we ask kids to do something unusual: to repeat what they just did (write a narrative), only this time, to do it better. The school curriculum often has kids traveling through a sequence of one-shot studies. In the writing workshop, we instead ask kids to cycle through the same writing process over and over, each time with greater independence and skill.

In this session, I try to rally students for the important work ahead, to inspire them, and to give them a taste for what is possible in personal narrative writing. I hope that by examining their own lives, they will begin to live with new alertness, seeing more, hearing more, noticing more, and caring more.

MINILESSON

Reading with a Writer's Eye

CONNECTION

Support your children's identities as writers by telling them anecdotes to show that their published writing affected their readers. Rally their enthusiasm for writing other stories that matter to readers.

"Writers, at our celebration yesterday, each of you became a published author. As you came in this morning, did you see your work displayed on the bulletin board? Did you pause to appreciate it again, or reread parts one of your classmates wrote?"

"This morning, I saw Ms. Manning come into school with her arms laden with books and boxes. She paused, her arms full, to glance at one of your pieces on the bulletin board; she planned to keep on walking so she glanced like this." I gave a fleeting glance. "Then watch what she did. After glancing at one person's story (I think it was yours, Joey, but I couldn't tell for sure), she stopped glancing and began reading (like this). Then she set her books and boxes down on the floor (like this), and read and read and read through the bulletin board. I watched her say, 'Ahhh . . .' at some parts, and laugh aloud at other parts. Watching her, I thought, 'This is so huge!' Writers dream of writing in a way that makes people stop in their tracks and go, 'Ahhh . . . .' And you've done that!"

"So from this day on, remember that you are writing for readers. Rise to the occasion by making your writing as true and as important as it can be, so your words make readers stop in their tracks and go, 'Ahhh.'"

COACHING

Your children will have just published their first pieces. It is important to use that experience to help them see themselves differently—to develop their identities as writers. I remember when I first studied writing with Pulitzer Prize–winning writer Don Murray. "Writers like you realize . . . " he said. I don't remember what he said after that because I was so blown away by the phrase, "Writers like you." Then a week later he wrote me a letter and addressed the envelope to "Writer Lucy Calkins." I found a discarded door in my cellar, set it between two file cabinets to make myself a desk, and began an intense regimen of writing that has continued ever since. Now I try to always remember that for me, being regarded as a writer allowed me to grow into that role.

If you wish to revise any partnerships or shuffle children's seating arrangements so that certain children are more accessible, the start of a new unit is a natural juncture for doing this.

At the start of a unit, the connection needs to set children up not only for that day's minilesson but also for the month's unit of study. It is always important to me at the start of a unit to promote the unit goals because I want them to be in the kids' hands as well as in my own. I have tried, therefore, to introduce the big concepts of this unit. I tell children that in this unit, we will return to personal narrative writing, but this time, our goal will be to improve the quality of writing. We will aim especially to write in ways that affect readers. To do this, we will learn from mentor authors.

Name the teaching point. In this case, tell children that to improve their writing, they can emulate published authors.

"Today, what I want to teach you is this: When we want to make powerful writing, one strategy we can use is to study the writing of authors we admire. We can read their writing and ask, 'What did this author do that I could do also in order to make my own writing more powerful?'"

On the next page, I include the text of "Eleven." This text will weave through this year long curriculum. Children will revisit it often and you'll find you know it by heart! Of course you may select another text as a touchstone. I refer to "Eleven" as a touchstone becaue it beomes a mentor text for the entire class.

Teaching

Show children that to emulate a piece of writing, we first search for an appropriate mentor text, then we read and experience the text we select. Then, we reread as writers to derive techniques worth emulating.

"In a few weeks, my friend is getting married, and she asked me to make a toast. I will need to stand up at the wedding reception, clink on a glass, and then, when everyone is quiet and looking at me, I'll give a toast to my friend and her husband. But what kind of thing should I say? Should I aim my words *to* her or should I address the crowd and talk about her? I need to know how toasts at weddings usually go, so I'm doing what writers the world over do: I am researching. I am asking people, 'When you've been to wedding receptions and someone gives a toast, what do they usually say?'"

"Today, we're going to begin a new unit of study on personal narrative writing, and this time, we're aiming to write even more powerful stories, stories that will make our readers gasp or nod or wince or laugh aloud or change themselves or even try to change the world. Before getting started, writers often read writing that resembles what we hope to do. We need to not only read that kind of writing, but to reread it, and reread it again. We are going to try that today."

"Earlier this year, we read Sandra Cisneros' story 'Eleven.' A section of the text resembles what we will write in this unit of study, so that's why I'm choosing it as our mentor text. Watch me as I reread the red-sweater excerpt. Notice, especially, that this time I'm going to study the excerpt like I'm studying wedding toasts. I'm going to ask, 'How does this kind of writing mainly go? What has the author done here that I could try?"

I read the excerpt aloud, as if I were reading to myself, trying to demonstrate experiencing the story as I read it. To show this, I acted out little bits of the text subtly; I became Mrs. Price, holding the sweater gingerly, and with disdain, between two fingers.

In this session, I will help students learn from a mentor text. As part of this, I want to teach children the process of reaching for such a source of help and of deriving their own lessons from a text. The truth is that whenever I am asked to undertake a new kind of writing, I search for examples that can help me envision the tone, structure, and voice that I want to assume. When I study a mentor text at this very early stage in the process, I'm not apt to notice the decorative details in that text; instead, I hope to gain an overall impression.

In this minilesson I mention that I'm investigating how wedding toasts tend to go so as to write one myself. On other days, I've talked about similar investigations of birthday cards—and of book dedications. I tend to choose tiny texts, and to refer to texts that kids interact with and may not even regard as texts worthy of study.

The decision to use "Eleven" as the mentor text was a tricky one. If the text is a personal narrative at all, it is a disguised one. (The narrator's name, Rachel, is not the author's name.) The truth is, usually before authors publish their personal narratives, they turn them into another genre. They may attribute their personal narrative to another character, embed the personal narrative into an essay, or recast it as fiction. I decided to use this excerpt from "Eleven" despite that ambiguity because it is written in ways that make it a perfect exemplar for kids. You might choose a different mentor text to use in this session. The text you select will travel through the entire unit so choose it with care and read it really well.

ELEVEN

By Sandra Cisneros

What they don't understand about birthdays and what they never tell you is that when you're eleven, you're also ten, and nine, and eight, and seven, and six, and five, and four, and three, and two, and one. And when you wake up on your eleventh birthday you expect to feel eleven, but you don't. You open your eyes and everything's just like yesterday, only it's today. And you don't feel eleven at all. You feel like you're still ten. And you are—underneath the year that makes you eleven.

Like some days you might say something stupid, and that's the part of you that's still ten. Or maybe some days you might need to sit on your mama's lap because you're scared, and that's the part of you that's five. And maybe one day when you're all grown up maybe you will need to cry like if you're three, and that's okay. That's what I tell Mama when she's sad and needs to cry. Maybe she's feeling three.

Because the way you grow old is kind of like an onion or like the rings inside a tree trunk or like my little wooden dolls that fit one inside the other, each year inside the next one. That's how being eleven years old is.

You don't feel eleven. Not right away. It takes a few days, weeks even, sometimes even months before you say Eleven when they ask you. And you don't feel smart eleven, not until you're almost twelve. That's the way it is.

Only today I wish I didn't have only eleven years rattling inside me like pennies in a tin Band-Aid box. Today I wish I was one hundred and two instead of eleven because if I was one hundred and two I'd have known what to say when Mrs. Price put the red sweater on my desk. I would've known how to tell her it wasn't mine instead of just sitting there with that look on my face and nothing coming out of my mouth.

"Whose is this?" Mrs. Price says, and she holds the red sweater up in the air for all the class to see. "Whose? It's been sitting in the coatroom for a month."

"Not mine," says everybody. "Not me."

"It has to belong to somebody," Mrs. Price keeps saying, but nobody can remember. It's an ugly sweater with red plastic buttons and a collar and sleeves all stretched out like you could use it for a jump rope. It's maybe a thousand years old and even if it belonged to me I wouldn't say so.

Maybe because I'm skinny, maybe because she doesn't like me, that stupid Sylvia Saldivar says, "I think it belongs to Rachel." An ugly sweater like that, all raggedy and old, but Mrs. Price believes her. Mrs. Price takes the sweater and puts it right on my desk, but when I open my mouth nothing comes out.

"That's not, I don't, you're not . . . Not mine," I finally say in a little voice that was maybe me when I was four.

"Of course it's yours," Mrs. Price says, "I remember you wearing it once." Because she's older and the teacher, she's right and I'm not.

Not mine, not mine, not mine, but Mrs. Price is already turning to page thirty-two, and math problem number four. I don't know why but all of a sudden I'm feeling sick inside, like the part of me that's three wants to come out of my eyes, only I squeeze them shut tight and bite down on my teeth real hard and try to remember today I am eleven, eleven. Mama is making a cake for me for tonight, and when Papa comes home everybody will sing Happy birthday, happy birthday to you.

But when the sick feeling goes away and I open my eyes, the red sweater's still sitting there like a big red mountain. I move the red sweater to the corner of my desk with my ruler. I move my pencil and books and eraser as far from it as possible. I even move my chair a little to the right. Not mine, not mine, not mine.

In my head I'm thinking how long till lunchtime, how long till I can take the red sweater and throw it over the schoolyard fence, or leave it hanging on a parking meter, or bunch it up into a little ball and toss it in the alley. Except when math period ends Mrs. Price says loud and in front of everybody, "Now, Rachel, that's enough," because she sees I've shoved the red sweater to the tippy-tip corner of my desk and it's hanging all over the edge like a waterfall, but I don't care.

"Rachel," Mrs. Price says. She says it like she's getting mad. "You put that sweater on right now and no more nonsense."

"But it's not—"

"Now!" Mrs. Price says.

This is when I wish I wasn't eleven, because all the years inside of me—ten, nine, eight, seven, six, five, four, three, two, and one—are pushing at the back of my eyes when I put one arm through one sleeve of the sweater that smells like cottage cheese, and then the other arm through the other and stand there with my arms apart like if the sweater hurts me and it does, all itchy and full of germs that aren't mine.

That's when everything I've been holding in since this morning, since when Mrs. Price put the sweater on my desk, finally lets go, and all of a sudden I'm crying in front of everybody. I wish I was invisible but I'm not. I'm eleven and it's my birthday today and I'm crying like I'm three in front of everybody. I put my head down on the desk and bury my face in my stupid clown-sweater arms. My face all hot and spit coming out of my mouth because I can't stop the little animal noises from coming out of me, until there aren't any more tears left in my eyes, and it's just my body shaking like when you have the hiccups, and my whole head hurts like when you drink milk too fast.

But the worst part is right before the bell rings for lunch. That stupid Phyllis Lopez, who is even dumber than Sylvia Saldivar, says she remembers the red sweater is hers! I take it off right away and give it to her, only Mrs. Price pretends like everything's okay.

Today I'm eleven. There's a cake Mama's making for tonight, and when Papa comes home from work we'll eat it. There'll be candles and presents and everybody will sing Happy birthday, happy birthday to you, Rachel, only it's too late.

I'm eleven today. I'm eleven, ten, nine, eight, seven, six, five, four, three, two, and one, but I wish I was one hundred and two. I wish I was anything but eleven, because I want today to be far away already, far away like a runaway balloon, like a tiny o in the sky, so tiny-tiny you have to close your eyes to see it.

> "Whose is this?" Mrs. Price says, and she holds the red sweater up in the air for all the class to see. "Whose? It's been sitting in the coatroom for a month."
>
> "Not mine," says everybody. "Not me."
>
> "It has to belong to somebody," Mrs. Price keeps saying, but nobody can remember. (Cisneros, p. 7)

In this session, I read aloud a fairly long mentor text. Usually minilessons contain only tiny excerpts for reading aloud. I'm diverging from the norm here because at the start of any new unit, it is important to try to motivate children for the big work ahead. Reading aloud a text that illustrates what we hope children will write is one powerful way to do this. For now, I won't dissect the text. I am helping them be absorbed by the story, and then I will help children step back to examine the text like writers.

"Do you notice how I try to take in what's happening? I try to read in a way that lets me experience the moment of the story." I continued reading with total absorption:

> I move the red sweater to the corner of my desk with my ruler. I move my pencil and books and eraser as far from it as possible. I even move my chair a little to the right. Not mine, not mine, not mine. (p. 8)

Putting the story down, I leaned in to talk directly to the class. "I can picture the story exactly. As I was reading, I practically felt like I *was* Rachel, moving the sweater to the corner of my desk with my ruler (so I don't have to touch the nasty thing)."

Demonstrate that you shift from reading and experiencing . . . to reading and extrapolating pointers about good writing.

"Now I'm going to pause, shift, and think, 'What do I notice about this story? What are the main things that Sandra Cisneros has done that I need to keep in mind if I'm going to write like this?'"

I want to show that there are different ways to respond to a story: as a reader, one who gets lost in the text, and as a writer, one who turns the text inside out, asking, "How did she do that?" My body language and tone will accentuate that I shift between two different ways of relating to the text, and between reading aloud and talking to the class. When doing the latter, I put the text down and lean as close to the class as possible.

My eyes scanned the text. Touching one finger to show I'm making a list and that I'm about to name the first item on it, I said, "She's written about an episode in her life that other people might not realize was a big deal, but that really did matter to her." I turned to the chart paper I had entitled Lessons from Mentor Personal Narratives and wrote:

Little actions such as touching one finger and then another when we progress through a list can make it much easier for children to follow what we say in minilessons.

Lessons from Mentor Personal Narratives

- Writers often write about a seemingly small episode—yet it has big meaning for the writer.

Again I scanned the story. "She writes it from start to finish with so much detail that I practically feel as if I am reliving the episode." Then I added, "One way she does this is by recording the exact words Mrs. Price said, which was probably how the episode started."

You'll notice that the techniques I extrapolate come not only from what I notice in the text but also from what I know children will need to do as they embark on writing another personal narrative. I won't, for example, point out the way an author has ended his or her narrative if I'm guiding children toward how to start their narratives! When I'm studying an exemplar text as a way to start writing that kind of text, I point out the overarching and essential characteristics of the text, and those that might influence how apprentice authors get started on their work.

Lessons from Mentor Personal Narratives

- Writers often write about a seemingly small episode—yet it has big meaning for the writer.
- Writers often tell the story in such a way that the reader can almost experience it from start to finish. It helps to record the exact words a character uses.

Debrief. Name what you have demonstrated in a way that is transferable to other texts and other days.

"Do you see how I reread 'Eleven' as thoughtfully as I could, and then, after a bit, I asked, 'What are the main things this author has done that I need to keep in mind if I'm going to write like this?' I'm not focused just yet on the little tiny details—on the repetition of 'not mine, not mine,' for example. Instead I'm trying to understand how her text mainly goes."

Active Engagement

Suggest children read first like readers (envisioning and experiencing the text) and then like writers (analyzing what the author has done). Ask them to list the main things the author has done and then share their lists.

"So let's try it. I'll continue to read, starting after the section in which Rachel pushes the red sweater to the corner of her desk. As I read, try first to simply experience this text, making a movie in your mind. Then I'll reread it, and this time, think about the story as a writer, trying to notice the ways the author has written that allow you to experience her story. Think, 'What are the main things she's done with her writing that I could do?' You'll have a chance to jot these in your notebook."

I resumed reading aloud, starting with this section:

> In my head I'm thinking how long till lunchtime, how long till I can take the red sweater and throw it over the yard fence, or leave it hanging on a parking meter, or bunch it up into a little ball and toss it in the alley. Except when math period ends Mrs. Price says loud and in front of everybody, "Now, Rachel, that's enough . . . ."

The Active Engagement section of minilessons begins with the teacher saying, "Let's try it." One trick is to name what students will be trying in a way that is transferable to other texts. So I didn't say, "Let's read 'Eleven,' picturing Rachel's experience with that red sweater." Instead I worded this differently so that what we are practicing is something that I hope writers do over and over, with lots of texts. "As I read," I said, "try to experience this text, making a movie in your mind." The truth is that children will be apt to do that if I make my own mental movie as I read aloud.

I read about Mrs. Price telling Rachel to put the red sweater on, and then I read this:

> I put one arm through one sleeve of the sweater that smells like cottage cheese, and then the other arm through the other and stand there with my arms apart like if the sweater hurts me and it does, all itchy and full of germs that aren't mine. (p. 8)

I gestured toward the text on chart paper, reminding children that the text was available for them to reread. Then I said, "Stop and jot. What did Cisneros do in her text that you could emulate?" After giving children long enough to generate a few items, I said, "Tell your partner what you noticed." As children talked, I listened for an observation that I wanted to highlight.

Ask children to report on their findings, and then add their observations to the class chart.

After a minute, I nodded at one child to repeat what I'd just overheard her saying. Jocelyn said, "She has a lot of feelings."

After I nodded to signal that another child could add on, Rafael added, "And she doesn't just tell that the sweater was disgusting and all, she showed it by describing it carefully."

I added their observations to the list, and now the chart looked like this:

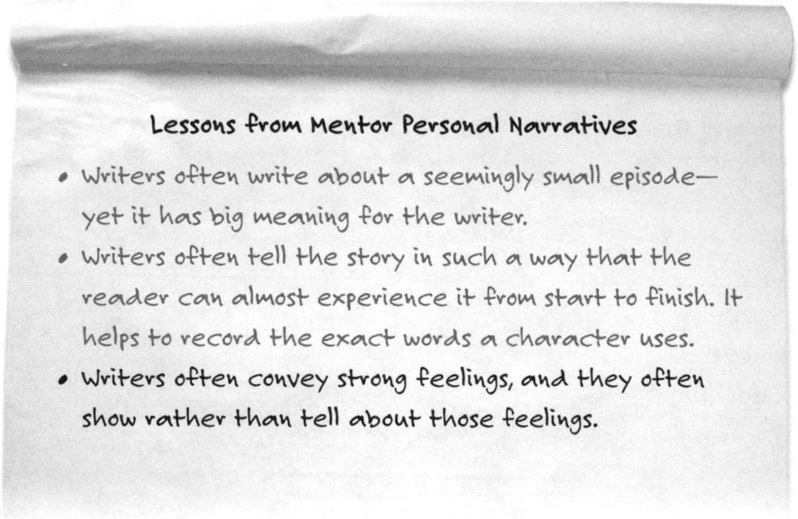

Lessons from Mentor Personal Narratives

- Writers often write about a seemingly small episode—yet it has big meaning for the writer.
- Writers often tell the story in such a way that the reader can almost experience it from start to finish. It helps to record the exact words a character uses.
- **Writers often convey strong feelings, and they often show rather than tell about those feelings.**

Practice reading aloud. Mem Fox once taught a group of us to read (and storytell) well. She cautioned us that instead of aiming to read expressively, we'd be better off to aim toward truly experiencing the text as we read it. When I read that it's an "ugly" sweater, if I am seeing the ugly thing, then my voice will reflect the ugliness of it. When I read about putting one arm in one sleeve, I need to mentally slide one arm into that sleeve so that as I speak, my voice allows listeners to also feel as if they are sliding their arms into that sweater, full of germs that aren't even theirs.

You may, of course, select a different text to thread through this unit, and I'd certainly advise this for your children's second cycle, in a subsequent year. The reason I like "Eleven" is its clarity. The decision relates to your image of good writing. Some teachers of writing (and I am one of these) lean toward an image of good writing that highlights clarity, detail, order, simplicity, and others prefer writing that is lush, poetic, descriptive, and decorative. Select a mentor text that matches your goals for your children, and hope that children study in progressive years under the tutelage of teachers with different preferences.

Notice throughout all of this that I use silent gestures often to cue children. I gestured to the chart paper to remind children to read it. I nodded (instead of calling out) to draw more voices into the conversation. When we use gestures instead of our voices to manage children's behavior, we are using less visible and concrete scaffolds, thus helping children transition toward proceeding with independence.

There is no question but that you could elicit lots more observations from the class community and you could spend half an hour making a gigantic list of all that children notice in the text. I wouldn't do so because the goal here is to demonstrate the strategy of studying a mentor text and noticing features worth emulating; the goal is not to produce a gigantic list. In fact, the great reading researcher, Marie Clay, once visited our classrooms and confided that she wonders if any list of more than five items is worth much—an intriguing thought! In any case, I'd keep the list brief now so that you can soon send children off to do this sort of work on their own.

LINK

Reiterate the teaching point and send children off to study mentor texts.

"So writers, today we launch a new unit—our goal will be to write personal narratives that make even more readers, like Ms. Manning, stop in their tracks! We learned today that writers read first as readers, trying to experience the story. Then writers read as writers. Just as chefs taste a great apple tart and then think, 'What was the recipe?' and seamstresses turn a particularly interesting dress inside out to study the seams and hems, thinking, 'What pattern did she follow to make this?' so, too, writers read the work of other authors, asking, 'How did she write this? What did this author do that I could try?'"

"Today and for the rest of your life, whenever you want to gear yourself up for an important writing project, I hope you remember to study texts that are like those you want to write. I've put a small folder of personal narratives on the middle of your tables. Instead of writing, today, let's read. Read these first to experience them, then read them again to study the main things the author has done. List what you see the author has done that you can try in your writer's notebooks, and get ready to talk together about your lists. We'll work silently for about fifteen minutes, and then we'll talk."

Don't hesitate to put texts that children already know into the folders on their desks. For example, they studied Shortcut *in the first unit of study—include it! You may want to retype* Shortcut *(and any other picture book you hope children will study) onto a single sheet of paper so that children have a copy of the text that they can mark up as they study it. Be sure to include "Your Name in Gold" if you plan to discuss it later (as I do). You'll find it listed (along with many other possible mentor texts) in the Bibliography.*

Writing and Conferring

Studying Mentor Texts

Today, prepare to gasp at the texts your children are reading and do so in a way that draws children into the reading. If a child points in a half-hearted way to a section of a text as you circulate, pretend the child has just jumped up and down with excitement over the words and that you are joining in. "Oh my gosh!" you'll say. "You are right. This is so powerful, isn't it?" Then read that section aloud. Read it like it's worth a million dollars. Don't question the child's judgment, and for now, don't interrogate the child to get him or her to produce a defense for the selection. At least at first, don't even analyze the text to unpack the writing techniques that it illustrates. Instead, begin by reading the texts deeply and well. This will help children to also read in such a way that the texts can make a difference to them. Read the selection aloud so that the hairs on the back of your neck prickle. Read it slowly. Gasp at it. Read it again.

Then after you have joined the child in reading at least a section of the text, model how a reader sometimes turns back to name the effect the passage created. Speak in true words, naming what the passage did for you and avoiding hackneyed phrases like "made a picture in my mind." Instead say something like, "When I read this, I realized I have done the exact same thing. And when I read these words, I was doing it in my mind." Or you might say, "This part gave me a hollow feeling. The words are so stark. 'Not mine. Not mine. Not mine.' It sounds like *amen* or *goodbye*."

Encourage the child to say what he was thinking or feeling or noticing. Help draw words out of the child through gestures and body language; listen, nod, respond in ways that say, "Yes, yes, I know what you mean, say more . . . ." Don't worry today about whether your conferences follow the usual architecture of conferences or whether you are explicitly teaching anything. You will teach *implicitly* today. You'll help children immerse themselves in the sort of text you hope they will soon write—and meanwhile, you will create a drumroll for a unit of study that essentially asks kids to go back and do what they did before, only better.

MID-WORKSHOP TEACHING POINT **_Rereading Texts_** "Writers," I said, standing among the children as they worked. I waited for all eyes to be on me. "When someone asked the great poet Robert Frost, 'How do I learn to write?' Frost said, 'Read *Anna_Karenina*, read *Anna Karenina*, read *Anna Karenina*.' He could have said, 'Read "Eleven," read "Eleven," read "Eleven,"' or 'Read *Shortcut*, read *Shortcut*, read *Shortcut*.' The point is that to learn from a text, we need to not only read it, but to reread, and reread, and reread it."

"Would you reread a section of a personal narrative text that you've already admired, and this time try to see more? Read the words aloud in your mind and listen to them. Think, 'What has this writer done that I can emulate in my writing?' In a bit, you'll have a chance to talk with your partner about what you noticed and admired."

SHARE

Discussing the Genre of Personal Narrative

Set children up to talk about their general sense of the genre, deduced from looking at many personal narrative texts.

"Writers," I said, and paused until all their eyes were on me. "Let's gather in the meeting area to talk about the incredible observations you are making. Bring your folders of mentor texts and your writer's notebooks, and sit with your partners." Once children had gathered, I said, "We're going to talk with our partners, but first let me help you prepare for those conversations. Our goal now is to think and talk about these texts in ways that help us write our own true stories even more powerfully than we ever have before. So I think it is important to look, think, and talk about the overall design of the writing we've just read. Here's my question: What were all these writers doing? Another way to put it is this: What is the shared form that you saw in this writing?"

"Would you reread and jot notes to get ready for partnership conversations on this topic: What is it that all of the narratives have in common?" I allowed time for children to quickly scan the stories they'd just read. After a few minutes, I asked them to discuss this topic with their partners.

You may wonder why I'm asking children to study personal narrative writing as if it's a new genre, when in fact they just finished a unit in which they wrote this way. I think that often in life, we do something and then later we reflect on that familiar action. I taught minilessons for several decades before undertaking a study of effective minilessons, which led me to design what I now refer to as the architecture of minilessons.

The endeavor I ask children to undertake here is not easy. It isn't clear to me that most eight and nine year olds can extract the common features across an assortment of short texts. However, the fact that I've invited children to try something which may prove difficult for them is okay with me, as long as they'll still benefit from the effort.

Reconvene the class. Solicit and chart the shared characteristics they saw in personal narratives.

"So writers, during our minilesson today we began a list, Lessons from Mentor Personal Narratives. What observations have you made that we could add to our list?"

Caleb said, "Well, 'Your Name in Gold' really is two small moments. It first tells about when the girls read the cereal box and saw you could send away for your name in gold. Then it jumped and told about when the package arrived in the mail. So it was two small moments, stuck together."

Ori agreed: "And *Shortcut* told about when the kids walked on the train tracks before the train came, then when the train came, and when it rattled off."

There is nothing magical about these particular texts I reference. I like "Name in Gold" because it is simple and straightforward—and shows that focused personal narratives can contain a few closely related moments. The sisters read the cereal box advertisement for a name-necklace, one makes off with the coupon to the other's disgust. In the end, it turns out the one sibling sent for her sister's *name in gold.*

I nodded. "This is a huge discovery! These authors zoomed in. But they didn't just write about one moment—the name plaque arriving in the mail. Author A. F. Bauman set that moment up by first writing about an earlier moment, when the girls read the cereal box's offer to send one name in gold. And you are right, Crews also didn't write just about the one moment when the train came, did he? He first told about walking, carefree, on the tracks with his friends, didn't he? It is as if his picture book included a Before Moment, then a Super Important Moment."

"Writers, I'm thinking we should definitely add your insight to our chart."

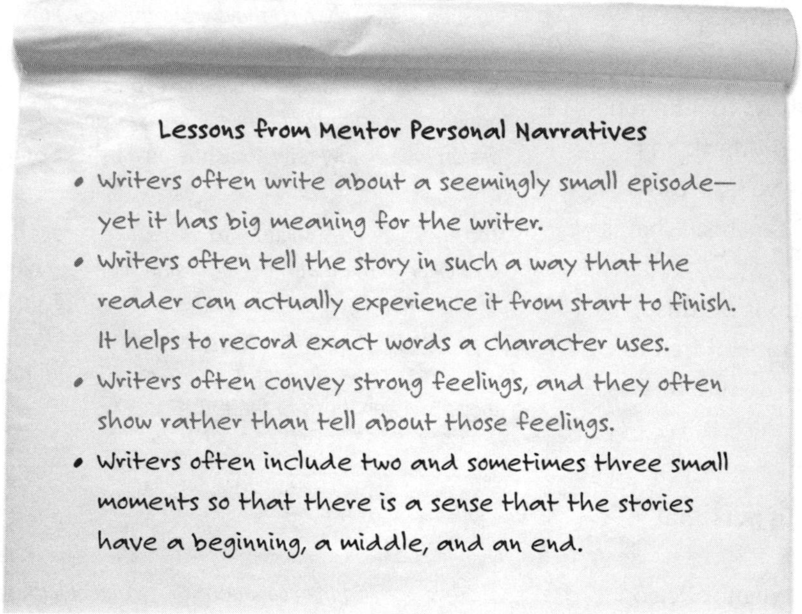

Lessons from Mentor Personal Narratives

- Writers often write about a seemingly small episode—yet it has big meaning for the writer.
- Writers often tell the story in such a way that the reader can actually experience it from start to finish. It helps to record exact words a character uses.
- Writers often convey strong feelings, and they often show rather than tell about those feelings.
- **Writers often include two and sometimes three small moments so that there is a sense that the stories have a beginning, a middle, and an end.**

Remind children of the strategy that can help them today and every day: Writers can learn writing techniques from great literature.

"Now we have made a list that you can look at when you are thinking about how your own personal narrative will go. More than this, I hope you have learned that always, you can do what writers do—look at literature similar to that which you want to write and let it help you figure out what to do!"

If students haven't noticed this particular aspect of personal narrative, the last item on the list, you will need to point it out as your own observation, after you have added their observations to the chart. One of the strongest ways to help children write more sophisticated narratives in this unit is this time you'll encourage them to build personal narratives which follow a story arc—with moments leading up to (and perhaps following) the main small moment of their story. You will build on this item in later lessons, so you need to be sure it's mentioned here.

Notice that in Unit 1 I taught children to zoom in on a single moment, and in this upcoming unit, I teach children to outgrow that somewhat rudimentary notion of focus. I believe that our teaching will often progress in such a fashion. After all, we teach beginning readers to point under words as they read . . . and then we teach them to stop pointing under words as they read. This doesn't mean that it wasn't helpful that children did, for a passing interval, point as they read. Similarly, expect in other ways that I'll teach in overly simplified ways that are later made more complex.

The Lessons from Mentor Personal Narratives *chart is likely to have similar, if not nearly identical, items to the* Qualities of Good Personal Narrative Writing *chart from the previous unit. This is intentional. Children are likely to need various ways to think about these qualities of good personal narratives. This session offers children a new approach to the same topic. Children can learn from this session that they can always turn to writing they admire to find ways to emulate good writing.*

HOMEWORK ***Studying Mentor Texts*** Painters visit art museums, and stand before the giant canvasses, studying the techniques of the masters. Scientists apprentice with researchers, working alongside them in laboratories. Writers, too, learn from studying mentors. We find texts that resemble the text we want to write, and we study those mentor texts.

It takes imagination to learn from a text that another author has made because we need to look at the text and think, "What kind of life did this writer lead which allowed her to write like this?" We wonder what sort of entries she may have collected in her writer's notebook. We speculate over whether she wrote a timeline first, or tried several lead sentences. We won't, of course, know the answers to those questions, but it is important to look at writing we admire and to think about the processes the writer probably used in order to write like this.

Tonight, would you read another narrative by Sandra Cisneros, this one called "Papa Who Wakes Up Tired in the Dark." Think about the sorts of entries Cisneros probably collected in her notebook. Why do you think she decided to write about this moment? Do you think she made a movie in her mind in order to write this?

Because you'll read "Papa Who Wakes Up Tired in the Dark" as a fellow writer, you'll no doubt want to star parts that are especially beautiful and to think, "How did she write this part?" Write all over the copy of this text that I'm giving you. Tomorrow you'll have a chance to write your own entries! Be thinking about moments that you, like Sandra Cisneros, can capture on the page.

TAILORING YOUR TEACHING

If you think your class needs some inspiration and motivation as they approach another unit of personal narrative writing . . . you could also seize this opportunity to teach children how to turn "Eleven" or the touchstone text you select into a symphony share. After giving children a few minutes to find and reread favorite parts, say to them, "I'm going to be the conductor of an orchestra. When I point my baton at you, would you read aloud a tiny excerpt, an excerpt you especially like? Read the excerpt in such a way that it gets through to us. Look up to show me you've found your excerpt and then I'll start conducting. Your excerpt can be just a sentence or a phrase." When I did this recently, I began the recitation by saying aloud, "Powerful Writing, by Sandra Cisneros," as if this were the title of the improvisation. The title adds a touch of extra dignity to the event. Then I pointed to one child and another. I didn't respond verbally to what a child read—instead, I moved to the

If you suspect that children will have a hard time making generalizations about the content and structure of the genre, it might help to set examples of personal narrative writing against examples of another genre of writing. Comparing personal narratives to short stories or short essays or short newspaper articles will make features of narrative writing pop out to young readers. Of course, if the genres being compared are similar, more emphasis will fall on the details of what makes personal narrative writing unique. When the two kinds of writing being compared are vastly different, the biggest differences will be the most pronounced. When choosing texts to contrast with personal narrative writing, keep in mind that generally the shorter the texts, the more easily readers can grasp a sense of the form of the whole.

This is from Cisneros' The House on Mango Street, *which is a book that you'll return to often for examples of powerful narrative writing. "Papa Who Wakes Up Tired in the Dark" could be your touchstone text for the entire unit—it is beautiful!*

next and then the next so their voices cascaded together. If a child chatted about his or her response, I intervened and asked the child not to do this; then we redid that one section. Soon the room filled with voices:

"with sleeves all stretched out like you could use it for a jump rope."

"I said in a little voice that was maybe me when I was four."

"'Not mine,' I finally say."

I find that the work required to pull this off is worthwhile because this symphony share is a ritual you can return to often over the year. While in this instance, children read lines they love from a published text, another time, you may instead ask them to select and read details from their own writing or instances of alliteration or strong action words. Just be sure to allow children to prepare before they perform by finding instances of whatever is being celebrated within their own or a published text.

If you decide to extend this work . . . you may invite children to join you in a search for either well-written personal narratives, or for texts that illustrate narrative craft so well that they can be instructive in this unit. Just as the red-sweater excerpt from "Eleven" functions well as an example of the narrative craft, children may also decide to study chapters in *Because of Winn-Dixie*, by Kate DiCamillo, for example. You may share a few examples and then ask children to help you search for others, compiling a basket of texts that resemble those they aspire to write. The day wouldn't follow a traditional workshop structure—and the children would benefit from the break.

ASSESSMENT

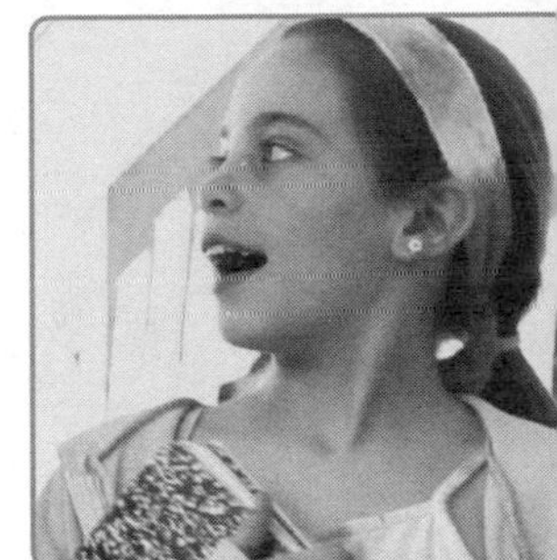

It has been said that we see and hear not with our eyes and ears but with our beliefs. The list of things that a child sees in a mentor text will reveal more about the child than about the text. Study your children's observations of published mentor texts. Ask children to study also a text written by another child, making observations about what the child has done (see CD for suggested texts). Your children's observations will reveal what they know about good writing. Of course, these observations will also reflect previous instruction. If many of your children report seeing similar things in mentor texts, these may be qualities of good writing that previous teachers have valued or that your students have come to believe you value. You may need to allow children more time to see past their first observations.

Very often I find, for example, that teachers have emphasized writing descriptively, and children are quick to admire any instances in which an author has used his or her senses or written with figurative language. But often children are *not* taught to read with an eye toward other qualities of good writing that have particular power to lift the level of their own work. You'll want to observe whether your children are carrying the work from the previous unit with them. For example, do they notice focus, commenting on whether the author has written a focused Small Moment story rather than writing all about a topic? Do they notice how the author has included true and exact details from within a scene? Do they see that the story develops in a step-by-step sequential fashion on the page?

Save your children's notes about the stories they read and, toward the end of the unit, ask children to reread the narratives they read today, again jotting down what they notice about the authors' craftsmanship. They should be able to see many techniques they didn't observe at the start of the unit, and this should provide you with a great sense of satisfaction. In a sense, this simple activity will convey to you whether your instruction is lifting children's sense of standards, giving them more informed ideas about effective narrative writing. Even if some of your children end this unit still unable to turn their images of good writing into realities, simply developing a richer image of what they are working toward when writing a story is a huge accomplishment. *[Fig. I-1]*

Meanwhile, of course, it is important for us, as teachers, to become much more skilled at reading writing. When you gather with your colleagues, try doing what you ask your children to do. Read a story and talk together about the characteristics of the writing that make the story an effective one. Put two narratives alongside each other, and try to find words for ways in which both texts incorporate a similar form. Resist the tendency to use prepackaged language. For example, it would have been helpful if I asked myself, "What exactly do I mean when I say, 'This story has a beginning, a middle, and an end'?" If I can expand on that cliché, I can make it more personal and meaningful for me and for my students.

Ingredients For a Small moment

1. one focus/small amt of time (stretched out)
2. action
3. sensory details/images
4. stk in the momen(present tense)
5. *what is the big thing? so what?
6. Some dialogue (not much)
7.

Fig. I-1 Ilana reminds herself of the ingredients for a Small Moment narrative

STARTING WITH TURNING POINTS

IN THIS SESSION, YOU'LL REMIND STUDENTS TO USE STRATEGIES THEY ALREADY KNOW FOR GENERATING NARRATIVE WRITING. YOU WILL ALSO TEACH THEM THAT WRITERS THINK OF FIRST TIMES, LAST TIMES, OR TIMES OF IMPORTANT REALIZATIONS TO GENERATE WRITING.

GETTING READY

- Strategies for Generating Personal Narrative Writing chart from first session
- See CD-ROM for resources

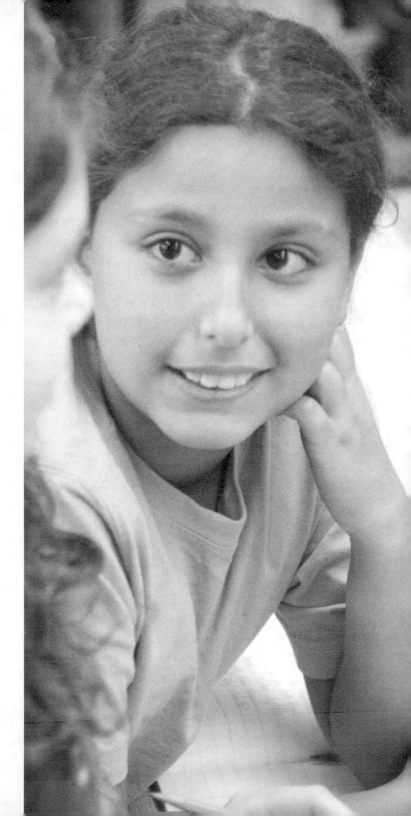

Although the preceding session *was the start of this unit, because children spent that day reading rather than writing, today's minilesson actually launches the writing work in this second unit of study. Approach this session knowing that your minilesson will need to set children up for the earliest stages of their writing process. As you plan today's minilesson (and the initial lessons of all units), you will need to help children consolidate, carry forward, and draw upon the lessons they have already learned. This will be especially important in this unit because children will be writing personal narratives again. Teach children that the strategies they learn during previous writing workshops will be useful throughout their lives. Of course, as children develop facility with these strategies, the strategies themselves will no longer be the focus of their attention. Instead, writers will be able to use them almost automatically, concentrating on new writing goals.*

When I introduce a strategy, I make a big deal of it: I lay out every part of it, turning it into a mechanical, step-by-step operation. This may feel odd at first, a bit unbalanced, but I believe that when we teach any complex activity, we need to explicitly lay out each step with exaggerated attention, keeping in mind that soon, the learner will master the procedure, repeating it as one flowing, almost automatic activity. For example, the tennis coach will show the novice how to grasp the tennis racket, then how to turn the racket so that it fits properly in the hand. But before long, the learner just grabs for the racket, swiftly taking—but no longer fussing over—the same steps.

In Launching the Writing Workshop, *we helped children develop a set of strategies for personal narrative writing and we asked them to carry these in their mental backpacks. In this unit, you'll help children use those strategies to more powerful effect. You'll teach a few new strategies, but this time, you'll focus less on the strategies and more on writing narratives like those the class is studying, narratives that contain more than a single small moment—narratives that have a story arc. The early lessons in this unit will help children generate not only topics for writing but also fleshed-out story ideas—topics with a ready-made plot line. This will help children write stories that revolve around (but are more than) accounts of single, small moments. That is, the narratives that children begin generating today should begin to feel like real stories—stories that resemble those your children have been studying.*

Minilesson

Starting with Turning Points

Connection

Tell children that in this unit, they will be writing even more powerful Small Moment stories—and one way to do this is to start with turning points.

"Writers, yesterday we pored over stories that resemble those we hope to write and we asked, 'What did this author do that I could try?' We especially looked at the way in which all the stories have a shared form. They all contain more than just a small moment, they have writing leading up to the main small moment in the middle, and then they sometimes have more moments to make an end. For example, in "Your Name in Gold," you noticed that the story starts with a scene at the breakfast table when Annie and her big sister both read the cereal box and both yearn to be the one to send the coupon off for a golden name plaque, and the story ends with a second small moment, a second scene (as writers call it) in which the big sister gives Annie her name in gold. We also read other stories—like *Shortcut* and 'Papa Who Wakes Up Tired in the Dark'—and afterwards, we realized that stories often have a shared form."

"In the stories we read, there is a beginning—and then something happens to change things, and then there is an end. The moments that change things are all different, but all are important: In one, the big sister does a surprising act of generosity; in another, the girl realizes that it could have been her own papa who died; in another, the train almost flattens a group of kids. In all of these moments, the character feels or learns something important. The stories we studied (and the stories we will be writing) are Small Moment stories, and if you study them even harder, you will see that they all include some kind of turning point."

Coaching

It is all too easy to begin our minilessons with an empty introduction: "Yesterday, we began our unit on writing powerful personal narratives," or "Yesterday we read and talked about mentor personal narratives." There is nothing terribly wrong about starting a minilesson like this, but if leads are important in children's writing, they are also important in our minilessons. And those ho-hum introductions may send this message to kids: The beginning of a minilesson is old hat, so you can tune out till later. Why would we want to convey such a message? Don't we risk having kids tune out for the whole minilesson? Instead think, "What can I say at the start of a minilesson that recaptures some of yesterday's learning but also consolidates and packages that learning so that it's ready for the road, or adds new nuance and energy to that learning?" In this instance, I try for the latter. I am also angling my account of the previous session so that I highlight one of the more complex and rich lessons, a lesson that I definitely want in the forefront of children's minds as we go forward.

Remind children that they already have a repertoire of strategies for generating narrative writing, represented in charts that can become vitally important tools for them.

"Today, as we begin to work on new pieces of writing, I want to remind you that *you already know* strategies for coming up with stories that make readers sigh and laugh and pull in to read more. Last month, you wrote two personal narratives and this month we'll work on the same kind of writing again! As writers, we each carry with us an invisible backpack full of all the strategies we've ever learned, and we pull them out as needed. It's not an accident that the charts from our first unit are still in the room. You'll look at those charts often throughout the whole year to remind you of strategies you've already learned. Later today, when it is time to generate narrative entries, I bet you'll use this chart to remind you of the strategies you might use."

Sometimes I see teachers disguising the fact that children will recycle, in this unit, through the same process they experienced earlier, once again writing personal narratives. Don't downplay this! Instead, seize on the important opportunity you have to teach children to draw on yesterday's and last month's teaching as they continue their work. Until children learn to do this, they can't be independent writers. The image of an invisible backpack is one I use again and again. Substitute your own metaphor, if you prefer, but find a way to help children learn to draw on all they know, not just the most recent lessons.

Strategies for Generating Personal Narrative Writing

- Think of a person, place, or thing that matters to you, then list clear, small moments you remember. Choose one to sketch and then write the accompanying story.

Note that the first bullet in this chart now consolidates three strategies introduced individually in the first unit: focusing on a person, place, or object. For conciseness, you too may want to group these items as I've done before adding to the list.

Name the teaching point. In this case, teach children that when writers want to generate ideas for personal narratives, they often think of turning point moments.

"Today, before you start generating personal narrative entries, I want to teach you one more strategy that I often use when I want to write personal narratives. This is a strategy that especially helps me write entries that can become powerful stories. Specifically, I find it helps to list moments in my life that have been turning points for me. These are often first times, last times, or times when I realized something important."

Notice that I do not phrase the teaching point like this: "Today we will think of turning point stories." That wording would have simply assigned children a task. That is not my goal! A minilesson is not a forum for telling children what we want them all to do in the upcoming workshop. Instead, it is a place for explicitly teaching children the skills and strategies of good writing—skills and strategies we want them to call upon as needed not only today, but always. In today's minilesson, I am hoping to teach children one more technique that they can carry with them in their invisible backpacks of strategies.

TEACHING

Demonstrate the step-by-step sequence of using the strategy. In this case generate ideas for personal narratives by listing first times, last times, or times when you realized something important.

"Let me show you how I use the strategies of thinking of first times I did something, thinking of last times I did something, and thinking of when I realized something important, because these are all ways for me to think of turning point stories."

"In order to come up with a first or last time, I take something—anything I do all the time. So I pick ice skating. Then I think, 'When is the *first time* I ice skated?' And suddenly, I remember a time (it might not have been the very first time, but it was an early time) when I skated out to an island, pushing a little red chair in front of me so I wouldn't fall. I write that time on my list, knowing I might come back and tell the story of it later." I jotted a phrase representing the episode on chart paper. "In order to come up with a last time I did something, I go through the same steps . . . and this time, I end up remembering the last time I saw my grandfather, on a visit to the nursing home."

"I can also think, 'What moment can I recall when suddenly I realized something important?' That's harder! But I think about 'Your Name in Gold,' and I think Anne wrote about that moment—her name in gold—because that's when she suddenly realized her sister really cared for her. And in 'Papa Who Wakes Up Tired in the Dark,' Sandra described the moment when she hugged and hugged and hugged her father because in that moment, she suddenly realized it could have been *her* dad who died!"

Don't bypass this lesson! It works like a charm to ask children to think about first times, last times, and times when they realized something important. When children think about these turning points, they automatically generate story ideas that have a before and an after, or a beginning, middle, and end. In other words, finding topics in this way helps children build a story arc because the arc is inherent in the story. This is most obvious in the "times when I realized something" stories. For example, a child might tell about how he'd always taken his dad for granted. Then a turning point happened, and he appreciated him. Another child may have thought a particular teacher would be terrifying, but then a turning point happened and the child realized his fears were unfounded. Last- and first-time stories also often have a before and an after, or a beginning, middle, and end. For example, first-time stories often begin with a prelude: "I always wanted to do such and such," and then the stories progress until the crucial moment happens. This way of finding topics puts a tension into the personal narrative—an element so many good stories contain—even though the writer may not yet be completely conscious of crafting to create the tension.

Debrief. Remind children of the purpose for the strategy. In this case, remind them that thinking of turning points can help them generate ideas for personal narratives.

"When I want to pick a topic for a personal narrative that will make a really good story, one that will have the shape of a story—a beginning, a middle, and an end—and one that matters, it often helps to think about turning point moments. And now you've seen that to do this, I sometimes brainstorm first times, last times, and times when I realized something important. My brainstorming leads to a list, and then I choose one moment from the list that I believe is the most significant to write about in detail."

While you teach children qualities of good writing, keep in mind that those same qualities can meanwhile transform our own minilessons. One quality of good writing that we have not yet highlighted for the kids is cohesiveness. By the end of this year, you'll see that I teach children how they can create a more cohesive text by repeating an important phrase at the beginning, middle, and end of a narrative, or by having images or symbolic objects recur. Cohesion is also important in our minilessons. You'll notice that I repeat the teaching point several times in a minilesson, and also that I carry phrases, images, and titles from one day's minilesson into the next.

Active Engagement

Ask your children to think of turning point stories they could write and to jot those ideas in their writer's notebooks so they have a list of story ideas for later.

"Let's try it. I'm going to suggest some general topics, and you try to think of a turning point story you could write. If you think of one, jot it down in your writer's notebook so that later, you'll have a list of ideas you can come back to." I posed one idea, then another, leaving time after each item for children to scrawl their thoughts into their notebooks.

"Think about the first time you did something that felt, at the time, like it was hard for you, like swimming across the pool, or climbing to the very top of a mountain, or taking the subway by yourself."

"Think about the first time you did something that now you do every day, like seeing your younger brother, or coming into this classroom, or walking to school from your apartment, or playing a sport, or reading a book."

"Think about the last time you saw a person (or a pet) who died, or the last time you saw someone who left you."

"Think about the time you realized something about yourself, or about a person you know well."

"Think about a time you realized something almost happened to you—something that would have changed your life."

"Thumbs up if you found it helpful to think about first times, last times, and times when you realized something," I said, revealing the more specific Questions to Ask to Find Turning Points chart I had written.

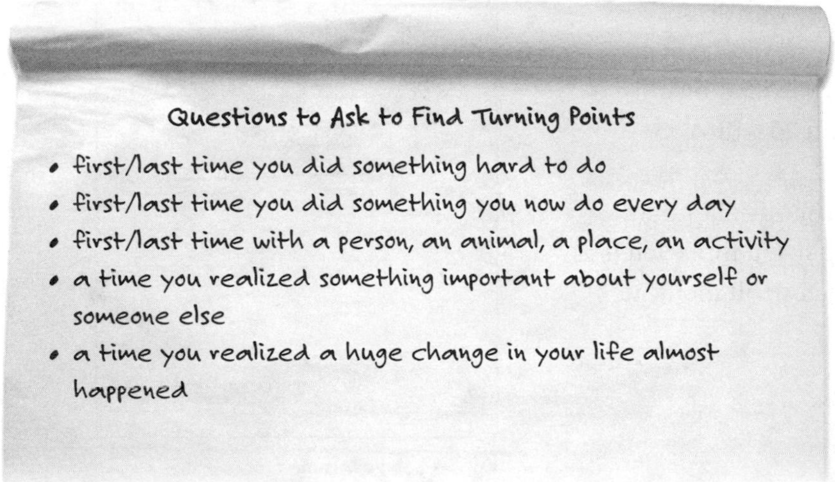

Questions to Ask to Find Turning Points

- first/last time you did something hard to do
- first/last time you did something you now do every day
- first/last time with a person, an animal, a place, an activity
- a time you realized something important about yourself or someone else
- a time you realized a huge change in your life almost happened

Keep your suggestions simple, common, and general. Your goal is for children to be able to prompt themselves the way you are now prompting them. For a strategy to be useful, the writer has to be able to use it independently, without a teacher, later. Therefore make sure your prompts are the sort that kids can internalize and use for themselves.

Don't underestimate the importance of leaving little pools of silence after each injunction. Give children time to think and to jot. The best way to do this is to have your notebook on hand, and to take a second after each injunction to do your own very quick thinking and jotting.

In this minilesson, you may wish to highlight the fact that the process of brainstorming possible story ideas involves five minutes, not a full workshop! Explain that writers shift between brainstorming, selecting, and writing.

LINK

Remind children that writers draw from their growing repertoire of strategies. Add the turning point strategy to the Strategies for Generating Personal Narrative Writing chart, and therefore to your children's repertoire.

"So writers, I hope you remember that you carry with you an invisible backpack full of strategies, including all the strategies you learned earlier this year for generating personal narratives. And today you learned one more strategy to add to your backpack. You learned that if you want to turn a small moment in your life into a really good story, it can help to start by thinking of turning point moments, and more specifically, to think of first-time or last-time moments, or times when you realized something important. I'll add that to our chart over here."

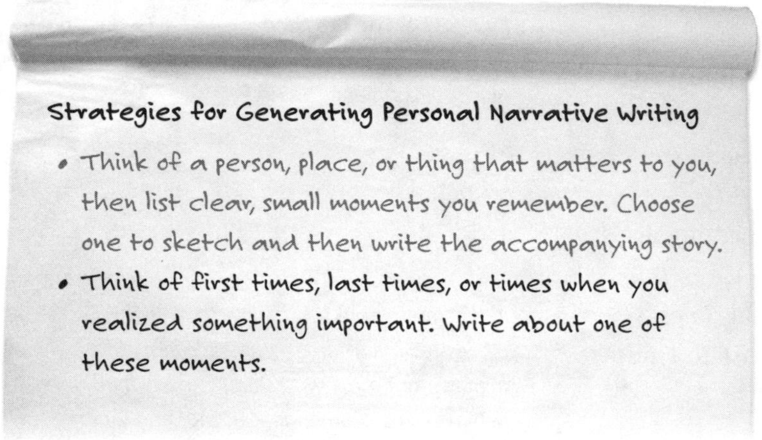

Strategies for Generating Personal Narrative Writing

- Think of a person, place, or thing that matters to you, then list clear, small moments you remember. Choose one to sketch and then write the accompanying story.
- **Think of first times, last times, or times when you realized something important. Write about one of these moments.**

"As you gather entries today, draw on any strategy from this chart. Remember that it should take you just a few minutes to jot a few quick lists of ideas for entries, and then you'll need to select an idea from your list and write it. You may have time to write two entries (as well as some lists) today."

"Give me a thumbs up if you think you'll choose to write about a first time, last time, or a time when you realized something important. Give me a thumbs up if you think you'll start with a person, a place, or an object, and then list and choose between small moments connected to that." Children so indicated and I sent them off to work.

Although these strategy "backpacks" are invisible, your charts are very visible. Be sure to add each strategy to your chart of Strategies for Generating Personal Narrative Writing.

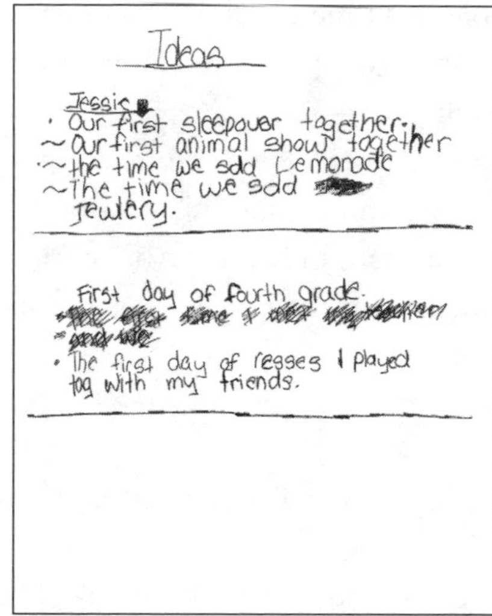
Ideas

Jessie
· Our first sleepover together.
~Our first animal show together
~the time we sold Lemonade
~The time we sold jewlery.

First day of fourth grade.

· The first day of resses I played tag with my friends.

Fig. II-1 Sophie's list of possible narratives

·The first day of sience and talking about hurican Katrina

My little brother ~~Sage~~
·the time he went to school in his pajamas
·The time he ate a wasabi pea
·The time he through-up during a show fear facter
·The first time he went to school

Fig. II-2 Sophie lists more possibilities

Writing and Conferring

Generating Energy and Writing

When you launch a new unit, you'll want to rally the children to do the new work, creating a burst of energy around it. You hope that by the end of the day, lots of children have used the new strategies you've taught and that their energy for the new unit is high. Because I always want to be sure the first minilessons in a new unit empower children, I scanned this session's teaching plans in advance, asking, "What problems can I anticipate the children might encounter today?" I don't want any problems to interfere with children's sense that the upcoming work will be do-able and exciting. I did not expect that children would have trouble with today's work because it is not very different from the work they did during Unit 1. However, some children may simply list turning points, not shifting from listing to writing, so I entered this work time ready to make a quick whole-class interruption, if necessary, to clarify that once a child had listed some moments, the challenge is to take one and write it as a story in his notebook—a story that resembles those he's been studying.

As children generate ideas for their writing, you'll remind them to draw on what they have already learned. Recalling the strategies for generating narratives shouldn't be too difficult. A bigger challenge will be to make sure children recall the qualities of writing they learned in the previous unit. For example, if Jacob worked hard during Unit 1 to focus his story on a smaller moment, you will want to act totally astounded if he forgets all that he learned in the first unit now and returns to writing about a huge, broad topic. If Maria learned during the last unit to write with detail, you'll want to act as if you can't comprehend why someone with her talent for detail would now be writing with generalizations. In your conferences, convey your expectation that children will use their accumulated knowledge every time they write.

If you know certain students are struggling, immediately give them the help they'll need to get off to a great start in this unit. Convene a group of your least experienced writers and read with them the chart of strategies for generating personal narrative writing. Help them select one strategy, then say, "Let me show you how that strategy works." With your help, the kids could (for example) each think of the first time they did something. Prompt each child to orally list and choose between a few story ideas;

MID-WORKSHOP TEACHING POINT

Making Planning Boxes "Earlier today you learned a few new strategies for generating true stories, and I've loved seeing your stories about first times, last times, or times when you realized something important. But I want to remind you that you needn't draw only on this list of new strategies. Remember how Cisneros' character points out that when she is ten, she is also nine and eight and seven? And that is true for us as writers as well. When we are in our *second* unit of study, we are also in our *first* unit of study, because as writers, we grow in layers like onions, or like trees in rings, with one unit of study inside the next."

"You'll want to draw on your full repertoire of strategies, and to do this, you'll want to use stuff—old charts, old entries and rough drafts, finished writing—to get you thinking about strategies that worked for you that you'll want to carry with you into this new unit."

"When I want to remember strategies that I've used before, I don't just sit at my

continued on next page

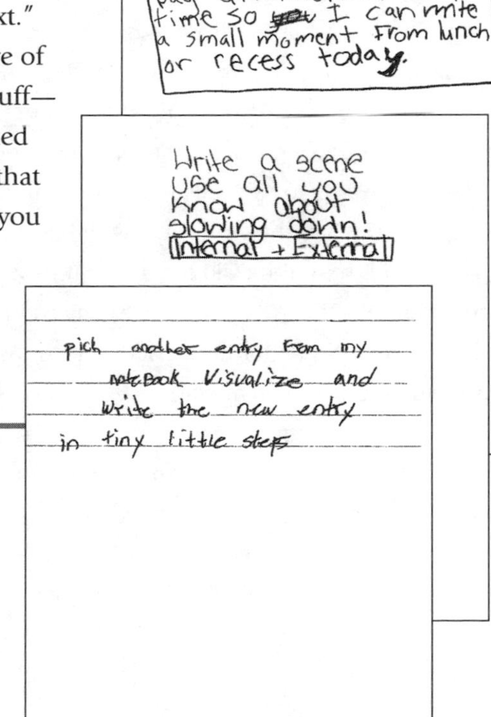

Figs. II-3, II-4, and II-5 Examples of Planning boxes

listen for and steer children toward story ideas that sound like they will pay off. Don't take too long helping children to generate story ideas because you'll also need to help them get those stories started.

Once every child in the group has a story idea, help them frame their writing as stories, not summaries. Try working with one child while the other children watch. Ask, "What were you doing at the very start of this event?" Once the child specifically describes her opening action, help her say more: "Then what?" Be prepared for the child to speak in generalizations, and help her speak in details. "What exactly were you playing?" The child's story should not have sweeping statements such as "I was playing and he yelled at me," but should instead be specific: "I was playing Frisbee with my dog, Banjo. Banjo grabbed the Frisbee. Then my Dad yelled, 'Cut it out!'"

The child will probably articulate her story one sentence at a time; once you have lured the start of the story out of the child, say her story back coherently, synthesizing the fragments into a flowing lead. If the lead you articulate is what the child wants to say, repeat it but this time say a phrase and wait while she writes it. Say the next phrase, and wait. After a bit, have the child reread what he or she has written. Then say, "Keep going." Once the child has said what comes next, signal for her to add that to the page. That child should be off to a great start.

Meanwhile, the other children in the small group will be ready for you to nudge them to use these same questions and prompts to help them with their writing. In this manner, you can get your strugglers off to a strong start. Plan to use their work soon as examples for other kids to emulate. You will totally alter their experience of the entire unit of study if you give these children an early boost toward success.

continued from previous page

desk and stare into space. Instead, I look back on my experiences as a writer and remember strategies that have helped me improve my writing. For sure, I reread old charts." I referred to the Strategies for Generating Personal Narrative Writing chart.

"As I look over old charts and the writing I've already done, I get ideas for the strategy I want to try next. I give myself an assignment for what to do next, and I record the strategy I will use in a planning box in my notebook." I showed children how most of the pages in my notebook begin with a little planning box. Leaning close to the children, I said, "Here's the important thing. Writers do not just plan *what* we are going to write about. We also plan *how* we're going to go about writing. Right now, would you reread what you've written, look over your charts, and think, 'How will I go about writing my next entry?' If you haven't already reused a strategy from our first unit of study, pick one to reuse today. And before you write (today and from this day on), make and fill in a planning box for yourself in your notebook. Then get going, following your plan."

What I did not say, but thought, was this: The fact that a child must take a moment to record his or her plan before proceeding makes it much more likely that children do make plans as writers. They are less apt to simply proceed as if on autopilot.

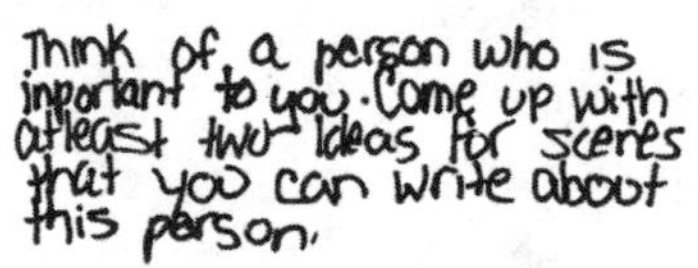

Think of a person who is important to you. Come up with atleast two ideas for scenes that you can write about this person.

Fig. II-6 Sophie's planning box

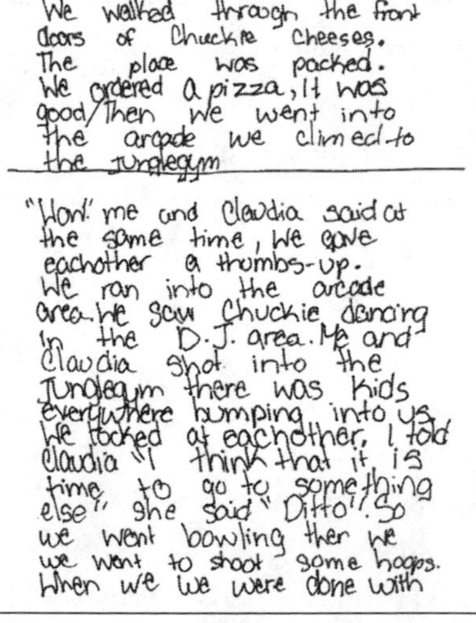

We walked through the front doors of Chuckie Cheeses. The place was packed. We ordered a pizza, It was good/Then we went into the arcade we climed to the Junglegym

"Wow!' me and Claudia said at the same time, We gave eachother a thumbs-up. We ran into the arcade area. We saw Chuckie dancing in the D.J. area. Me and Claudia shot into the Junglegym there was kids everywhere bumping into us. We looked at eachother, I told Claudia "I think that it is time to go to something else" she said "Ditto". So we went bowling then we we went to shoot some hoops. When we we were done with

Fig. II-7 Sophie's writing based on her plan

SHARE

Noticing Features of Personal Narratives

Ask partners to share and discuss their own writing just as they did the day before with texts written by published authors.

"Writers, yesterday we read folders full of mentor texts written by famous authors, and we talked about all those texts, noticing what most of those authors tended to do. Today we have new texts that we can look at—texts you all have written. Would you and your partner get together, and partner 2 (thumbs up so I can see that you know who you are), please share the entry or the entries you wrote today with partner 1, and then talk together about that writing. What is it that you've done? What were you trying to do? How is the form of your writing similar to (and different from) the form you noticed in the folder of mentor texts? Talk deeply and read closely, and in a few minutes, I'll bring us back to talk as a group."

If students are skilled at discussing their writing, you may choose to ask them to look at the writing they did in the previous unit as well as the writing they've done today. If children can assimilate the information about personal narrative writing offered by a whole folder of their own writing rather than just one piece, their conclusions will be deeper and more advanced.

Ask one partner to share an entry, and the other to share observations of it. Then debrief in a way that reminds writers of the lessons they can hold on to.

After a few minutes, I convened the class. Joey read his entry: *[Fig. II-8]*

> Jumping in the pond really late at night
>
> Me and John were going to jump in the pond really late at night. John kept on telling me, "Come on! Jump!" I just could not. John kept on encouraging me to do it. He said, "You can do it, come on. Nothing is going to happen."
>
> I had to do it. I jumped. I closed my eyes and tried to think of good things. Splash. "I did it!" I yelled.
>
> John ran up to me and said, "Great job. You did it! You're the best."

Fig. II-8 Joey

Joey's partner Felix said, "He told about one moment, and he had the beginning before the jump and all."

Joey added, "And I showed I was nervous, I didn't just tell it."

I nodded. "Yes, you noticed that like the other personal narratives we read, your story has more than just plop, there's the moment, right? Although the climax of the story is the moment when you jumped into the pond, you led up to it, didn't you? Just like a diver often has a three-step approach before diving in! And Joey, you also spiced up the way that you told the story, adding dialogue and showing your feelings. Doing these things will serve you well for a long time, Joey." Turning to the entire class, I said, "All of you can do these things that Joey has done. You can consider having a beginning as well as a middle to your story, keeping in mind Joey's prelude and a diver's three-step approach to the dive. You, like Joey, can spice up the way you tell your stories, too. And do whatever else you learn from studying great personal narratives! So writers, give yourselves a thumbs up for all the hard work you did today. I can tell this is going to be an amazing unit of study."

The concept that personal narratives generally have a moment leading up to the Big Moment (and another time I'll emphasize that stories also have a moment leading away) is a concept we will keep coming back to in this unit. Eventually, we will talk with students about story arcs, and help them find the story arc in their own personal narratives, probably by adding a moment before the Big Moment (the rising action) and a moment after the Big Moment (the resolution or falling action). For this share, if you know there is a student who has been noticing features of personal narrative related to these concepts, it will be helpful for you to choose her to share her thinking and work.

HOMEWORK ***Emulating Writers' Lives*** We can learn from authors' *texts*, like we did yesterday, and we can also learn from studying authors' *lives*. We can research how an author did whatever we are trying to do. For example, if we are trying to come up with story ideas, we can find out how certain authors came up with their own story ideas. Since you all are working on getting story ideas, I want to tell you about how two authors we know got their story ideas. Then, you'll have a chance to write a planning box for the writing work you plan to do this evening.

When Cynthia Rylant was asked about how she gets her ideas, she said, "We are talking about art, thinking about art, and creating art every single day of one's life. This is about going fishing as an artist, having relatives over for supper as an artist, and walking the aisles of Woolworth's as an artist." (1994) I think Rylant keeps a writer's notebook, and often, as she lives her life, she opens the notebook and writes the story of catching a fish, shopping for slippers, or of other tiny little events that make up her life. It sounds like she collects ideas all the time; even when she is also doing other things, part of her mind is on writing.

Robert McCloskey, the author of *Make Way for Ducklings,* was in Boston in his car one time and the traffic stopped. "What's going on?" he thought, wondering if there had been an accident or something. So he got out of his car to look, and walked ahead a few cars—and saw a long line of ducks crossing the highway. The traffic on all sides had stopped while each little duckling waddled along. McCloskey said to himself, "I could write a story about this! I could tell about the day I was driving in the traffic, then everything stopped, and I could tell about how I got out of my car and watched . . ." That story became *Make Way for Ducklings.*

If these stories of Rylant's and McCloskey's lives have given any of you an idea for how you could live your life as a writer, please jot these ideas in your notebook.

I anticipate that some of you will write that, like Cynthia Rylant and Robert McCloskey, you could carry your writer's notebooks with you, recording little things that happen in your life. I think you are ready to do just that. Many of you will probably notice that writers pause and pay attention to details that others might just walk past. We see ducks crossing the road and instead of just thinking, "Come on, come on! I'm in a hurry!" we get out of our cars and watch the line of ducks quacking across the street. In school tomorrow, we can perhaps add this idea to our Strategies for Generating Personal Narrative Writing chart: Carry your writers' notebook with you, paying attention to details and thinking, "I could write a true story about this."

You have lots of options, then, for ways to come up with personal narrative entries tonight and evermore. When you decide which of these strategies you want to use (and you can invent a new strategy instead of using one of these) record it in a planning box on the next blank page of your notebook and get started!

TAILORING YOUR TEACHING

If your students would benefit from spending a bit more time reviewing the strategies for generating personal narratives from the first unit of study . . . you could reteach each of these strategies. Be sure to reference the earlier instruction rather than acting as if these are new strategies. For example, you could say, "Earlier this year we learned that one strategy writers use to generate ideas for writing is that we think of places in our lives that matter to us, then brainstorm small moments that we experienced in these places." Then you could proceed to retell how one child in the class did this effectively, weaving little pointers into your description of what the child did. Alternatively, you could demonstrate (role-play) the writer who begins by thinking of a place, a person, or an object, or you could cite the example of a child or a published author who used a strategy well. You won't know, for a fact, how an author went about generating the idea for a story, but you could say, "I'm pretty sure Ezra Jack Keats got the idea for this story by . . ." For example, you could suggest that *The Snowy Day* probably came from thinking first of a place—his neighborhood. The idea for *Peter's Chair*, on the other hand, could have come from noticing an object: a small child's chair.

If your students are skilled at using the strategies for generating personal narrative that you've already taught . . . you may also decide to teach children that *they* can create their own strategies for generating writing. Children are inventive, and sometimes you need only share what one child comes up with. Other times, you might guide a child in applying a strategy for generating writing. Once a child has used the strategy successfully, that child can teach the rest of the class how the strategy works. Remember to go to unlikely children who aren't usually in the academic spotlight; consider, also, going to a child who has some social power in the classroom—other children may be more apt to learn from her. You might start your minilesson like this: "Writers, I want to tell you about something smart Felix has done. He has come up with a new strategy for getting writing ideas—we will need to add it to our list. The strategy is this," and I wrote: "Listen to other people's stories and let them remind you of your own" on the Strategies for Generating Personal Narrative Writing chart. You could easily demonstrate the strategy. "I'm like Felix," you might say. "Oftentimes, when I listen to someone else's story, I think, 'That reminds me of something that happened to me,'" and show how one writer's idea acts a springboard for your own. Then you could suggest, "Right now, while we're here on the rug, let's all try Felix's strategy. Let's all let one person's ideas nudge us to think of new ideas. Will partner 1 share a story—choose one—and partner 2, will you listen really well? Then partner 2, say, 'That reminds me of a time when . . .' and tell *your own* story, a story that comes to mind just now as you listen." This minilesson could also be condensed into a mid-workshop teaching point.

COLLABORATING WITH COLLEAGUES

I know that during the first unit, I encouraged you to spend time writing together with your colleagues. If you resisted taking that plunge then, you have a new chance to do so now. My hope is that all of the talking you've been doing with your children about writing will lure you toward the idea of your own writing. I promise you, you won't regret it if you and your colleagues devote a grade-level meeting or two to your own writing workshop. My mother recently had seven hours of back surgery, and I returned to the old family manse to help her in the week after her surgery. I won't forget that first moment, after we'd carefully maneuvered things to get her into the kitchen, walker and all. She shifted onto the edge of the kitchen chair, pulled herself up by leaning on her walker, and said, "So now I'll try going to the bathroom," and she started shuffling off toward the john. As I watched my tough, all-powerful mother inch from the kitchen toward the bathroom, I thought, "Is she going to need my help?" And I thought also about how I'm not ready for a change of roles, and how odd it felt to have this woman who is the strongest force in my whole life in a vulnerable position.

Later, at my desk, I began to write the story of just that one small moment. All the techniques that we talk about become so dear and so huge when we use them to bring our moms to life on our pages, and to wrestle with what it means for us to grow old, to need each other, to face those huge life issues.

If you and your colleagues are reluctant to actually write entries alongside each other, at least use the strategies I've suggested to generate ideas you *could* write, and storytell one or two of these to a partner. That, alone, will give you a feel for this work's vibrancy and significance when our own life stories are at stake.

If you storytell together, I know that after leaving your meeting, in the privacy of your own home or your classroom, many of you will write.

So write. Write alone, without your colleagues, or write with each other. And write about your mother, your son. Write about your last times, your first times, and about the turning points that have given shape to your life. Your teaching will be utterly and totally different if you take the plunge and try all that you are asking your children to do. As you write, don't aim to write *well* so much as to write *true*. Don't aim for colorful or fancy words. Aim to put the truth of your story on the page, using the words that come first and most easily to you. You'll find that without trying to write well, you'll end up doing just that.

If you share your writing with your children, something magical will happen between you and them. I promise. Don't wait—that magic will mean more than any minilesson!

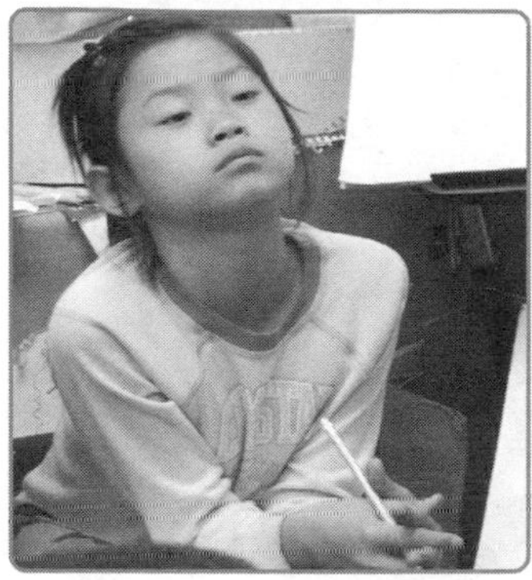

STARTING WITH STRONG FEELINGS

IN THIS SESSION, YOU WILL TEACH CHILDREN THAT WRITERS CAN GENERATE PERSONAL NARRATIVE WRITING BY CHOOSING A STRONG FEELING AND WRITING THE STORY OF ONE *PARTICULAR* TIME FEELING THAT FEELING.

GETTING READY

- Chart paper listing a strong emotion and several instances when you experienced it; second example ready to share
- Your own Small Moment story, based on a strong emotion, ready to "compose" on chart paper
- Strategies for Generating Personal Narrative Writing chart
- When to Use Paragraphs in Narrative Writing chart
- See CD-ROM for resources

When children grow as writers, *this growth is not represented simply by greater and greater mastery of the conventions of English. Growth as a writer has many facets. One is that as children work within any genre, they progress from writing in simple versions of it toward writing in more complex versions of that genre.*

When children first learn to write narratives, they usually aren't writing narratives at all. That is, as they strive for narrative writing, they usually first produce all-about or attribute entries in which they list their thoughts and ideas and feelings about a personal topic. With some instruction, young writers can shift toward writing a simple narrative, one in which the writer (the central character) does one thing after another after another. These narratives are chains of actions that often are connected only sequentially with each other. That is, there may be no cause-and-effect relationship between the events. The connection is mostly a temporal one; the main character does one thing and then the next thing: "I went to the beach, then I went to McDonald's."

As writers develop a more complex understanding of story, their writing revolves around not only a central event but also around a person who has feelings and motivations. In a personal narrative, that person is almost always the writer, presented as someone who has wants or hopes or ambitions or worries that lead the character into a sequence of actions. Because of something inside a character, one action leads to another; something happens and sets in motion a reaction.

The previous minilesson and this one both appear to provide children with strategies for generating personal narratives, but in fact, these minilessons also represent efforts to scaffold children toward telling and writing stories that are more shapely and more complex than those that involve a simple chain of events. For example, today's strategy for generating story ideas leads children to begin thinking about true stories by focusing on a time when a character (the writer) had motivations (which we refer to as strong feelings). The specific feelings I suggest—worry, hope, embarrassment, sadness—are all ones that likely mean the character will encounter trouble (as characters tend to do in stories). I haven't highlighted the role of trouble or the traditional structure of stories yet because I'm trying to scaffold children so that they suddenly find themselves telling well-structured little stories before I tell them that this is what they are doing!

MINILESSON

Starting with Strong Feelings

CONNECTION

Celebrate the way children share their entries with each other, and celebrate that the children are living like writers.

"Writers, I love the way those of you who arrived first in the meeting area opened up your notebooks and showed each other what you wrote last night. I listened in as you shared some of those entries, and I am totally impressed with the way you lived like writers last night. I remember at the start of this year, I read Naomi Nye's poem to you. She wrote, 'Maybe if we re-invent whatever our lives give us, we find poems,' (1990) and she challenged you to live in a way that lets you find poems and stories, too. But back then, some of you came in the next day saying, 'Nothing happened that I could write about last night.' Ipolito, do you remember saying to me, 'All I do is watch TV. Watch TV, feed the pigeons, watch TV; that's it.' But you ended up taking your writer's notebook up on the roof while you fed the pigeons, and you realized significant stories were hiding there, didn't you?"

"I walked down the street the other day with a photographer friend of mine, and every few steps, he'd point to something that could make a great picture. Because he is a photographer, even if he doesn't have his camera with him, he's always seeing possible photographs. And in the same way, you all live your lives seeing possible stories everywhere. Thucydides, a historian in ancient Greece, once said, 'Stories happen to those who tell them.' Because you all are writers, stories happen to you!"

Name your teaching point. In this instance, tell children that you will teach them another strategy writers use to generate powerful personal narratives.

"Today I am going to teach you one more strategy that writers use to generate personal narratives. This one is especially good for generating entries that can be turned into really powerful true stories. We know it is easier to write well if we are writing about small moments that are, for some reason, important ones. So usually, we'll want to recall times when we wanted something badly or felt something strongly. It sometimes works to think first of a strong feeling—worry or hopefulness, embarrassment or sadness. We can write a feeling on the top of a page, and then ask ourselves, 'Can I remember one *particular* time when I felt that feeling?' Then we write the story of that time."

COACHING

Even if you aren't 100% supportive of everything that your children are doing as writers, it is important, as Dr. Benjamin Spock often advised, to "catch them in the act of doing something good" and praise whatever they've done that merits support. Writing is a risky enterprise, and all of us who do it feel vulnerable. A little positive support goes a very long way toward increasing our energy for writing. So if a few children read aloud the entries they wrote at home last night, make a big fuss over how the class as a whole is changing. Do this even if it is only partly true.

It helps to liken writers to painters, photographers, runners, teachers . . . because this is a way of helping more children see this as a just-right role!

Earlier, you and the children read published personal narratives and realized that usually these are stories of small moments that convey really big feelings. Often we suggest children start with small moments that they somehow, for some reason, recall. Today's strategy suggests that writers can generate story ideas by thinking first not of the small moment but of the big feeling, going from that feeling to a tiny time when the writer remembers feeling that way. Whether you start big and go small, or start small and go big, the resulting topic will be both detailed and enormous.

TEACHING

Tell children about a time when you needed help generating ideas and reached for this strategy. Share what you did, then demonstrate to show the step-by-step sequence.

"Before you came in this morning, I was thinking I should get going on my own entries, but I wasn't sure what to write about. So I decided to use a strategy that writers use often, especially when we want our stories to have significance right from the beginning. Specifically, I wrote down a feeling I have sometimes—I just picked any feeling—and then I tried to list small moments I could remember when I had that strong feeling." I showed children that I had written the word *worry* on chart paper, and listed several times when I felt that:

Worry

The time I knew my mom had gone to see the doctor. The phone rang and I answered it, worried over what the news would be.

The time I came home, collected the mail, and saw that one envelope held a report card. "Oh no," I thought.

"So watch me while I use this strategy again—I will take another feeling, write it down, and think of small moments when I felt it." This time, I wrote *embarrassment* and started brainstorming in front of the children, recording vignettes.

Embarrassment

The time when my dress ripped and I had to go to the party with scotch tape holding my clothes together

The time when the kids told me the dress I was wearing looked old-fashioned enough to serve as a costume in the Civil War play

"After I take a minute to gather a few ideas, I select one that seems the most significant to me. I'll take this second one because I think it says something about who I am even now, and that's a sign that it is significant! First I'll make a movie in my mind of what happened, and think, 'Who said something or did something that could get this started, that would make a good lead?'"

I captured the small moment linked to worry in a few sentences that show the specific step-by-step sequence of the phone ringing and me answering it which conveys to children that the lists I'm advocating are still of small moment stories. I'm not planning to write an entry in which I summarize all that I feel when I am worried! Instead, I will recount one small episode. It's the marriage of a strong feeling and an episode (one which evolves through a sequence of actions) that will lead to a powerful narrative.

When possible, I try to use stories that are either from my childhood (because I know these are evocative for kids) or that could happen in a child's life. My mother, in fact, just went to the doctor, in my adult life, but this could easily be a child's topic as well. I deliberately try to share stories in which I admit my vulnerabilities because I know that writing is a risky, revealing thing to do; I try to create a place of safety and compassion in the room by being willing to share hard, though appropriate, parts of my own life.

Soon I was writing on a pad of chart paper, voicing each word as I scrawled it down. I wrote the text in one solid paragraph so that I could go back later to teach about paragraphing:

> "Those of you with parts in the play, stay after class to talk about your costumes," Miss Armstrong said just before the bell rang. I smiled as I packed up my books. Eliza, Becky, Richard, and I were to be the stars. We'd probably need to stay late often. We'd probably go to each other's houses on Saturdays to study our lines. I knew Eliza's house because, many times, the school bus had drawn to a stop in front of it and she and a whole group of girls had thronged off the bus. I always wondered what they did at Eliza's and now I'd find out. I pulled my chair over to where the others had already gathered. Eliza ripped a page from her spiral, and said, "It's from the 1860's, so we'll need antique costumes . . . oh!" She giggled and pointed at me. "You won't need a costume. You can just wear the dress you have on!"

The text I wrote is really too long for any minilesson and especially for this one, which is not really about writing entries but specifically about generating topics. Sometimes I know my minilesson is problematic in one way or another and I let it be anyway, as we all will at times. Nonetheless, you should know that I try to refrain from writing long entries in front of the class because the long bits of writing usually distract from the main teaching point of the minilesson.

I paused at this place in the story (not before it) because I wanted to return to the plot line before I stopped, lest my story contain too much internal thought and not enough plot. In general, I hope children write a sequence of occurrences. One advantage to the length of this particular bit of writing is that I can now use this same piece of writing to teach paragraphing. For these reasons, I rationalize the fact that I let the writing go on a bit long. But the real reason I did this is that the piece, to this day, makes my heart ache. And I'm a better teacher if I can share my heartaches with young writers.

Debrief by reiterating the sequence of actions involved in using this strategy to generate personal narrative stories.

I paused. "Do you see how I first wrote a feeling, and then listed small moments when I felt that feeling? Then I took another feeling. Soon I decided I had one that was significant and would make a good story—and I began writing the story-idea out as a real story, just like the stories we've read. I didn't worry about doing my best writing yet. Instead I kept my mind on my subject and got down to writing. (I think I'm already getting somewhere, because now I see it's really about two big feelings—hope and embarrassment.)"

I added this new strategy to our class chart.

Although I do not dwell on the fact that my story actually contains two feelings—hope and embarrassment—I believe this is worth exploring. In a story, the main character changes, so it makes sense that the character will experience more than one feeling. In our final unit of the year, you'll see that I revisit this concept. For now, I just mention it. Because I am an adult and also am someone who has been writing for decades, there will be lots of things I know and think about effective writing that I decide to not mention or mention only lightly. If I think most of the class is not ready for a concept, I don't talk much about it because then children will learn to tune me—and the concept—out.

Active Engagement

Set children up to try the strategy, reiterating the moves students will have to make by sharing one child's work.

"So let's try it. Open your notebooks to a blank page. Let's take . . . um . . . let's take hope. Write that down. Now, think back over your life to very particular times when you were hoping for something," I said, and let there be silence while children recorded the feeling in their notebooks and started brainstorming times they felt this. "You may have been hoping for a present. For recognition. For someone to come, to call, to say yes. If you write something general like, 'hoping for a bike,' think also of a very specific time when you had that feeling. Then record the actions you did: 'Looking through the Sears catalog, I stared at the bike I wanted, then tore that page out and put it on our refrigerator door.' Once you list one time, go back into your memory files and come up with another very specific time you felt that feeling."

After two minutes, I intervened. "Writers, listen to Leath's list," I said, and read her list aloud. *[Fig. III-1]*

Hope

I was hoping for an award for all my practice and hard work I have done for swimming.

I was hoping to be chosen to represent my little league baseball team.

I was hoping for my mom to finally accept me keeping a dog.

I was hoping for the best birthday party ever.

I was hoping for my mom to make the best ribs and strawberry cheesecake for my school picnic.

Hope

- I was hoping for an award for all my practice and hard work I have done for swimming
- I was hoping to be chosen to represent My Little legue baseball Legue
- I was hoping for my mom to finally exapt me keeping a dog
- I was hoping for the best birthday Party ever.
- I was hoping for my mom to make the best ribs and strawberry cheese-cake for my school picnic.

Fig. III-1 Leath's list of topics are in sentences

"Do you see how Leath used the big emotion to help her remember specific times in her life when she's felt that feeling?"

Strategies for Generating Personal Narrative Writing

- Think of a subject (or a person, place or thing) that matters to you, then list small moments you remember. Choose one to sketch and then write the accompanying story.
- Think of first times, last times, or times when you realized something important. Write about one of these moments.
- Carry your writer's notebook with you, paying attention to details and thinking, "I could write a true story about this."
- **Think of a strong feeling, then list Small Moment stories pertaining to that feeling. Choose one to sketch and then write about.**

Notice that when I'm asking children to try a strategy during this component of the minilesson, I deliberately do part of the work for them, leaving for them the work that I think they especially need to practice. Because I bypassed topic choice and gave them an "exercise topic"—hope—I know they'll spend less time hemming and hawing before they get started.

LINK

Restate today's teaching point in the context of the children's writing strategy repertoire in particular and writing life in general.

"So today, we'll continue writing entries that could grow into stories like those we read. Remember to record the strategy you will use to generate writing in your planning box before you write. I've put some examples of planning boxes on the bulletin board, if you want to see them. You already know lots of strategies for collecting Small Moment stories and *any* of these can help you today if you need help getting started." I pointed to the Strategies for Generating Personal Narrative Writing chart. "If you are having trouble getting started, I especially encourage you to try the strategy of writing an emotion on a page of your notebook, then listing moments when you felt that emotion. Then take a very significant one of those moments, and write it as a story. Today, let's write for half an hour in absolute silence, so we can do the important work of putting our true stories on the page. Then we will read our stories to our partners, and after that, we'll have a chance to write even more."

Figs. III-2 and III-3 Planning boxes

Writing and Conferring

Letting Observations Inform Your Teaching

Until now, I've talked about assessment as if it is something you do at home when sitting with a stack of your children's writing. It's crucial to pay attention to these drafts, but you can also assess during the workshop itself. You can especially assess on days like this one, when your children should have a large enough repertoire of strategies to be able to carry on with some independence. By now, most of your children should be able to choose topics for their entries, compose entries, and finish one entry and begin the next. This should enable you to take some time off from conferring and leading small groups and instead assess by observing.

When you survey the room during work time, notice, first, your students' levels of engagement. This is not a minor detail! If some children seem disengaged, resolve to study the situation so that you can address the underlying issue rather than simply nipping at their feet. Watch, also, to see what seems to derail or distract your writers. Does the layout of your classroom mean that children need to walk across the room to get another sheet of paper, and does that walk leave disengaged writers in its wake? Notice what your children do when they look up from the page. Hopefully, they spend a fair amount of time rereading. If they don't, make note of this.

It's all too easy for us to spend all our time *fixing* problems. As teachers, we very much need to study, as well as to fix, problems, and then to step back and think about solutions that are deeper and more long term than those we can imagine and execute amid the hurry of our teaching.

For example, you may find that some children always seem to be without a writing tool. Chances are good that these writers prefer to spend their time sharpening pencils or searching for pens rather than writing. One response is to provide a can full of sharpened pencils at each table, but another response is to study these writers' engagement during writing time to see what *does* draw them in. Does the threat of needing to stay in for recess if they

MID-WORKSHOP TEACHING POINT **Remembering to Paragraph** "Writers, the stories you are writing today are really powerful ones. What you're doing, which is what I did with my Miss Armstrong story as well, is you are letting your words flow quickly on the page. You are fired up over your stories, and you are writing fast and long. That is great."

"But just like we talked about in the last unit, since you and I want readers to really take in our writing, we need to chunk our writing into paragraphs. Paragraphs give readers pauses in which to envision what we've said, allowing them to take in one thing we've said before the next thing happens. In general, we use new paragraphs when—" and I pointed to a new chart I had prepared, and read from it.

When to Use Paragraphs in Narrative Writing

- new character comes along
- new event happens; new idea is introduced
- new setting
- new person speaking
- time moves forward (or backward) a lot

"But those guidelines don't tell us exactly what to do—we need to make artful decisions. Watch while I reread my Miss Armstrong story, dividing it into paragraphs, and then you'll be able to do the same with your entry."

continued on next page

"haven't had a chance to write a page" seem to spur the child on? Does the child profit from continuing to make a timeline and to rely on it as a scaffold? Would the child accomplish more on the word processor? My suggestion is to ask the writer. Say, "What could I do, or could *we* do, that would make writing time go better for you?" Ask, "What makes writing hard for you?" And when a child names a problem, try to first *understand* the problem rather than simply rushing for a short-term remedy. "Can you tell me more about that?" you might ask.

A second suggestions is this: You may have some children in your class who write at the level of many first graders. So visit a first grade and notice all the ways in which paper choice and writing tasks are designed to scaffold such a writer. Could you provide some of that support to your struggler?

When you observe your writers, expect that these observations will inform your mid-workshop teaching points. The ones I give are embedded in classrooms other than your own. You'll find that your own class is like an orchard of fruit trees, waiting to be harvested.

continued from previous page

As I reread, I said aloud my reasons for paragraphing where I did.

> "Those of you with parts in the play, stay after class to talk about your costumes," Miss Armstrong said just before the bell rang.
>
> I smiled as I packed up my books. Eliza, Becky, Richard, and I were to be the stars. We'd probably need to stay late often. We'd probably go to each other's houses on Saturdays to study our lines. I knew Eliza's house because, many times, the school bus had drawn to a stop in front of it and she and a whole group of girls had thronged off the bus. I always wondered what they did at Eliza's and now I'd find out.
>
> I pulled my chair over to where the others had already gathered. Eliza ripped a page from her spiral, and said, "It's from the 1860's, so we'll need antique costumes . . . oh!" She giggled and pointed at me. "You won't need a costume. You can just wear the dress you have on!"

"There isn't a rule that will tell me where to make that second paragraph. When Miss Armstrong talks at the start of the story, I'm already there in the room (even though the story doesn't say so), which means that when I pack up my books, I don't qualify as a new character entering the scene. I made a paragraph there because the spotlight now shifts onto me, but also because I know my story won't have lots of actions and I'm trying to get readers to realize that the little movements I make will comprise the action in this story."

"So each of you please reread what you've written, and be sure you are making artful decisions about where to paragraph!"

SHARE

Retelling Family Stories

Congratulate writers for writing personal narratives of significance. Tell children that another strategy for generating personal narrative stories of significance is to retell our family stories.

"Writers, can you gather?" I said. "You all are writing up a storm, and the stories you are telling are poignant ones. I think during our first unit of study, some of you took the phrase *small moments* literally and wrote about moments that were so tiny that they didn't really matter. You'd want to write about playing dress-up with the seaweed at the beach but to write a small moment, you'd tell just about getting a drink of water: 'I opened my mouth. I drew my mouth near the water fountain, I pushed the button, and the water spurted up.' The problem was this: You weren't necessarily telling important stories. But today, in this room, I saw many of you writing really important stories. They are still focused, but you've come to realize that when we writers say we are writing about small *moments*, we really mean small *episodes*. Small episodes that carry big meanings."

Use the fact that this unit is similar in structure to the last unit to continually point out to children the lessons they've learned and the growth they've achieved. They are the kinds of writers who get better and better—they are going places!

"Watching you work, I remembered another strategy that helps me when I want to generate entries for true stories. I think about the stories that I enjoy telling. In my family, we have stories that we tell and retell and retell. When relatives gather, we bring out the muffins, and we bring out the stories. Usually we tell trouble stories."

When you choose a family story to tell, try to choose one that will remind listeners of their own family stories. Choose something memorable and vibrant—let it put zest and humanity into the classroom as well as the yearning to tell stories.

Demonstrate telling a family story that could become a personal narrative entry.

"For example, the other day my brother, Hugh (who is a single father) told one of his many trouble stories about how he messes up, trying to be the perfect parent. Last week, the parents at his daughter's school were supposed to bring cookies to the class celebration. Hugh isn't the best cook, but the night before, he bought sugar dough, sliced it up, made cookies, and covered them with a loose piece of plastic. The next day he went to work but left early, hurried home, grabbed the little plate of cookies, and raced into the classroom in time to join all the mothers at the celebration. Just as the last child was performing, Hugh looked over to the counter where his cookies sat. He noticed the chocolate chips on his cookies . . . and then thought to himself, "Wait. I didn't make chocolate chip cookies! I made sugar cookies!" The performance was just

Notice that I tell this story in a step-by-step fashion, using all that I know about personal narrative writing. I could have summarized instead of storytold. I could have written, "Last week Hugh made cookies for Eliza's school event, but he realize after he'd brought them into the class they were covered with ants." Instead, I storytold, hoping that by doing so I could let children experience the event . . . and learn from the model.

ending. As the children thronged toward the food, Hugh reached his arm to the buffet table, pulled out his plate of cookies, and looked down to see that his contribution was teeming with ants. He whisked the plate away, breathing a sigh of relief to have somehow avoided yet another crisis in his life as a single father."

Set children up to share their own family stories. Add this strategy to the chart.

"I bet some of you have stories that are told and retold in *your* families, and I bet that your stories, like mine, might be trouble stories about times when you narrowly escaped mess-ups. If you are thinking of a story that is told a lot in your family, give me a thumbs up," I said. Since five children had stories, I created informal storytelling groups and set these children up to captivate their audiences. After a few minutes, I interceded. "Writers, the stories you are telling now, and any of the family stories that you tell and retell, can be ones you record in your notebooks. (When you do record them, remember to give readers space to think by writing in paragraphs.) Let's add this to our chart," I said.

True story ideas

- when I almost died in the ocean
- When my Mom and my Dad got deforst
- when my sister almost ranaway
- The first time I realized my mom couldn't afford what I wanted
- The last time I saw my Mom and Dad together
- The first time I got a dog
- One time when my sister recorded me sleeping with my mom and dad
- One time I got lost in the air port

Fig. III-4 Rafael's list of topics

- Meeting Takeshi in the airplane
- in airplane play gobble snake with the Takeshi
- first time I got a basket ball in the hoop
- first time I went on a go kart
- first time I went on the double loop roller coaster.
-

I was shivering in the long line to the double loop roller coaster. "Are you sure about this," I asked my sister in a worry voice. My sister said "If your scared you don't have to go on." But I really wanted to go on but I was a little scared to go on it by hearing the voicese of the people scream. But while I was thinking if I should go

Fig. III-5 Takuma shifts from listing to composing

In my family, we do actually refer to these as trouble stories. I write about the importance of sharing our trouble stories in my book for parents, Raising Lifelong Learners: A Parent's Guide.

Strategies for Generating Personal Narrative Writing

- Think of a subject (or a person, place or thing) that matters to you, then list small moments you remember. Choose one to sketch and then write the accompanying story.
- Think of first times, last times, or times when you realized something important. Write about one of these moments.
- Carry your writer's notebook with you, paying attention to details and thinking, "I could write a true story about this."
- Think of a strong feeling, then list Small Moment stories pertaining to that feeling. Choose one to sketch and then write about.
- **Think of the stories that your family tells and retells to each other. Write about one of those.**
- Keep an ongoing list of story ideas in your writer's notebook.

HOMEWORK ***Making and Using Topic Lists*** Writers, I love the feeling that your minds are bursting with stories, because this means that during writing time, you aren't just *thinking up* stories, you are *selecting* the stories that you feel will especially work. Just to make sure you are brimming with possible stories, would you take some time tonight to gather a list of possible stories on a special page of your writer's notebook? That way, if you ever finish an entry and, for a moment, can't think of something to write about, you can always also draw from your very own well. Here are some more ideas that can help you find your own stories.

- Take a topic from your life: your hair, your glasses, your hobby, a pet, a relative, one part of school, your home. Make a timeline of things that have happened connected to that one topic. Choose one dot from one timeline, and write that story.
- Start free-writing a list, using a recurring phrase. It could be *I remember,* but be sure to remember very specific, sensory moments: "I remember the sound of the last bit of milk being sucked from my school milk cartoon." "I remember standing at the edge of the mountain stream up to my ankles in freezing water." "I remember putting my head inside my sleeping bag and trying to warm myself up with my breath."
- Alternatively, you could start with a more specific phrase such as "At my cousins, I . . . " or "Sleep-overs mean . . . " and then list different ways to complete it. After creating a list, reread what you have written, circle one item, and then begin to write this as a story.

"Writers, collect your lists in your writers' notebooks, and from this day forward, you will always have more possible ideas than you need." I added this to our chart.

TAILORING YOUR TEACHING

If you notice that many of your students' notebook entries seem uninspired, lacking significance or power . . . you might want to teach them to follow the strategy that poet Georgia Heard once heard when she was learning to draw. Her instructor suggested that she fix her eyes on a subject—say, a tree—and draw fast and furiously, never once glancing away from the subject. The drawings that result often contain a life force that is remarkable. You can teach the students to apply the same kind of focus to the stories they are working on. You'll suggest that a life force, or power, can emerge in our writing when we keep our eyes (and minds) intently on the mental movie of our memories as we write them.

Assessment

For now, look over your students' writing with an eye toward the essentials of effective personal narratives. Above all, make sure that they are letting their stories develop on paper in a step-by-step fashion. You don't want to see them summarizing or swiping at or commenting on events. Instead, you want to sense that each writer is reliving an event as he or she writes. Instead of writing, "I went to the ball game and it was fun," you hope the child writes, "I paid for my ticket and walked into the stadium. I found my seat and sat down."

Then, too, check to make sure the kids are writing about fairly focused events. If they are writing about a whole day or the whole afternoon, the writing will sometimes feel like a list of generalizations: "I went on the swings, then I went on the slide. Then I went for lunch." Of course, the child who zooms in to tell the story of hurting herself on the monkey bars will still need a set up (presumably approaching the monkey bars) and a resolution (perhaps talking or thinking about the monkey bars after the incident is over). That is, out of a commitment to focus, see that children don't take the expression "small moments" too literally!

Look, also, at the volume of your students' writing and at the typical length of their entries. For grades three through five, you should expect that most kids will write entries that are about a page long, and soon most of them should be able to write at least a page a day in school (and eventually, more than that) and an equal amount at home. If your kids' entries tend to be only half a page long, it will be hard for them to write well because good writing requires detail, dialogue, development—and all of these require some breathing space on the page. So if their entries are brief, teach toward the goal of faster writing and more stamina. And be sure you are giving enough time for actual writing during writing workshop!

When I study Marco's writing, *[Fig. III-6]* it seems to me that he's written two drafts here about lunch in the park, and has tried to write the second version of the story in a more step-by step, stretched-out manner. The resulting story is not yet an especially effective one, but I still do notice that instruction has influenced Marco. Whereas his first draft began with the crucial moment—the picnic lunch where there is no food for him—in the next draft, Marco attempts to stretch out the moment. He continues his narrative writing in a step-by-step fashion. He even includes direct dialogue—another example that instruction has affected him. Although the "story" is really a chain of events, without the elements that make for a story, it is organized sequentially in a step-by-step fashion and some details are included.

When I went to central park with my cousin and we played baseball. First we all ate but me because by mistake I told my mom that I wasnt hungry so she didnt bring me enything. Then I got really really hungry but when I started to play baseball I didnt care about my hungernis

I steped in my godmothers car with my sister and my cousin. Then we went to pick up my mom so we can go to central park. After we picked up my mom we drove off to central park. But then we hade to wait outside because my godmother went to podke her car. So then we waited and waited and waited until finally my mom said "lets go setting up the chairs wail we wait for her." Then after that my godmother finally came so then we all started to eat but me. Because when we were picking up my mom from her house by mistake I told my mom I wasnt hungry so she didnt bring me enything. But then when I started playing baseballs with my cousin I didn't really care about my hungernis.

Fig. III-6 Marco's entry

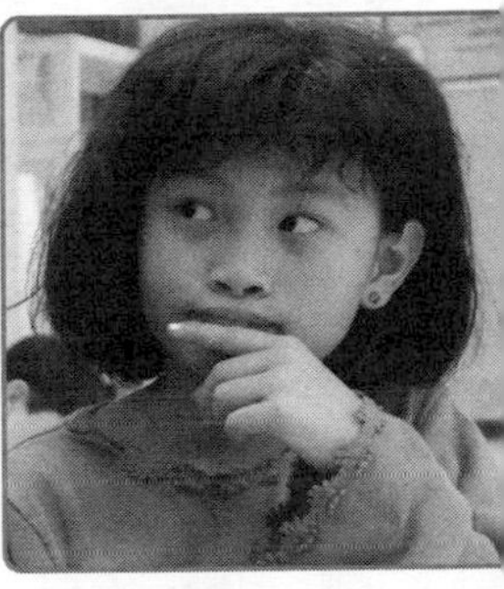

Next, I study Adam's writing. *[Fig. III-7]* Like Marco, Adam has written an entry which shows that he understands that narratives are organized chronologically by time, with one event leading to the next and the next. Neither writer is simply compiling all that he knows that pertains to the topic on hand. Instead, both children have tried to narrow in on an event, and to recreate that event sequentially on the page. Early stories are often written as chains of events rather than as an integrated, cohesive story, and both of these boys have written narratives that are chains of events. One thing happens, then the next, then the next.

In time, Adam will learn to think, "Who is the main character here? What is he—(in this case, what am I)—really wanting? What gets in the way? What's the main event of the story? How is that one event developed?"

Pay attention to Adam's entry. His notebook in the autumn of the year was filled with entries like this one. At the end of the final book in this series, you'll follow Adam's process as he writes a heartbreaking and poignant story about his brother's departure for college. It will be important for you to remember, when you read his final piece, what his writing was like at the start of the year.

When my son Miles was three, he planted popcorn in his sandbox. A month later, tiny lime-green tufts of grass poked through the sand in his sandbox. Then we moved. As Miles and I walked through the old house one last time, he stood beside his sandbox, tears welling. "But I'll never see it grow into a cornfield," he cried. Teaching is like that. We plant seeds, we see the lime-green tufts poke through the soil . . . and we rarely have the chance to see our plans grow into a cornfield. When teaching writing, however, the growth is palpable and dramatic.

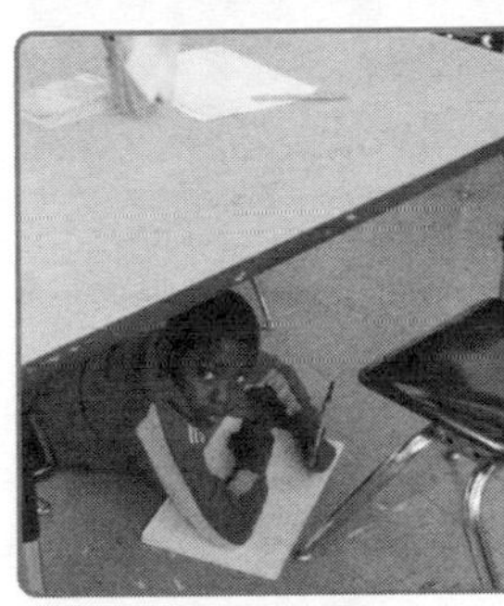

First we all climbing into the car
to go to Degenirro's a pizza
Parlor. When we got there
we went into the bathroom
to wash our hands. When we
finished washing our hands
we all picked out a bottle
of Soda. Then we sat down
at a table and talked.
It was my friend who used
to live in tenafly's birthday
So he had alot of us over
to his house. When we got
the pizza pie we were
all hungry we each ate
about two pieces of pizza.
All of us left then
we filed back into
the cars and we drove
to an ice cream parlor
called coldstone. we got to
pick an ice cream and
a couple of toppins to
mix in. It was really good.

Fig. III-7 Adam's entry

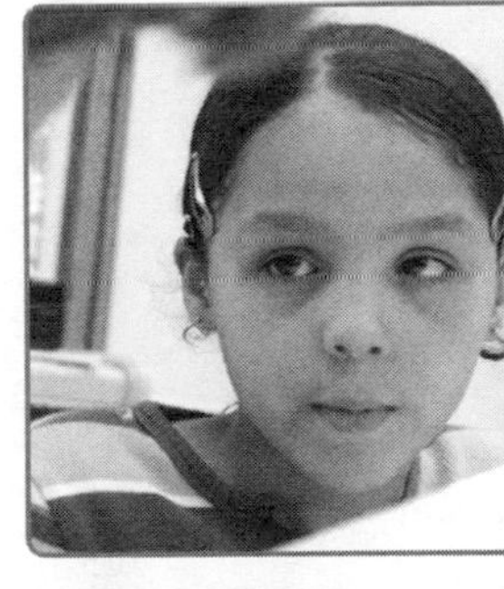

SESSION IV

YESTERDAY'S REVISIONS BECOME TODAY'S STANDARD PRACTICE

IN THIS SESSION, YOU WILL GUIDE STUDENTS TO SET GOALS FOR LIFTING THE QUALITY OF THEIR NARRATIVE ENTRIES BY USING ALL THAT THEY'VE LEARNED SO FAR ABOUT WRITING WELL.

GETTING READY

- Qualities of Good Personal Narrative Writing chart from first unit
- Student example demonstrating an item from that chart
- When to Use Paragraphs in Narrative Writing chart from previous session
- Student example that demonstrates focusing on the subject and writing fast and long, using true, exact details
- Student example that demonstrates paying attention to the details of life
- Overhead projector and markers
- See CD-ROM for resources

Those of us who teach writing often say *that we are helping children cycle through the writing process. And it is true that throughout a year and across children's school years, we give them the time and support to cycle again and again through the process of rehearsal, drafting, revising, and editing.*

But when we teach writing, our aim is actually not just for children to cycle through the writing process; our aim is for children to spiral through that process. With each new cycle, we hope that the level of work our children do increases. And this happens not just because they accumulate knowledge and experience. Children's work becomes progressively more sophisticated in part because we explicitly teach them to incorporate yesterday's lessons into today's work.

By this time in the year, you'll be very aware that our teaching accumulates, with one day's minilesson often building on previous minilessons, and with one unit of study building on previous units. The cumulative nature of this curriculum will be very clear to you—but it is probably less clear to your children.

Today, your goal will be to remind children that as they draft entries in this new unit of study, they need to draw upon all they've learned in the previous unit. If a child's final draft from the last unit was written in paragraphs, then you'll wonder why her early drafts in this unit are not written similarly. If she stretched out the heart of her story during revision in the first unit, you'll suggest that this time, she can do that work as she drafts.

In this way, you'll give children a spiraling process for ratcheting up the level of their writing work.

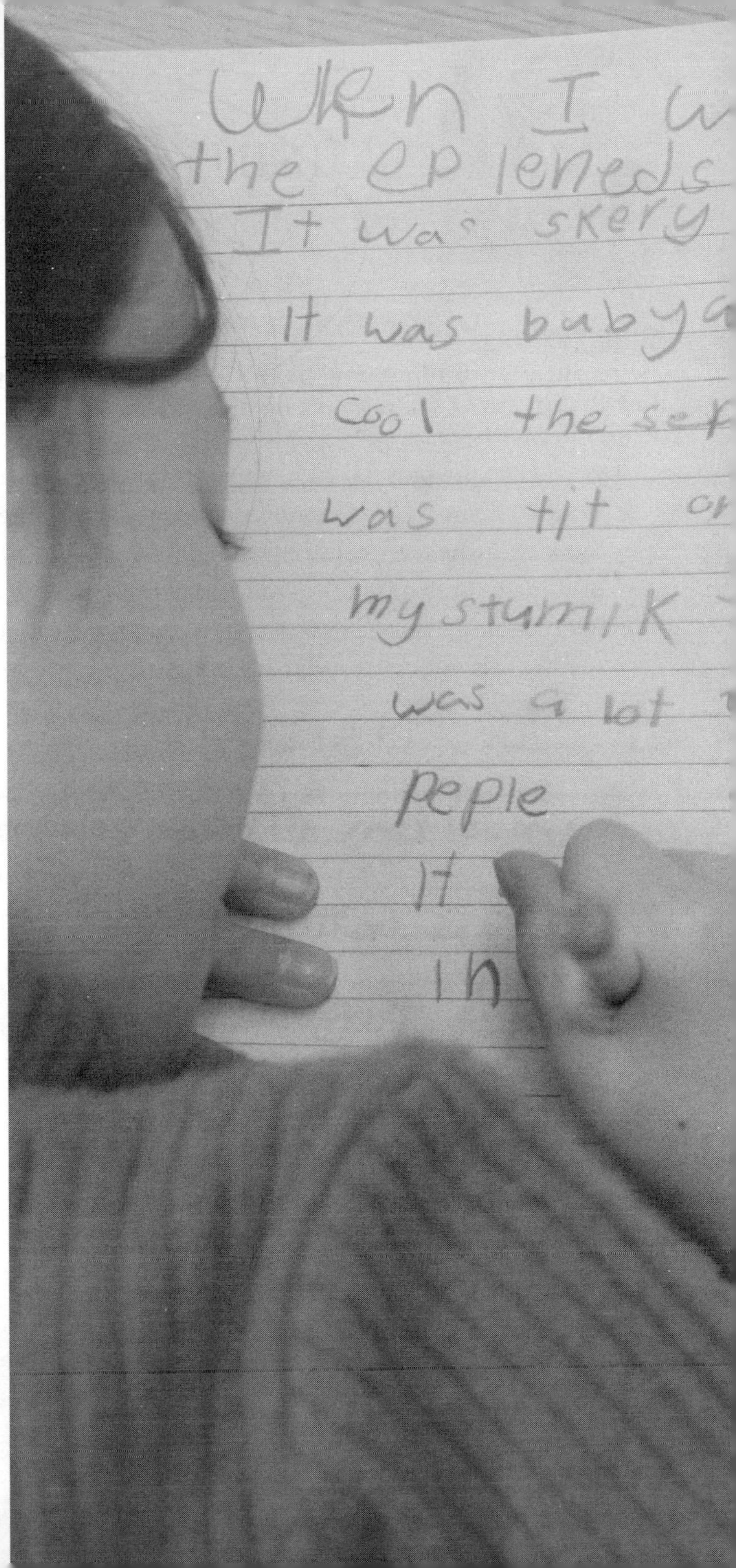

Minilesson

Yesterday's Revisions Become Today's Standard Practice

Connection

Point out that children now have a repertoire of strategies for generating writing ideas, but that many of them aren't needing these strategies as they now come to school brimming with ideas.

"Over the past few days, you've learned lots of strategies for generating ideas for true stories. I know you can continue to use those strategies—and others that you learned earlier this year—whenever you are unsure of a topic for writing. I also know that more and more of you are coming into the writing workshop already brimming with ideas for your writing—and that often you don't need a strategy to jump-start your writing. Your life itself sparks your writing . . . and that's true for lots of writers."

Name your teaching point. Specifically, tell children that what they once did through revision and editing can now become part of planning and drafting.

"Today, instead of helping you think about *what* to write, I want to help you think about *how* to write. And specifically, I want to teach you this. Everything that you did to revise and edit your last piece of writing can now move forward in your writing process, becoming part of what you do naturally as you write an entry or a first draft. What was at one time a revision and editing strategy ends up becoming part of planning and drafting."

Coaching

It is important for you and your children to keep in mind that the strategies they've learned for generating writing are all tools a writer can call upon when needed. But the truth is that for many, many writers, the challenge is never to come up with ideas for writing . . . the challenge is only to choose between all the possibilities. So expect to only devote a couple of days in any unit to teaching strategies for generating writing, and be ready to shift towards teaching strategies for writing more effectively.

Over and over you will notice that I use parallel construction. "Today, instead of helping you think about what to write, I want to help you think about how to write." I do this because minilessons are an oral genre. Effective speakers often use repetition and parallel construction. Think of Martin Luther King's "I have a dream" speech or John F. Kennedy's famous words from his inaugural address: "Ask not what your country can do for you; ask what you can do for your country." This parallel construction makes what we say easier to remember and therefore easier to take to heart.

TEACHING

Show children how one child studied the first paragraphs of her first publication, gleaning from it lessons she could incorporate into upcoming drafts.

"Remember that earlier we talked about the importance of studying authors and the texts they write? Well yesterday, Sophie studied a really important author. She studied herself."

"She went in the hall to the bulletin board and took off the tacks holding her published story on the wall. And she read her story over, reminding herself of all that she already learned as a writer."

"Let me show you how she did this," I said. "Sophie got some paper, and as she read her last publication, she paused whenever she reached something which she'd done on purpose, and she jotted down the strategy she'd used, the goal she'd reached towards."

"So she read this." I showed her text using the overhead projector: *[Fig. IV-1]*

> Tic- toc, tick toc. I was sitting anxiously in my seat. I was wondering when Mrs. C was going to line us up to go home? I was looking at the clock every 5 seconds to see if it was 3:00 yet. I knew that my grandma was picking me up from school that day. I hoped that when my grandma picked me up, we could get ice cream together. I couldn't wait for her to come to get me.

"After reading her first paragraphs, Sophie made this list." I revealed a copy of it on chart paper:

- Indent! Write in paragraphs
- Zoom in on a small moment
- Start at the beginning
- Start with dialogue or small action
- Follow the timeline step by step
- Tell what I was thinking

Research has shown that we need to explicitly teach toward transference. That is, we can teach all the strategies and qualities of good writing that we can imagine, but none of this amounts to a hill of beans unless we also teach children to draw on what we have taught when they are actually writing on their own.

The idea that children are expected to make a planning box before they begin an entry, and to record in that box whatever they intend to do, might seem an unnecessary step, but it is more significant than many people realize. If children learn to pause before writing, reflect on their options, review what they have been taught, and make a conscious decision about how they'll proceed, it is much more likely that they will access what they've been taught long enough for these strategies and qualities to become habitual.

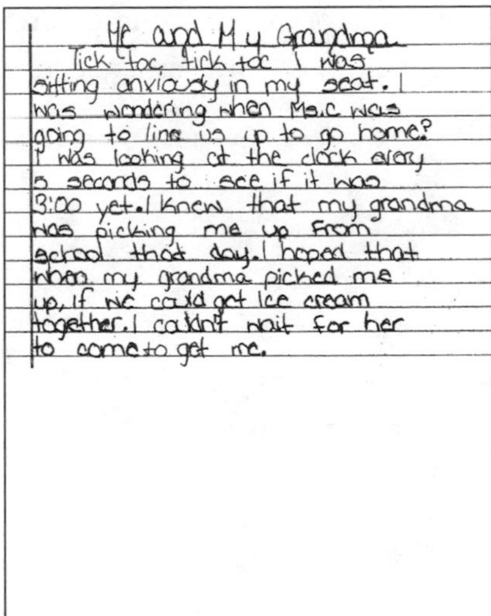

Me and My Grandma

Tick toc, tick toc I was sitting anxiously in my seat. I was wondering when Ms. C was going to line us up to go home? I was looking at the clock every 5 seconds to see if it was 3:00 yet. I knew that my grandma was picking me up from school that day. I hoped that when my grandma picked me up, if we could get ice cream together. I couldn't wait for her to come to get me.

Fig. IV-1 Sophie's entry

Active Engagement

Recruit children to help the child study the next sections of her publication, gleaning more lessons. Then ask them to help the child apply these to her new entries.

"Then she read on. As I read aloud the next two paragraphs in Sophie's story, be thinking about other things that she's learned to do, things that she also added to her list":

> I looked at the clock it was 5 to 3:00. I heard somebody call my name "Sophie!" Joy ran through my body. I heard my grandmas voice a smile shot on my face. I got my bookbag and walked out the door. She looked so beautiful. When I looked into her eyes I remembered all the good times we have together and I knew that we were going to have a great time together today.
>
> I went to give her a hug and when I got there I wrapped my arms around her. I felt so happy to be with her. When I hugged her I squeezed her as tight as I could. She squeezed me back. When I hugged her I had a feeling it felt like I was just safe with her. "Mimi, thank you for picking me up from school today." "No problem Sophie."

"Tell each other things that Sophie has learned to do, as evidenced in her first publication," I said, and the room erupted into partner conversations. After a minute, I elicited a few suggestions from children and added to the list:

- Indent! Write in paragraphs
- Zoom in on a small moment
- Start at the beginning
- Start with dialogue or small action
- Follow the timeline step by step
- Tell what I was thinking
- Show not tell feelings
- Write with precise details

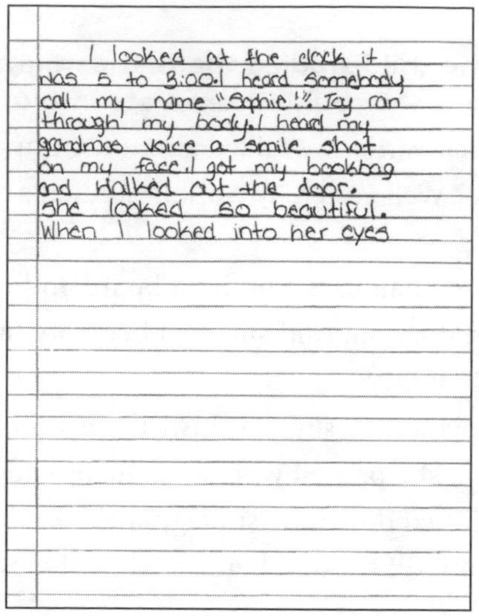

I looked at the clock it was 5 to 3:00. I heard somebody call my name "Sophie!". Joy ran through my body. I heard my grandmas voice a smile shot on my face. I got my bookbag and walked out the door. She looked so beautiful. When I looked into her eyes

Fig. IV-2 Children studied the first page of Sophie's story booklet in order to practice deducing what she's learned to do.

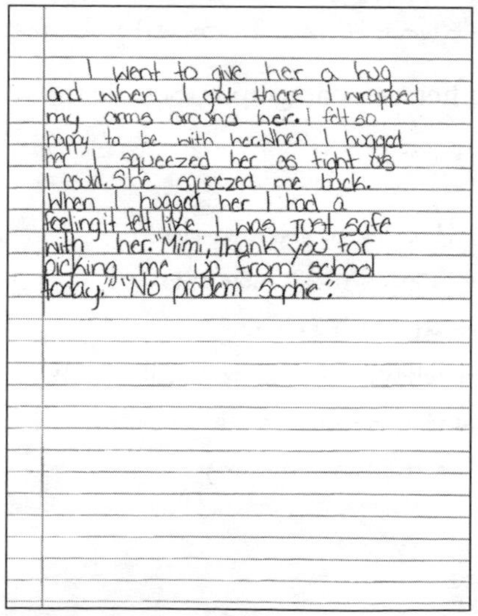

I went to give her a hug and when I got there I wrapped my arms around her. I felt so happy to be with her. When I hugged her I squeezed her as tight as I could. She squeezed me back. When I hugged her I had a feeling it felt like I was just safe with her. "Mimi, Thank you for picking me up from school today." "No problem Sophie."

Fig. IV-3 Children also studied the next page of Sophie's narrative from the first unit.

"Writers, eyes on me. I need to tell you what Sophie did next because it is hugely important. She opened up her writer's notebook to an entry she'd just recently written and she did this—watch!" *[Fig. IV-4]* (I looked back and forth, slowly, between the publication and the entry, the publication and the entry.) Then I added, "After a few minutes, she said, 'I can do better,' and she began a new draft of her Chuck E. Cheese entry. Let me show you the start of it—that's as far as she's gotten—and will you check and see whether Sophie is incorporating many of the things she learned in our first unit of study into this entry? *[Fig. IV-5]* Is she writing in paragraphs? Does she seem to zoom in on a small moment or two? Start with action or dialogue? What else do you notice?"

In this session, you'll notice that during the active engagement children practice what I've taught using what I call "an exercise text." That is, I set them up so they can try what I'm suggesting writers do, trying this on a text other than their own. Later they will transfer and apply this with some independence to their own text during the writing workshop. When I teach classes full of reluctant and struggling writers, I alter these minilessons so that children do the work on their own texts instead of on exercise texts, as this makes it easier (and more likely) that they'll do the work at all.

Link

Rename your teaching point: Writers can draw from all we've learned from past writing experiences and apply those lessons early in the process of writing future texts.

"Writers," I said, waiting for the children's attention. "I often end my minilessons saying, 'From this day forward, for the rest of your life, remember that writers . . .' and you know this is an important task—to remember the lessons you've learned so that you can grow stronger and more skilled as writers. But I want to tell you that becoming stronger and more skilled as a writer takes more than just remembering—it takes action. You have to take what you've learned and do it, use it, again and again until it's easy enough for you that you can learn something even newer and even more challenging. So go ahead, make some plans and take some action!"

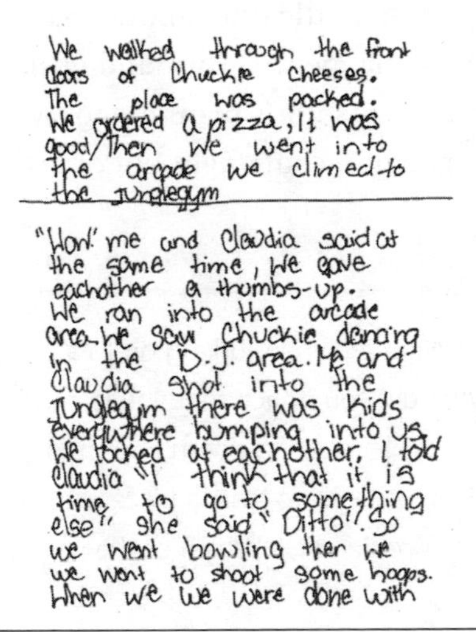
We walked through the front doors of Chuckie cheeses. The place was packed. We ordered a pizza, It was good/Then we went into the arcade we climed to the Junglegym

"Wow!" me and Claudia said at the same time, We gave eachother a thumbs-up. We ran into the arcade area. We saw Chuckie danaing in the D.J. area. Me and Claudia shot into the Junglegym there was kids everywhere bumping into us. We looked at eachother, I told Claudia "I think that it is time to go to something else" she said "Ditto!". So we went bowling ther we we went to shoot some hoops. When we we were done with

Fig. IV-4 Sophie contrasted her first publication with this entry and resolved to improve her entries

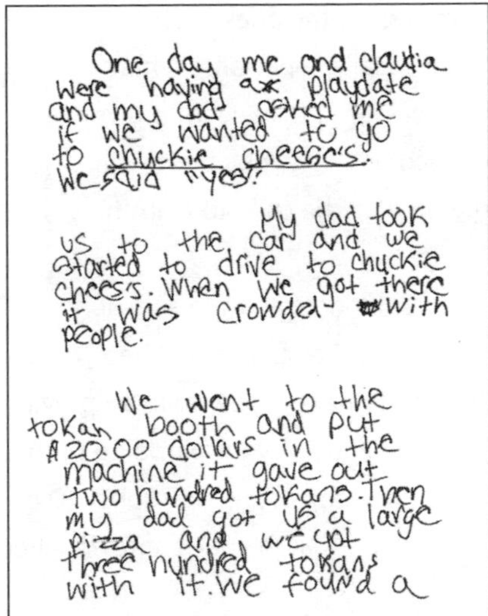
One day me and claudia were having a playdate and my dad asked me if we wanted to go to chuckie cheese's. We said "yes"!

My dad took us to the car and we started to drive to chuckie chees's. When we got there it was crowded with people.

We went to the tokan booth and put $20.00 dollars in the machine it gave out two hundred tokans. Then my dad got us a large pizza and we got three hundred tokans with it. We found a

Fig. IV-5 Sophie lifted the level of her entry, incorporating lessons from Unit One.

Writing and Conferring

Participating in a Writing Conference

Your minilesson today set children up so they should be able to talk to you in conferences about what they are trying to do as writers. After you ask, "What are you working on as a writer?" and follow up with, "Can you show me where you've done that?" you'll want to consider how effectively you think the child has done the work he or she set out to do. You'll want to know the child's assessment as well. "How are you feeling about what you've done?" you can ask. Plan in advance to ask the child to elaborate on any generalizations. "What do you mean when you say you feel okay about it?" you might ask. "What do you like that you've done? What don't you like?"

When children have trouble with your questions, try to ascertain if the trouble is the way you have worded the question or if the child has simply learned that whenever he or she resists, you'll go away. Don't let a child shrug off your questions; instead, try rephrasing the question. Say, "The question I am asking you is really important. What's making it hard for you to answer?" You may need to give the child a few minutes to reread and to think about what you've just asked, then come back to the child to learn his or her thoughts.

You may need to help children understand the sort of answers you imagine them providing. For example, when you ask a child, "What are you working on as a writer?" if the child doesn't seem to have a clue, follow up by asking, "What did you notice that you learned in our first unit of study? What did you see yourself doing in that publication?" If the child doesn't seem to have an answer, you could ask more supportive questions. "Did you, like Sophie, learn to start a piece with small actions or dialogue? Did you do that in your entries?" Alternatively, you could ask, "Which of the

MID-WORKSHOP TEACHING POINT **_Paragraphing_** "Class, I want to share with you what Jake learned when he looked back at his last publication. He realized he'd learned to write in paragraphs and decided that now as he writes his entries, he wants to keep in mind that paragraphing matters," I said and gestured to the When to Use Paragraphs in Narrative Writing chart from the previous session. "It's not the paragraphs alone that Jake cares about—he knows he tends to write one sentence describing the first thing that happened in his narrative sequence, and then one sentence describing the next thing, so he's written in his planning box that he's trying to write a whole paragraph (even if it's just a little one) about each new event in his story, so that he really gets out more of what happened. This kind of elaboration is something Jake did late in the game for his last piece, so he's planning to try it sooner in this piece. One of these days, his writing is going to come right out of his brain in full paragraphs!"

continued on next page

qualities on our list [point to it] are you thinking you want to work towards in your next entry?" If the child isn't sure, use the child's work to clue you in, and take a guess.

Children will probably name goals but be unclear about the strategies they could use to achieve those goals. If a child says he's working on writing it so that readers can picture the story, support this intention. "That is such a huge goal!" you could say. If the child is less clear how he is achieving that goal, you could show him how you go back and make a movie in your mind of what happened, drawing on telling details from that movie. "If I was to write about this writing class," you might begin, and then proceed to show how you'd go about starting your entry.

"So why don't you try this when you write your new entry," you could say, and coach the child to recall some part of the episode and to articulate a detail. "You can add that to your entry, just like I added details to my story about how Eliza teased me about my out-of-fashion dress," you might say.

If in another conference, a child tells you she is trying to paragraph, ask if Cisneros has helped her. Show her that once you decided to work on paragraphing your story, you first reread a mentor text, attending only to the paragraphing. Don't go into all the reasons you found—one is enough for a start, but slyly choose one that you know will pay off for the child's own writing. Remember, if every gesture to paragraph the child makes is not necessarily well informed, it still is important if the child is now thinking in paragraphs.

Make sure that you not only support the child in attaining her writing goal, but also support her in drawing on all she knows to reach her goal.

continued from previous page

Then I said, "To figure out where his paragraphs should go, Jake did something I'd like to teach you to do."

"Choose any page of a book and sort of squint your eyes so you can't exactly see the print. Instead of the print you might see gray blocks that get longer and longer as they move down the page—or shorter and shorter. It's kind of like standing on a rooftop and looking down at the streets and blocks below. They look all organized. You can't see any little details like curtains on the windows, or the bike on the fire escape, but you might notice a kind of pattern in the sizes of the paragraphs. Sometimes just the look of the paragraphs—the bunches of words on the page, the white spaces in between them—helps to shape the story the way the author wants it. *Everything* counts in writing! Now read the page for real and notice how the paragraphs organize and separate the parts of the story the way the streets organize and separate the houses and buildings and city blocks. You can try with your own entries, too."

SHARE

Using Precise, Engaging Details

Demonstrate for children studying a mentor author's work to learn ways to achieve a writing goal.

"Writers, I love the plans that you gave yourselves today. I have one hint that can help you do whatever you aspire to do. This is the hint: Whatever writing goal you take on for yourself, a mentor text can usually give you examples of ways to get there! Marco's goal is to keep his eyes glued onto what really happened, mentally acting it out, writing with exact, true details that reveal what the scene was really all about."

I pointed to the copy of "Eleven" written on chart paper. "Marco can look at 'Eleven' and see the ways Sandra Cisneros goes about writing with true, exact details. Cisneros' mind was probably fixed on Rachel sitting next to that sweater. In Cisneros' mind, she could see Rachel sitting herself in that hard little school chair. Cisneros probably envisioned exactly how the scene went. She probably thought about what Rachel noticed when she looked at that red mound on the corner of her desk. Cisneros' mind was fixed on Rachel and how she would act, and Cisneros aimed to write details that would tell the truth."

> I open my eyes, the red sweater's still sitting there like a big red mountain. I move the red sweater to the corner of my desk with my ruler. I move my pencil and books and eraser as far from it as possible. I even move my chair a little to the right. Not mine, not mine, not mine. (Cisneros 1991, p. 8)

"Studying 'Eleven' can give Marco inspiration about how he, too, can write with true, exact details."

"Marco already knew that in his next entry, he would be writing about a *first time*, and specifically about the first time he took his puppy to obedience class and put him in a 'sit-stay' line with all the other dogs. But after he looked back at this chart, Marco decided that when he wrote his entry, he was going to work especially hard to keep his eyes on the sit-stay event and to include true, exact details, trying to see and hear and recreate what happened. He said, 'When I tried that before, it felt as if I was *acting the story out* in my head as I wrote and that really worked for me.' Marco wrote those plans in his planning box. This strategy started out as a class lesson, but it is becoming a part of who Marco chooses to be as a writer!"

HOMEWORK *Living Like Writers, Paying Attention to the Details of Our Lives*

Writers, teachers often describe the writing process by saying writers first rehearse for writing (making leads and timelines and plans), then draft, then revise, and then edit and publish their writing.

But when *writers* describe their writing process, we don't always start by talking about desk work—about entries, leads, or timelines. Instead, writers start with life work. Remember how Cynthia Rylant talked about going fishing as an artist, walking the aisles of Woolworth's as an artist, and having relatives over for supper as an artist?

She *could* have said, "Writing is playing dodge ball as a writer, watching a rainstorm blow in as a writer, going to Starbucks as a writer." Zora did just that. She went to Starbucks *as a writer*, and she saw more, heard more, felt more because of that. You might think, "What's there to see, to notice, at Starbucks?" But listen to this entry Zora wrote last night and continued today: *[Figs. IV-6 and IV-7]*

Trips to Starbucks

Whenever my family goes to Starbucks I sit in the same chair. It's a ragged old chair in the corner where the men play chess. Its arms are shagged with gold cloth and patches of red and silver. Its legs are chipped and have the smell, old, stained in. There is dust on top of the chair and if you sit in it and pull this long pole back, you fly back also. When you sit in that chair you feel as if you are gliding on air. Like your worries about the big multiplication test that you know you are having on Monday because your teacher forgot to give it to you on Friday vanishes in thin air. That smell of coffee beans grinding is just what you need on that Saturday when you're sitting in that same old ragged chair with gold cloth and patches of red and silver, with chipped legs, and the smell of old stained in.

When your mom gets that Double café mocha or whatever. With the hazelnut and orange extract. And the half low fat soymilk with the whip cream that has no flavor, cappuccino (she's on a diet, you know) with a couple of sweet and low sugars it will make it taste just like a milkshake with coffee ice cream. You ask your

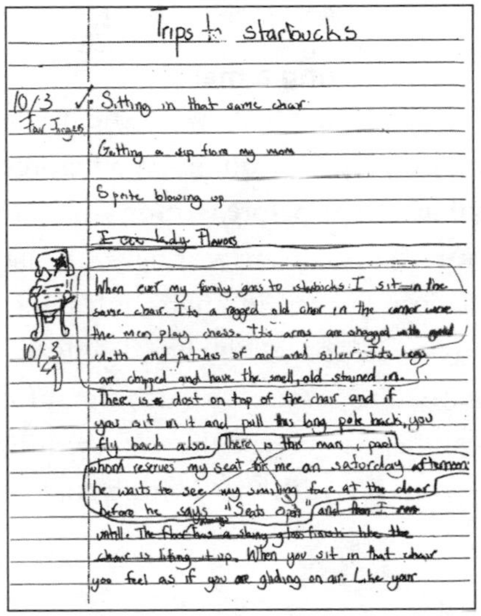

Fig. IV-6 Zora

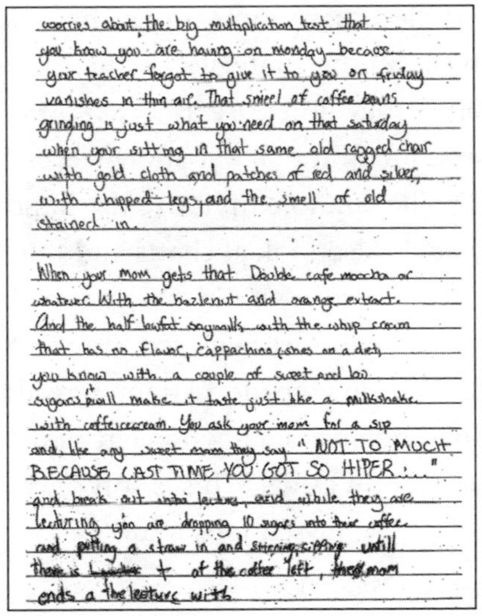

Fig. IV-7 Zora

mom for a sip and like any sweet mom they say "NOT TOO MUCH BECAUSE LAST TIME YOU GOT SO HYPER . . ." and break out into lecture, and while they are lecturing you are dropping 10 sugars into their coffee and putting a straw in and sipping, sipping until there is 1/4 of the coffee left, then mom ends the lecture with ...

Do you see that Zora is applying what she has learned about being a writer to the earliest, earliest, earliest parts of writing, even before it gets near a notebook? Zora is doing the part of writing that comes before writing—noticing the world! And she's noticing in true, exact details, just like you were writing your first drafts using true, exact details. She has taken this goal back even farther into herself. It's like she put a planning box in the corner of her mind, not just on her page! She has details here that she could only remember if she tried to catch them, tried as a writer to catch them for writing down later. And that's what she did! Try that—put a goal, maybe the same writing goal as Zora, in a planning box in your mind and live your life with that writing goal.

TAILORING YOUR TEACHING

If your students need support to try the new strategies they're learning . . . you can suggest they use the class charts almost like checklists as they reread their entries. As they reread, they can check off the strategies on the charts that they use often, so that it's easy to see which strategies they don't use as much. After rereading a few entries, they can make a plan to use some of the newer strategies either as they revise an older entry or begin a new one. You'll want to emphasize the importance of trying new strategies by saying something like, "I also look at charts and think about strategies that I never got a chance to try, that I might try now." You could look back at the chart and say, for example, "I never reread old entries and let them remind me of new stories. I have a feeling that would work for me. So I am going to plan on rereading all the entries I have collected so far, letting them jog other memories. I'll write 'reread old entries' in a planning box on the next page." You might add, in an aside, "This is sort of cool because I really am acting like I'm my own job captain, giving myself jobs to do!"

Strategies for Learning from Previous Writing

- Reread old charts and think about strategies that have already worked for us.
- Reread old charts and think about strategies we have yet to try that might work.
- Give ourselves self-assignments, writing things we plan to do in our notebooks.
- Look back over old writing, noticing what we did in revision that we might want to do earlier.
- Look back over old writing, noticing what made our writing strong that we want to remember to do, and noticing what got us into trouble that we want to avoid.

MECHANICS

In the previous unit, I suggested you write a letter to parents letting them know that you care about their children's control of the conventions of written language. Before long, it will be time for parent-teacher conferences, and you can be sure that some parents will bring up this topic. The fact that those conferences are coming soon should nudge you, then, to do some work you need to do in any case.

So do this: In your mind, sort your children into clusters based only on their issues around the conventions of written language. Perhaps you'll group children like this:

1. Children in the first group are so swamped with problems that you hardly know where to begin. They have problems with spelling, handwriting, punctuation, stamina, syntax, making sense, length—the works.
2. Children in the next group write quickly and generally write with 90% accuracy (although at first you thought they were worse because their errors stand out). These children make all the common mistakes that many kids do: mixing up *to*, *too*, and *two*, forgetting to double consonants when they add endings, and so forth.
3. These children are English language learners who are literate in Spanish and use their knowledge of Spanish to help them write in English. While this has helped them in some ways, it also creates its own set of problems. For example, a fair percentage of the errors these children make in English result from relying on their knowledge of Spanish in ways that don't work for English. These children sometimes put an adjective after the noun it modifies, mix up their gender-related pronouns, struggle with tenses other than the present, and spell phonetically (which works in Spanish but not in English).
4. Children in this group write with fairly correct conventions. They concern you not because they make errors but because they are not using complex sentences or vocabulary. You worry that their zeal to be correct and in control has led them to cling to safe terrain. As a result, much of their writing reads as if it is a list. They don't seem at home with literary syntax, and they don't use a diversity of connectors, relying almost entirely on *and, so,* and *then.*
5. These children have an easy command of the conventions of written language. Some seem to be trying new things and pushing themselves to experiment, to create effects on the page, to use mentor texts as models; others do not, but all of these children seem to have this aspect of writing well under control and avoid making errors.

You may have clusters of children who fit into other groupings. I'd sort children according to whatever groups you see emerging, and then look closely at the work of at least one representative child from each group. Consider whether that one child's progress (or lack thereof) is representative of the others from that group as well. Ask yourself, "What progress am I expecting from this group of children?" Based on your answer, you should be able to think about how your teaching thus far has or has not been appropriate for each group, and you'll begin to become accustomed to gauging whether a child is or is not making dramatic progress in the control of written conventions.

Chances are good that you will need to begin working regularly, for five or ten minutes a day, with some of these groups of children. You might think that, right off, you'll want to zero in on the children who are so swamped with problems that you hardly know where to begin. If you do decide to work with these children, you may work first on their use of end punctuation. The first step is not for them to reread their entries, inserting punctuation, but instead for them to get some sense for the rhythm of writing with punctuation. Help these children think in sentence-long bites instead of word-long bites. "Say your thought," you nudge. "Now write that fast, without stopping, and then put a period." They do this. "Now say your next thought." They do that. "Now write that fast without stopping and put a period." Meanwhile, asking these children to rehearse for writing by saying the story across their fingers, or across several pages, can help them focus on large chunks of the story instead of on small bits. This can help them avoid losing the thread of their story amid the complexities of the individual words they are trying to write. Composing the stories aloud first can also help; students find ends to their sentences. This can keep them from writing idea after idea, connected simply by the word *and*.

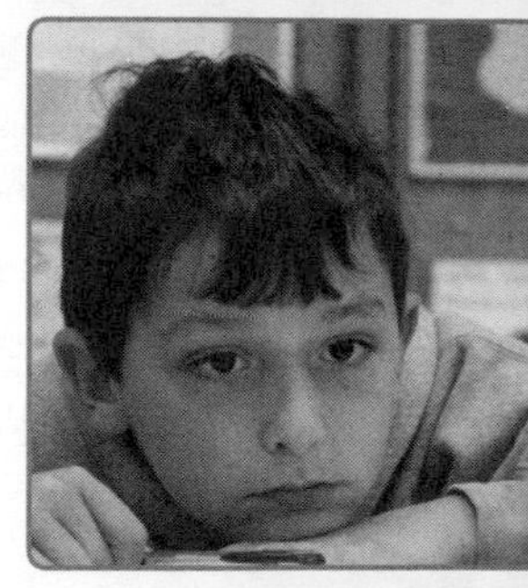

But you may find that children who struggle the most with mechanics are getting better in leaps and bounds, leading you to suspect that above all they needed chances to write and to be respected as writers. You might, for example, help children in the fourth category (above) make the transitions from run-on to simple sentences—a transition that can set them up so they are ready to next learn to write with subordinate clauses.

If children write in a structure of subject, predicate, conjunction, subject, predicate, conjunction, on and on, in one run-on sentence after another, then it is hard to help them introduce commas and clauses into that writing. And if kids aren't composing their writing with commas, they probably aren't composing their thoughts with subtle relationships between them, with one slightly less important thought, another slightly parenthetical, another deserving of a full breath. Those different levels of importance and relevance are there, of course, and may even be intended, but many children aren't yet crafting their writing to reveal them. Adding commas hither and yon to make the writing correct after the fact does not help children learn to tease out these relationships.

The first step, then, is to help children see that strings of simple sentences linked with the words *and* or *so* don't work. Then once these children have begun to write in simple sentences, it is powerful to show them that authors use clauses and more complex transition words to convey their ideas. We need to help children understand that relationships exist between parts of sentences as well as parts of stories. We can help them to learn that writing with commas and subordinate phrases can help them to convey what really matters. But these are tall orders!

You might, for example, gather some children in category four together and tell them that you often admire the way a certain author writes his or her sentences and sometimes try to revise your own writing under the influence of that author.

You might study Cisneros' artful use of sentences in "Eleven." She could have written:

> I don't know why I'm feeling sick inside. The part of me that's three wants to come out of my eyes. I squeeze them shut tight. I bite down on my teeth real hard. I try to remember today I am eleven, eleven.

Instead, Cisneros uses some connectors, such as *but, like, only,* and *and,* to make one fluid sentence.

> I don't know why *but all of a sudden* I'm feeling sick inside, *like* the part of me that's three wants to come out of my eyes, *only* I squeeze them shut tight *and* bite down on my teeth real hard *and* try to remember today I am eleven, eleven. (Cisneros 1991, p. 8)

Encourage children to learn from this aspect of Cisneros' craftsmanship as well as from her other qualities of good writing.

All of this work will help you to show the parents of your children that you are tailoring instruction based on what you see their child needing.

LISTENING FOR SIGNIFICANCE IN SEED IDEAS

IN THIS SESSION, YOU WILL TEACH CHILDREN TO BE STRONG LISTENERS, LEARNING TO DRAW OUT THE POSSIBILITIES IN THEIR OWN AND EACH OTHER'S SEED ENTRIES.

GETTING READY

- Monitoring My Writing Process checklist from first unit (with blank spaces for adding new strategies)
- Student copies of the Monitoring My Writing Process checklist (also with blank spaces for adding new strategies)
- Student seed idea that shows qualities of strong personal narrative that the class has studied so far
- Lined paper
- Set up place where two students can confer
- See CD-ROM for resources

I hope that by now, you and your children *have become accustomed to the rhythms of the writing process. I'm hoping that even before today, your children have been rereading their entries and thinking, "Which of these will I choose to develop into a publishable piece?" This process of collecting, selecting, and then developing is an important one for teachers, for writers, for human beings. It is tempting in life to try to do all things. We rush about as teachers, as writers, as people, trying to do and be everything. But in life, one thing we know for sure is that there will never be enough time. And so we, as human beings, are called upon to make choices. "Out of all that I could say and do and be," we think, "what matters most to me?"*

When choosing a seed idea, it's helpful for children (and for us) to be able to look at a quickly written, abbreviated, less-than-artsy entry and see potential. Some people can look at a room and imagine it redecorated, or look at a piece of raw marble and imagine a finished sculpture. Writers need to eye entries, seeing potential. This is a talent that teachers as well as children need to develop. What an art it is to be able to look at a fragment of an entry, the skeleton of a story, and imagine the tale it might become!

You'll want to remind children that they've traveled this road before, and that they already have strategies for developing a seed idea and for planning the draft they will soon write. Just as earlier you asked children to recall their strategies for gathering personal narrative entries, now you will ask them to recall their strategies for developing those entries in their notebooks prior to writing their stories. You will remind children that they can draft and revise timelines and leads, especially.

In Writing and Conferring, I emphasize the spirit that needs to be woven throughout this session.

MINILESSON

Listening for Significance in Seed Ideas

CONNECTION

Remind children that they are job captains for their writing and that they can use the writing process charts to guide them as they progress along a predictable course. Invite them to choose seed ideas when they feel ready.

"Many of us have organizers and calendars to make sure that we use our time productively, and earlier this year, we learned that writers often keep tabs on our writing process by charting our progress. Because we know that our writing process will generally proceed along a fairly predictable sequence of work, we keep a chart of the writing process near us as we work, and check off when we have completed each step in that process. (Of course, we'll need to revise this chart as we go to reflect all that we're now learning about the writing process.)"

Monitoring My Writing Process	First Piece	Next Piece
Gather entries		
Select and develop one seed idea		
Storytell to rehearse for writing		
Read published writing that resembles what I want to write		
Draft leads—try action, dialogue, setting		
Make a timeline		
Choose paper, plan story on pages, copy lead		
Write draft with each part on a separate page		
Reread and revise for clarity		
Draft endings—try writing with important ideas and images from the story, and with details that are reminders of the whole		
Revise and edit more now or decide to wait until later, or not to revise		

COACHING

This chart scaffolded children's work in the Launching unit of study, and will grow alongside them in this unit as well. Charts support students' independence as long as we reference them consistently and as long as they contain clear, concise language that becomes part of the class lexicon. We also emphasize "less is more." In other words, we use only a few charts, but use them often, with the expectation that students will do the same. This chart is the most important chart in many teachers' writing workshops.

"I want to remind you that you can decide when you are ready to move along in your process. When you are ready to choose a seed idea, you'll want to make a check in the first column on your chart to indicate that you have collected entries, and then you'll want to reread all your entries carefully, giving every one a chance, perhaps marking several possibilities, and finally selecting one entry as your seed."

You'll notice that although I talk up the idea of moving from gathering to selecting entries, I do not suggest that all the children choose their seed ideas today. First, I want to give children a sense that they are in control of their own writing process. Then, too, it would be hard for me to get around to every child in one day, so if half the writers continue to gather entries for another day or two, that will only make life easier. I have no hesitation saying at some point, "If you haven't chosen your seed idea, do so now."

Confide that for you, it's comforting to share writing decisions with a partner.

"For me, it is always a little scary to make a choice, to say, 'This will be the entry that I develop into a publishable piece.' Sometimes when I reread my notebook looking for an entry that's worth developing, I fret. 'I wonder if this is good enough,' I say to myself. When that happens, what I really need is a listener. I need someone who'll say, 'Tell me your story . . .' and who listens with such rapt attention that I find myself saying more than I thought there was to say and getting to the heart of my writing."

The fact that the writing process is cyclical means that we, as teachers, are freed from always needing to teach children what their next step should be as writers. We need only to reference that next step, and meanwhile we can teach them how to do that step especially well, or we can address the predictable problems they'll encounter. In both your conferences and your minilessons, be sure you don't let yourself get into the trap of reteaching steps and strategies that you know your children already know. Allow yourself to spotlight something new.

Name the teaching point. In this case, tell writers that in order to write a great story, writers need to become writing teachers for ourselves, listening raptly to our own stories.

"Today I want to teach you to become good teachers for yourselves and for each other, because each of you needs someone who can listen so deeply and so intently that you find yourself saying more than you thought you had to say. Good writing teachers listen, and allow writers—the writer in each of us—to uncover layers of an idea. Good writing teachers help us know we've chosen a good seed idea, and help us get started finding the words to write about that seed idea."

Teaching

Tell the story of one time when you listened so intently to a writer that you helped the writer find significance in a seemingly small moment.

"Has a friend ever gotten you talking—a friend who listens so intently that all of a sudden it's as if a dam broke inside you and suddenly you are telling the whole story, feeling words pour out as you talk? Writers need listeners like that. I want to tell you about one time when I was a good writing teacher because I listened, and then I'm going to help each of you become a good writing teacher for yourselves and each other. I remember one time when I pulled my chair alongside a fifth grader, Kenny. Most of Kenny's classmates had produced long narratives, but Kenny's writing amounted only to these lines."

> My Life Story
>
> I saw my father. We had coke, and then we had a hot dog.
>
> The end.

"Looking at his entry, I was tempted to say, 'Kenny, you need to produce more!' But I reminded myself that writers need listeners who are affected by our stories. So I told myself to really listen. I read what Kenny had written again and really tried to listen to it: 'My Life Story. I saw my father. We had coke, and then we had a hot dog. The end.'"

"This was, indeed, huge. And tragic. 'Kenny,' I said. 'This is huge. This is so important.'"

"Kenny looked at me, his eyes widening.' Yeah?' he said, tentatively."

"I asked Kenny to tell me all about his visit with his father. At first he just repeated what he'd already written—they had Coke and a hot dog—and instead of being impatient, I tried to really picture the moment. 'Kenny,' I said, 'I can picture it. You and your dad having Coke and a hot dog.'"

"Kenny nodded. And I waited. After a long silence, Kenny added, 'My dad showed me buildings.' Again Kenny paused, and again I waited. Kenny added, 'I still have the soda can."

"It was three years since Kenny met with his dad and ate a hot dog and soda. But all these years later, he is still holding the soda can and the memory of that afternoon."

"When I trusted that Kenny's entry was important, *Kenny* finally realized his story is important, and he began using words and details that showed what made that story so important. The reason I care about writing true stories is that for all of us, life amounts to just, 'We had Coke, and then we had a hot dog.' But when we write and think and talk about those moments, we find that a little story about having a soda with one's dad—or about a red sweater—is not so little after all."

You'll want to begin collecting your own stories and your colleagues' stories of young writers. We all have countless times, like this one, when a child struggles and then makes a breakthrough. As these teaching moments happen, you need to become accustomed to thinking, "I could write about this." You are lucky to be in the classroom every day because stories like this are all around you! Harvest them. Cherish them. Use them in your teaching.

When you turn these teaching moments into entries, keep in mind that you are essentially writing a narrative. Mine begins with a small action. I pulled a chair alongside Kenny. Soon the problem presented itself: Kenny's draft, unlike the drafts of his classmates, was tiny. In my story of this teaching moment, I include the internal story: Looking at Kenny's draft, I wanted to say, "Is this all?" This episode is shaped like a story. A teacher encounters a problem, tries for a solution, and finds a breakthrough—one that has universal ramifications.

Notice that I tell this story like a small moment, then I step back and reflect on what the story shows. This is one model for what you may want your children to do.

Active Engagement

Set one child up to share her seed idea, and use this as an opportunity to coach children in listening responsively to each other's writing.

"Writers, we not only need strategies for developing our seed ideas, we also need to respect our own words. We cannot write a good story if we don't respect the story we are trying to tell. The best way I know to respect our own words is to have a listener who really listens and who says, 'Whew! This is going to be huge!'"

"Let's practice being that kind of listener. Cindy is going to read an entry that she thinks might be her seed idea, and will you tell each other what you might say to her to show her that you are listening to her, just as I listened to Kenny." Cindy read her entry aloud. *[Figs. V-1 and V-2]*

I was standing in the middle of the kitchen arguing with my Aunt Blanca about some party she wanted to go to and to take me to.

"I'm going to call your Father and you're going to get into big trouble, you brat," Blanca said as she pushed my dad's phone number.

"Can I speak to Ramon Benitez?"

"Hello?" my dad said. Blanca threw her hands out at me and I snatched the phone.

"Dad, I don't want to go to the party!" I screamed.

"What?" my dad said, expecting something bad for Blanca to say.

"I don't know the people. I'm going to be so bored!"

"Sweetie, you have to—"

"No, I hate you! I hate everybody! Why? Because no one loves me or cares about me and no one listens to me." There was silence on the phone and in the house.

"Oh, my God! Cindy, I can't believe you!" Blanca said shaking her head.

"Shut up! Please shut up!" I couldn't believe my words! They had come out one by one. BANG! I dropped the phone. I closed my eyes. I swung my hands. My aunt was standing right next to the stove with the vegetables right on top. At that moment, I wished I could go back in time and change what I said and done.

When you teach children about the importance of listening, you may want to read aloud Byrd Baylor's I'm in Charge of Celebrations. *One could look at Baylor's subjects and shrug them off. She's writing about seeing a green cloud in the sky, that's all, and some dust blowing around in a spiral. But Baylor knows that we human beings have choices to make. We can pass by the details of our lives, hardly noticing them, or we can let a green cloud stop us in our tracks. "We're in charge of celebrations," Baylor says, and her advice is gigantically important.*

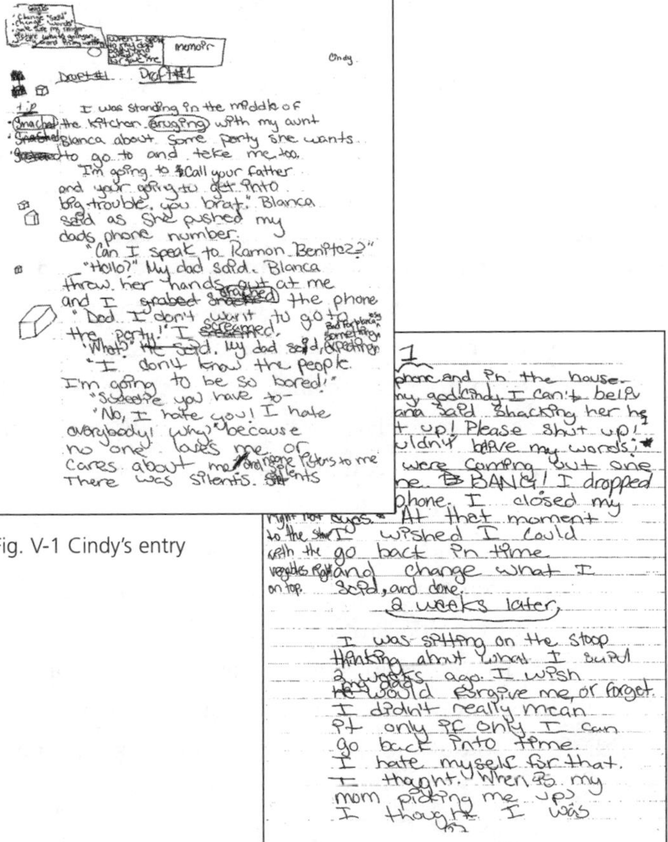

Fig. V-1 Cindy's entry

Fig. V-2 Cindy's entry page 2

"What could you say to help Cindy feel heard?" I asked. The room erupted into talk

After a moment, I called on one child to talk to Cindy, cautioning, "Remember, your job is not to ask questions. Your job is to let Cindy know you listened."

"I know how you felt because I once did that to my mom. It's like you love them, but you just get so angry sometimes that you end up saying mean things."

Mellora interjected, "Yeah. It's like you don't mean it, it just comes out, and then you regret it."

Cindy said, "Yeah. That's *exactly* how I felt. It was bad news, like I'd *never* live it down." She looked down at her feet as she spoke. "I hated what I'd done."

"Cindy, I hope what these listeners are saying is making you realize that you had feelings that day that are really an important part of what you want to say. You might reread your draft and figure out how you can expand the part about your sense of regret, if that's the main message." Then I turned to the whole class and said, "When a writer has someone who really listens to us, we often end up realizing the aspect of our story that moves us, that fills us with feelings. When we have a listener, and we take in our own story, realizing what it is that matters most to us."

Link

Remind children that when they are choosing their seed ideas they can be listeners for each other and themselves, using this as a way to find significance.

"At your desks, you will each find a copy of our Monitoring My Writing Process checklist," I said, holding up a copy to signify that children needed to record their progress on their own charts. "Writers, remember that as writers, you need to be job captains for yourselves. Some of you will collect entries for another day or two, and some of you will decide you are ready to choose your seed idea now. If you do choose a seed idea, and you think it'll help, say to your partner, 'Can we confer about this?' You'll probably want to leave your workspace and sit together in the meeting area, or in one of the conference areas I've set up in the margins of our classroom. Partners, be listeners who help writers want to write."

"Once you've chosen your seed idea and talked about it, you may want to draft a timeline, you may want to try some leads, you may want to start a draft. If you are starting a draft, do so outside your writer's notebook, on lined paper."

It is important to keep concepts we teach earlier alive. Even by making just a passing reference to job captains, planning boxes, or charts, we remind children of these concepts.

WRITING AND CONFERRING

Listening to Teach Listening

If I had a writing teacher's magic wand, I'd use it to make sure that every single writer had a private teacher on the day that he chose a seed idea. I'd tell all the private teachers to listen to the entries that kids have chosen and say, "Wow. This story is going to be huge," or "Whew. You've chosen an important story, haven't you?"

But because you and I do not have magic wands, the wisest thing we can do is to teach children to become listeners for each other. Teach children that in a good writing conference, the writer leaves wanting to write. The writer's energy for writing should go up. That is the single most important hallmark of an effective conference.

You'll want to move among children who have decided on their seed idea, and help them tell their stories so well that they give their partners (and you) goose bumps. Say to the child, "This is going to be an amazing story." Help the child believe that he or she is poised at the brink of a remarkable writing venture.

If you aren't sure how to get writers to tell the story well to you, remember what therapists know. They listen and then say back what they've heard. "It sounds like you are really mad at your mother," the therapist says, using the technique they refer to as active listening. You will see that the technique elicits more than a battery of small questions could possibly elicit. The important thing is not the fact that you say back what the writer has said. Instead, what matters is the listening. Listen with rapt attention to just a chunk of the story, then respond by reiterating or exclaiming over what you've heard and *then by not talking.* "You were really worried as you stood there, ready to jump into that pond, weren't you? And John kept saying, 'You can do it'?" Then wait. Be quiet. Let the writer talk. If you do want to prompt for more information, instead of asking specific questions, say things like, "I'm not sure I can picture it. Exactly how did it go? What did he say? What did he do? Oh! So he said . . . Then what?" Once a child has told the start of a story with voice and passion and detail, scrawl it down if necessary to hold on to it. Then say the start of the story back to the writer while he or she records it, and say, "You're off to a good start. Keep going."

Sometimes I make an even more pointed effort to rally a child's energy for the work ahead. "Takuma," I might say. "I have a feeling that this is going to be the most important story you've ever written. Do you feel that too? You're onto something here." Or I might say, "Sophie, I'm not sure you realize that the detail with which you're talking about your writing plans is very special. You are talking like you are a real published writer. I hope you take this talent of yours seriously."

MID-WORKSHOP TEACHING POINT **_Drawing on Strategies_** "Writers, I want to remind you that you have a backpack full of strategies for developing your seed ideas. Right now, before I go any further, would you list across your fingers three things writers do to choose and develop their seed ideas?" I watched as children whispered to themselves, moving along their fingers as they did so.

"You already know that to choose a few possible seed ideas, we reread every entry in our notebooks thoughtfully. We don't just flip past them; we give each entry a chance."

"Thumbs up if any of you remembered that now is also a good time for storytelling your seed ideas . . . great!"

SHARE

Reading Aloud Powerful Writing

Plan a way for every writer to read a bit of his writing aloud to the group as a means to celebrate children's stronger and stronger writing.

"Our goal this month is to write in ways that make readers stop in their tracks like Mrs. Manning did. I thought we would spend the next few *weeks* trying to put some powerful writing on the page, but you've *already* written entries that are powerful! Some of you selected entries which will become your seed ideas today, and you made wise choices! Remember earlier this year, I acted as the conductor of your orchestra? When I pointed my baton at you, you read aloud a tiny excerpt from your writing. We're going to do the same thing today; when I point to you, read aloud a tiny excerpt of the entry that you've chosen as your seed idea. You may read your lead, or you may choose the heart of your entry to read aloud. I'll give you a few minutes to look through what you've written and choose what you'll read. Practice reading your words in your head like they're precious jewels, so that you can do justice to them."

Soon I gestured with my "baton" and one child after another read aloud.

Khalid: *[Fig. V-3]*

> I balanced on the bike with my feet. I looked down the long hill. Gulp! I swallowed hard. Camillo pushed me. The wind was blowing hard. I kept going into the dark night. Would I crash? I was kind of scared.

After a few others, Sabrina read: *[Figs. V-4 and V-5]*

> I spent about three seconds in the air partly tripping and partly jumping. As I was in the air, I thought, please let me land on my feet. I don't want to fall with Mya in my hands. Mya is just a baby, what if she gets hurt? It will be all my fault if Mya gets hurt. I really don't want Mya to get hurt!

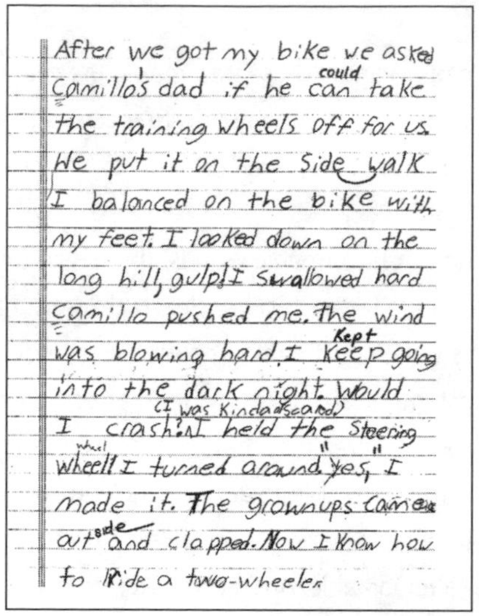

After we got my bike we asked
Camillo's dad if he could take
the training wheels off for us.
We put it on the sidewalk
I balanced on the bike with
my feet. I looked down on the
long hill, gulp! I swallowed hard
Camillo pushed me. The wind
was blowing hard. I kept going
into the dark night. Would
I crash? (I was kinda scared) I held the steering
wheel! I turned around "yes," I
made it. The grownups came
outside and clapped. Now I know how
to Ride a two-wheeler

Fig. V-3 Khalid

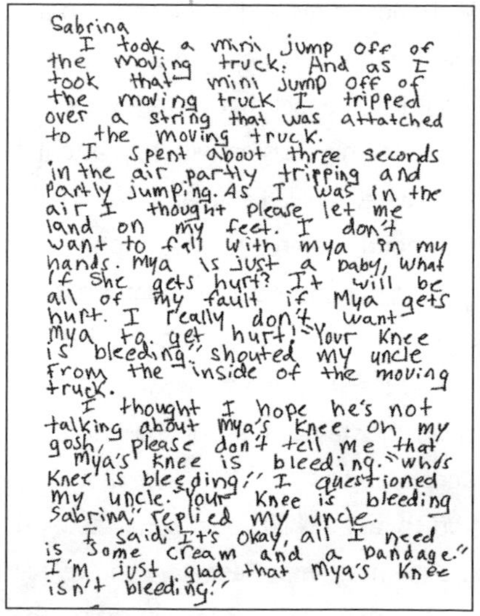

Sabrina
I took a mini jump off of
the moving truck. And as I
took that mini jump off of
the moving truck I tripped
over a string that was attatched
to the moving truck.
I spent about three seconds
in the air partly tripping and
partly jumping. As I was in the
air I thought please let me
land on my feet. I don't
want to fall with mya in my
hands. Mya is just a baby, what
if she gets hurt? It will be
all of my fault if Mya gets
hurt. I really don't want
mya to get hurt! "Your knee
is bleeding," shouted my uncle
from the inside of the moving
truck.
I thought I hope he's not
talking about Mya's knee. Oh my
gosh, please don't tell me that
Mya's knee is bleeding. "Whos
knee is bleeding," I questioned
my uncle. "Your knee is bleeding
Sabrina," replied my uncle.
I said "It's okay, all I need
is some cream and a bandage."
I'm just glad that Mya's knee
isn't bleeding!"

Fig. V-4 Sabrina

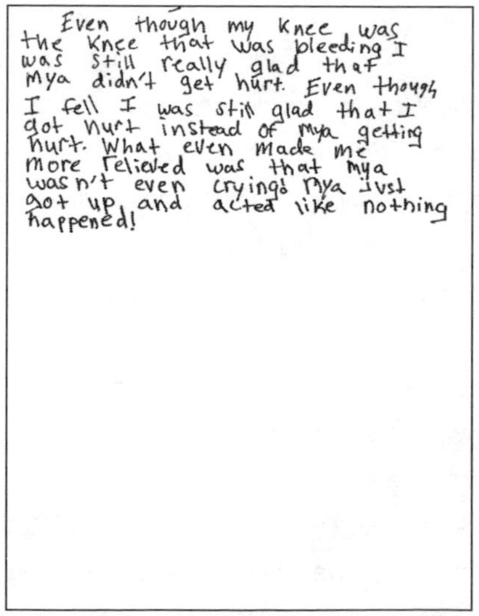

Even though my knee was
the knee that was bleeding I
was still really glad that
Mya didn't get hurt. Even though
I fell I was still glad that I
got hurt instead of mya getting
hurt. What even made me
more relieved was that mya
wasn't even crying! Mya just
got up and acted like nothing
happened!

Fig. V-5 Sabrina

After hearing five or six other snippets as well, I said, "Writers, this writing definitely gives me goose bumps. It gives us all goose bumps. Listening today, I realized that one thing you each did in these entries which makes your writing really strong is that you shifted between telling an external action, telling what you said, and telling an internal thought. Listen to Juliana's excerpt from her entry retelling the story of how she met her father for the first time and notice how she shifts between action, thought, and dialogue": *[Fig. VI-6]*

> I was looking at the people sitting at the bar. (action) There was a bald man with a mustache sitting by himself, and he smiled and waved. "He's not what I expected," I thought. (thought) But I guess he was waving at someone else because my mom led me towards the back and there was a blond man with glasses wearing jeans and a sweater who stood up when we got close. (action) "This is Chris," she said.
>
> "You must be Juliana," he said. (dialogue)

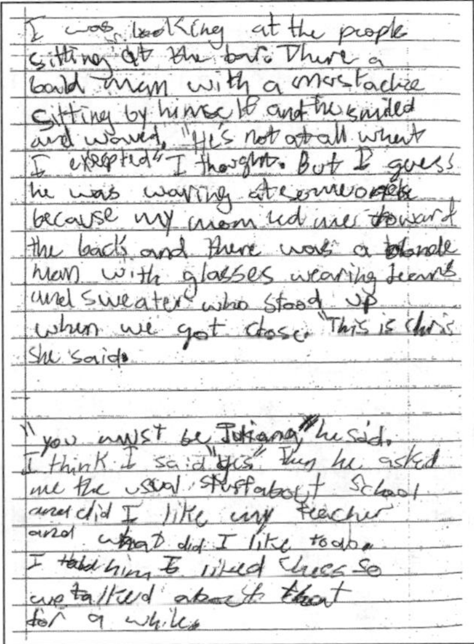
I was looking at the people sitting at the bar. There a bald man with a mustache sitting by himself and he smiled and waved. "He's not at all what I expected" I thought. But I guess he was waving at someone else because my mom led me toward the back and there was a blonde man with glasses wearing jeans and sweater who stood up when we got close. "This is Chris" She said.

"you must be Juliana" he said. I think I said "yes" then he asked me the usual stuff about school and did I like my teacher and what did I like to do. I told him I liked Chess so we talked about that for a while.

Fig. V-6 Juliana

"When you go from writing an entry to writing a draft, remember that this is one more strategy that you already know how to do as writers."

"Congratulations!"

HOMEWORK ***Collecting Details Related to the Seed Idea*** Once we have decided on a seed idea, we need to be like magnets, attracting details that pertain to our story. So tonight try to collect details that will help you write your personal narratives especially well. If I've decided to work on a story about when I got my new fish, I can't go back to that day—it is done—but I might spend time trying to describe this fish, putting words to the fact that it comes to me when I tap on the glass. I'll notice that the fish looks silvery sometimes, and orange at other times. I'll watch him closely. I can also go back and remember the time when I got him. Why did I pick him from all the other fish in the pet shop? How did he behave when I put him in with the other fish in my tank? How did my mother word that advice she gave me? Writers reach for the specific details that will help them develop their stories. Tonight, when you are home, collect those details.

TAILORING YOUR TEACHING

If you notice that students need extra help with stretching out key moments in their writing to reveal their importance . . . you might share examples by students who have done this successfully because students often attain concepts best through peer examples. For example, you might say, "Francesca selected her seed idea and made a timeline of it. The actual actions are simple ones. Her timeline goes like this:

- Phone rang
- Can I hamster watch?
- She's given the cage and hamster

"That's it! But pay attention to the way Francesca helps us appreciate that this moment is monumental to her. Watch the way she stretches this moment out, telling not just the external story but also telling the internal story of what she is remembering and wondering and noticing." *[Figs. V-7 and V-8]*

Hamster for a Day

I am picking up my black cold phone. I almost drop the phone at what I'm hearing. I am going to hamster sit Homer Rezler for 27 days. I feel half excited, half scared. I thought about my 13 pet worms that I got from Seattle, 3 months later they died. I don't know why. Maybe it was because they did not have the same soil? What if the same thing happens to Homer? I think. I know how hard it is to lose a pet. So I will try to be as careful as I can with him.

With a nervous look she handed me the cage and him. I felt brave that she chose me over anyone else to watch Homer. As I saw the half sad, half relieved look on her face I slowly picked up the cage. Homer was one of the cutest things I had ever seen in my life! With his little wet pink nose and orange soft fur. It was like watching a little tiny baby.

You could show students the internal events Francesca included at the start of her draft and ask them to locate and discuss with partners those she included in the second half of her draft. By naming Francesca's craft, they will be more able to apply it themselves.

2 Homework
Hamster for a Day
I am picking up my black cold Phone.
I almost drop the Phone at what I'm leaving,
I am going to hamstersit Homer (Rezier) Rentz)
for 27 days I feil half exided half scared.
I thought abut my 13 pet worms that
I got from Seattle, 3 months latter they
died. I don't know why. maybe it was
because the did not have the same
soil?? What if the samething happens
to Hommer, I think, I know how
hard it is to loose a pet. so I
will try to be as carefull as
I can with him.

privety
I am walking in to A strange new taxi with
a half nervos half exided feling in my
somoc. privety
"Pop" A Bonie with paper in it
goes. I walk over to the cold ocen watter
at Beach Haven Resort I remember

Fig. V-7 Francesca

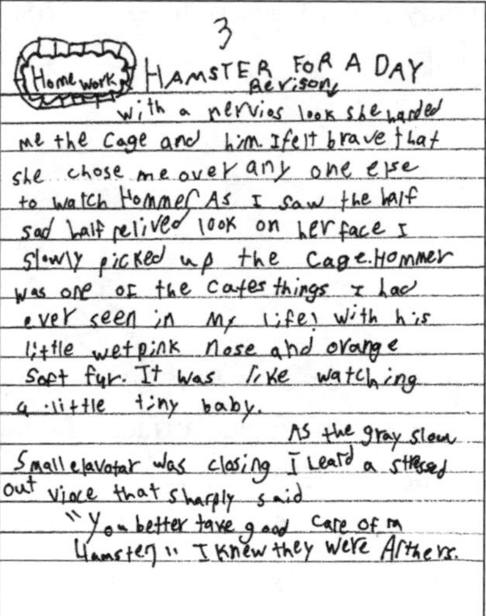
3
Homework HAMSTER FOR A DAY
Revison
with a nervios look she handed
me the cage and him. I felt brave that
she chose me over any one else
to watch Hommer As I saw the half
sad half relived look on her face I
slowly picked up the Cage. Hommer
was one of the cutes things I had
ever seen in my life! with his
little wet pink nose and orange
Soft fur. It was like watching
a little tiny baby.
As the gray slow
Small elavatar was closing I heard a stressed
out vioce that sharply said
"You better take good care of m
Hamster" I knew they were Arthers.

Fig. V-8 Francesca

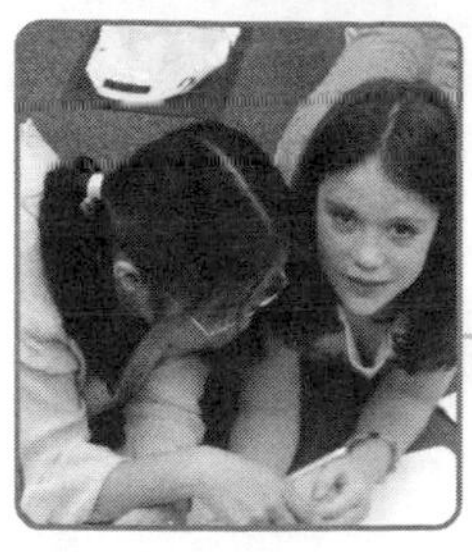

Assessment

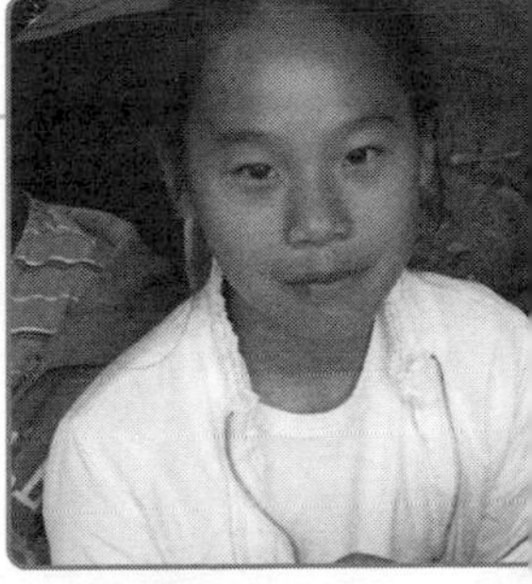

You will want to spend some time assessing your children's writing at this point so you can tailor the minilessons and strategy lessons you teach over the next few days to lift the level of their stories. The minilessons I suggest assume that children have graduated past the phase of writing all about their subjects. But I know from experience that some of the children will still be listing all their thoughts and feelings and memories related to a personal topic, a topic such as "The Soccer Game" or "Bowling at My Birthday Party." And their writing will look something like this:

> I love soccer. I'm good at it. I am good at making goals because I am sly. Once I went behind the other kids and got a goal in. They didn't see me. But one time I twisted my ankle. "Ow, did that hurt!"

You need to watch for children who still believe that texts like these are narratives. At the very least, a narrative—and this includes a personal narrative—involves a central character progressing through a sequence of events. If your children are instead gathering a pile of the thoughts and ideas and memories associated to a personal topic, then they are on the verge of writing an all-about or informational piece, not a narrative. They either need to go that way with the piece—chunking their information so one paragraph (or chapter) tells why the child is good at soccer, one paragraph tells about injuries the child has incurred during soccer—or they need to stop and ask a question such as, "What is one particular small event that I experienced during soccer that might make a good story?"

There are other essential lessons that I do not teach in this unit of study, but which you may decide to revisit. Perhaps your children are trying to write about the whole mountain climb, the whole day at the park, the whole soccer game, and they need to realize that any one of those topics contains dozens of focused stories. You may protest, saying, "Doesn't there need to be a place in life for a narrative that depicts the whole mountain climb?" and of course you are right. But to be effective, those narratives probably will comprise several vignettes (or scenes or small moments—those are all words for the same thing) linked together with tiny bits of exposition (as students noticed in "Your Name in Gold," back in Session I). Perhaps the whole-day-of-mountain-climbing story begins with a vignette about starting up the hill, then jumps ahead to depict the last strenuous moments of climbing, then leaps forward to retell the triumphant moment when you crest the top of the mountain and see the world spread below. For now, you may teach children who are still struggling with narrative form to write just one of those vignettes.

Be willing to look at your children's writing with honest eyes. Look through their command of spelling, through their use of adjectives, and try to see what they are doing as writers of narratives. Be sure they have learned to write focused narratives, and to storytell rather than summarize. If they're doing these things, the minilessons that follow will be helpful. If they are not doing these things, go back and find the minilessons from *Launching the Writing Workshop* that were designed to help with these skills. Draw on our list of mentor texts so that you bring fresh examples into minilessons, and try to understand what the challenges are that are derailing your children. Drawing on these resources, you'll be able to revise and reteach minilessons.

WRITERS ASK, "WHAT AM I *REALLY* TRYING TO SAY?"

IN THIS SESSION, YOU'LL TEACH STUDENTS THAT WRITERS ALWAYS CONSIDER WHAT THEIR STORIES ARE REALLY ABOUT SINCE THIS DECISION GUIDES ALL CHOICES IN CRAFTING AND REVISING NARRATIVES.

GETTING READY

- Excerpt of red-sweater scene from Sandra Cisneros' "Eleven," written on chart paper
- Whole-class common experience that can be told from various angles
- Monitoring My Writing Process chart
- Example of student writing before and after revising to reveal a particular meaning
- *Little by Little*, by Jean Little
- See CD-ROM for resources

***Once again, you will help students** shift between collecting entries and writing a draft. This is a good time to mentally back up for an aerial view of the curriculum, seeing how you are helping children spiral through the writing process over and over, each time drawing on a bigger repertoire of possible strategies and each time carrying a more complex knowledge of the qualities of effective writing.*

Knowing that your students—and your teaching—will continue to cycle through the writing process should help you realize that it is okay if your children do not grasp all the nuances of your teaching. At any one point, some children will be mastering a concept while others are still acquiring it. Those in the latter group will know the concept is important, but they will not yet be able to use it without your support. This shouldn't surprise you. Whenever we are learning to do something, we often understand the teacher's words long before we can master the trick of making our actions fit those words. I recall my mother teaching me tennis. Over and over she'd tell me, "Keep your eye on the ball!" and over and over I would want to say to her, "What do you think I'm doing? Watching birds?" But then one day I actually watched the ball spin toward me, and I saw it hover for a minute at the top of its arc. I saw my racket make contact with the ball—and I realized that until that moment, I had never before followed my mother's advice.

Today, your lesson is as essential as my mother's advice to me. It is, in a sense, the same message. You will be saying to children, "Keep your eye on your subject," and they will think, "What do you think I am doing? Counting elephants?"

Some children will grasp the power of this teaching today; others will not yet fully take in your words. Still, teach them with the full knowledge that this is enormously important and complex work. Because actually, everything else that a writer might do—drafting and revising a timeline, exploring different leads, considering which section of a story to tell in detail and which to summarize in passing—is contingent upon the writer first asking, "What am I really trying to say?" and then keeping his or her eye on that meaning.

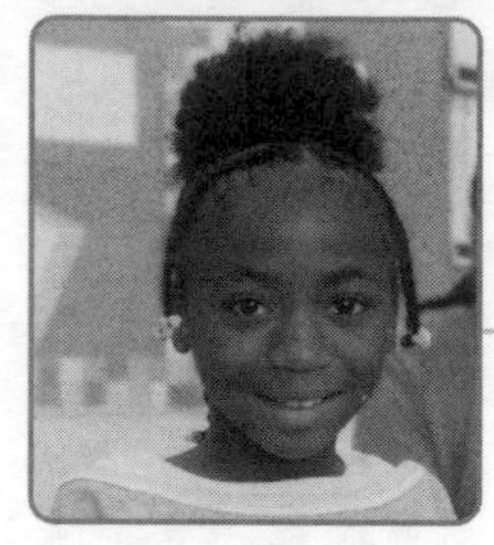

Minilesson

Writers Ask, "What Am I *Really* Trying to Say?"

Connection

Celebrate the stories you heard yesterday.

"Writers, yesterday many of you chose your seed idea, and you told your stories to each other in ways that made people gasp or laugh or want to hear more. The stories that I heard yesterday are incredibly significant ones. You all are doing hard and important writing work, aren't you! Because of the amazing, *big* stories I heard you tell yesterday, I believe you are ready for this: today I want to teach you one of the most important lessons I will ever teach you about writing."

Name your teaching point. Specifically, tell children that writers need to ask, "What am I really trying to say in this story?" and then let that question guide us as we develop seed ideas into drafts.

"Before you can decide which lead will work best for your story, or whether you want to stretch out one section or another, you need to decide what you really want to say in your story. You need to ask, "What is my story *really* about?" and to realize that the same story could be written to show very different things. You could write about going on a Ferris wheel, and your story could show that you conquered your fear of heights. Or you could write about the same ride on the Ferris wheel and show that when you are in a crowd of people, you always find ways to be alone. As a writer, once you have chosen the entry that will be your seed idea, you need to pause and think, 'What am I *really* trying to say in this story?' and then let your answer to that question guide your work as a writer."

Teaching

Tell children that their mentor author probably asked, "What am I really trying to say in this story?" Show that she could have angled her story differently.

"When Sandra Cisneros wrote 'Eleven,' I am pretty sure she remembered that story of the red sweater and thought, 'What is it I really want to say about that incident?' She could have written the story in a way that highlighted that the kids kept losing stuff that ended up in their coat closet, in which case she would have had Mrs. Price come out of that coat closet carrying a big pile—not just the red sweater, but also a whiffle bat and ball, some old coats, and maybe some left-behind lunch bags. Cisneros could have told the story to

Coaching

You may want to glance back across a whole series of minilessons, noticing the variety of ways in which I ask for children's attention. In the booming, crazy chaos of a classroom, commanding attention is no small feat. I do this by saying the opening word, "Writers," quietly, leaning toward the class, and by waiting until I see that I have their eyes before continuing. But I also try to find words that say, "What I'm about to say is really important." Today's lesson has a bigger than usual drumroll preceding it, and so I want to lean forward to you as well as to the children, to say, "Teachers," and I want to help you step aside from the chaos and take in the significance of today's lesson.

The qualities of good writing pertain to minilessons. I could have simply stated the generalization: Cisneros could have angled her story of the red-sweater incident to highlight any one of a range of meanings. Instead of simply telling kids this, I try to show it with examples that detail how Cisneros might have told the story differently.

emphasize that Mrs. Price was mean to Rachel; in that case Cisneros might have shown the teacher raging more, and made a bigger point of how Mrs. Price saw Rachel cry and instead of offering comfort, Mrs. Price turned her back on Rachel."

"Instead, I think Cisneros decided she wanted to highlight the idea that people have all different levels of maturity in themselves and different ones show up according to different situations. Even though Rachel is old enough to stand up for herself, when Mrs. Price says, 'Of course it is your sweater. I remember you wearing it once,' and puts the sweater on Rachel's desk, Rachel can't get words out of her mouth to protest. Because this part of the story matters a lot, this section is described carefully, with lots of words, in detail, and with paragraphs all to itself." I point to and read aloud the excerpt from "Eleven."

> Mrs. Price takes the sweater and puts it right on my desk, but when I open my mouth nothing comes out.
>
> "That's not, I don't, you're not . . . Not mine," I finally say in a little voice that was maybe me when I was four . . . Not mine, not mine, not mine, but Mrs. Price is already turning to page thirty two, and math problem number four. (pp. 7–8)

"When we write, we always need to ask ourselves, 'Which part of this story will I tell with lots of details, and which parts will I write only a little about?' One way to emphasize a part of the story that really says what the story is about is to take tiny steps through that bit, writing down every little part. Sandra Cisneros could have decided to pass quickly by the part of her story that involved putting on the red sweater. She could have written only a little about it, like this."

> "You put that sweater on right now," Mrs. Price said. I put it on.

"But instead, she decided that this section of the story could help convey what she really wanted to say about Rachel not having the courage to say, 'It's not mine.' So she took tiny steps through this partial episode and wrote every bit down as she went."

> I put one arm though one sleeve of the sweater that smells like cottage cheese, and then the other arm through the other and stand there with my arms apart like if the sweater hurts me and it does, all itchy and full of germs that aren't even mine. (p. 8)

It is a great treat to be able to rely on published authors as co-teachers, helping us demonstrate the skills and strategies of good writing. Cisneros writes so beautifully that when we borrow her text, inserting it into our minilesson, some of her magic rubs off on our teaching. But the challenge when using published texts is that we only have the finished product, and it's not enough to say to children, "Go and write like this." So we often need to imagine what a writer's process might have been, as I do in this instance.

As I teach this minilesson, I know that writing with great detail and in small steps is not always better than writing that traverses the terrain in big strides. But I also know that children come to us, writing in giant steps, and that it is definitely a good thing for a writer to vary the amount of detail according to the content of the story and its relative importance. The fact that I oversimplify the goal is acceptable to me. Later in the year, you'll see children learn a more nuanced sense of good writing.

During the teaching component of minilessons, you may use your writing or a child's writing or a published author's writing. Usually it helps to revisit the same piece of writing often because you can zoom in on specific sections, knowing that children can recall the entire text enough to contextualize the point you make.

You'll notice that to highlight the choices an author has or has not made in ways that guide children's choices, I often say, "This author could have . . . but instead she . . . "

Active Engagement

Invite children to retell a familiar event twice, angling the story differently each time to bring two different meanings to the event.

"What I hope you are learning is that, as a writer, once you have decided on a story you want to tell, you need to pause and think, 'What am I really trying to say?' Once you have decided on the meaning you want to convey, all other decisions will be affected by that decision."

"Let's try it. Remember yesterday when our window was stuck and we couldn't open it? Let's pretend we want to write that stuck window–story and we want to angle the story to show that it is really hard for us to get through even one read-aloud without interruptions because so many things in our room don't work. I'll start the story, and then partner 2s, you continue it. Everything you say doesn't need to be exactly true; you can take some poetic license."

> Yesterday, our teacher read aloud. It was so hot that sweat was rolling down our faces, so our teacher stopped and went over to open the window. She pushed. Nothing happened. Flakes of paint rained down. So she . . . (Did what? Partner 2s, continue the story.)

Notice that the for portion of the minilesson in which I debrief, my teaching can fall either at the end of the Teaching component or at the start of the Active Engagement component, or in both places.

I know that what I am asking children to do is not easy. This is why I get them started, telling a good deal of the story. I try to provide enough scaffolding that it's feasible for them to carry on where I've left off, and I know that even if they can't, they will probably learn from these added illustrations of my point.

Intervening after a few minutes, I called for children's attention to revert to me. "Let's say that instead, we want to tell about that same episode but this time, we want to show how we all work together as a community, solving our problems by helping each other. How could we tell the same story? I'll start it, and partner 1s, add on."

> Yesterday our teacher read aloud. She looked out and saw that we had sweat rolling down our cheeks. So she knew she had to help us. She went over and tried to open the window. It was stuck. Soon Ori had jumped up . . . (partner 1s, continue the story.)

I listened in as children carried on, telling their partners about how first one, then another and finally four children gathered around the window, pushing with all their might until, with a groan, the window creaked open.

I could have chosen a more accessible example. I could, for example, have asked children to describe entering the classroom that morning, putting their things away and convening in the meeting area. They could tell this as if they came to school in high spirits, looking forward to the day—or as if they came to school in a depressed mood, dreading even the writing workshop.

"You told the same event really differently, didn't you?" I said. "You told the story of that event once to show that nothing works very well in the school, adding details about the paint flakes raining down on us and the hissing radiator that won't stop whining and groaning. Then you told the story of the same event a second time, this time showing how we jumped up to help each other, and how, when we all worked together, we could get that window to creak open. You brought out different details in each story because you were aiming to show something different in each version."

This is a writing lesson, but of course it is also a life lesson. The truth is that as teachers, too, we need to remember that we are the authors of our lives. It will always, for each of us, be My Life, by me.

LINK

Reiterate that writers need to pause and ask, "What am I really trying to say?" and then revise and craft the stories to convey that chosen meaning.

"So, from this day forward and for the rest of your life, when you decide to work on a story, remember that one of the first and most important things you can do is to pause and ask yourself, 'What am I *really* trying to say in this story?' Let's add that to our Monitoring My Writing Process checklist as one important way to develop our seed ideas." I took a moment to add "Write an entry about what I am *really* trying to say in this story" to our class chart.

I'm convinced that until a child has decided what she wants to highlight in a story, it's fairly likely that her revisions won't actually improve the text. The single move to decide on one's meaning makes enormous contributions. As I've said before, this lesson is only the beginning of teaching children how to write and revise their stories based on what those texts are "really" about. At first, children may not have the experience to know how to answer that question—thinking about it is a start, however, and we will teach them more about this in later units.

Monitoring My Writing Process	First Piece	Next Piece
Gather entries		
Select and develop one seed idea		
Write an entry about what you are really trying to say		
Storytell to rehearse for writing		
Read published writing that resembles what I want to write		
Draft leads—try action, dialogue, setting		
Make a timeline		
Choose paper, plan story on pages, copy lead		
Write draft with each part on a separate page		
Reread and revise for clarity		
Draft endings—try writing with important ideas and images from the story, and with details that are reminders of the whole		
Revise and edit more now or decide to wait until later, or not to revise		

"After you have chosen your seed idea, you will want to do that—write an entry about what you are really trying to say, and that will help you determine what goes on your timelines and what details to include in your story." Then I said, "If you want to see an example, I have an entry one of my students from last year wrote *[Fig. VI-1]* and I'll leave copies at our writing center."

What's the big thing/really important?

I want the reader to know that my father and I are so intensely into the game that we're nervous and biting our lips. I want the reader to know that I am hoping with all my heart that Soriano gets a hit, or even a homerun. I think the big thing of the story is leading up to the hit and how everyone's very tense.

How am I going to show this?

I'm going to show more of my surroundings, and what the people around me are doing. Also, show mine and everyone's actions more thoroughly, so the reader gets a sense of all the tension even more, so the reader is tense or excited.

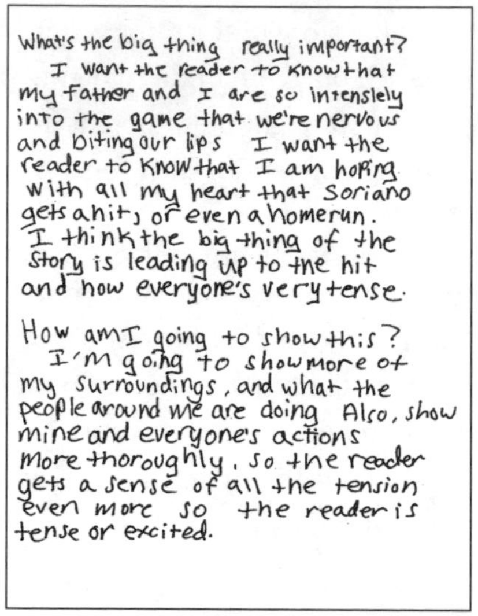

What's the big thing really important?
I want the reader to know that my father and I are so intensely into the game that we're nervous and biting our lips I want the reader to know that I am hoping with all my heart that Soriano gets a hit, or even a homerun. I think the big thing of the story is leading up to the hit and how everyone's very tense.

How am I going to show this?
I'm going to show more of my surroundings, and what the people around me are doing Also, show mine and everyone's actions more thoroughly. so the reader gets a sense of all the tension even more so the reader is tense or excited.

Fig. VI-1 Notice how this writer reflects on what it is he really wants to convey in his piece.

Writing and Conferring

Teaching Children to Confer with Each Other

I pulled my chair alongside Sophie. "How's it going?" I asked her.

"Good," she said, her intonation suggesting that in fact she was in a quandary.

A rule of thumb that guides me when I do research in a conference is the advice that journalism students are often given: to get information, you need to give information. If I detect something in a writer's demeanor or her drafts and can name what I see, letting my further questions stand on the shoulders of that knowledge, that will usually yield more insight. So this time I said to Sophie, "You say you are doing well, but your voice isn't convincing. Are you in a quandary, in a puzzling situation?"

"I can't decide what my entry is really about," she answered, "'cause it's just about going to Chuck E. Cheese's with Claudia and I told what we did,' cause we had pizza and we got tokens and we did this squirt gun game and all."

"What a time you guys had!" I answered. "And you are so wise, trying to decide what the main thing is that you really want to show in your story. Writers do exactly what you are doing – and it's a hard question for all of us. What have you done so far to figure it out?"

"I was rereading it and voting – you know, one check for the pizza, two for the games, like that."

"Let me see if I understand," I said. "You've been rereading your draft and you have a coding system to decide which episode, which moment, from the dinner was the most important one. Is that right?"

Sophie nodded.

"I love that you aren't just sitting here holding your paper expecting that the answer about what really matters to come out of thin air!" I said. "It is smart that when you found yourself in a quandary, in a puzzle, you thought, 'So how could I go about solving this?' and then you came up with a plan for proceeding. That is so like you, Sophie, to be such an active problem solver!"

MID-WORKSHOP TEACHING POINT **_Angling Writing_** "Ori's seed idea tells the story of a Saturday morning when he got up early and brought his little brother downstairs, fixing him breakfast. Ori's first version of his story went like this." [*Fig. VI-2*]

> This Saturday I woke up at 7:17 am. I rolled out of my bunk bed and crouch to the hall when I see that my little brother, Alon, was lying in my mom's extremely large, brownish bed with my dad. Mom must be in the bathroom, I think to myself. I crawl into bed when my mom comes out of the bathroom.
>
> "Good morning Ori," she says. She goes in the bed on the left side next to Alon. "Alon, do you want to go downstairs?" I ask.

"So today, before working on leads and starting his draft, Ori took the time to write an entry in which he asked, 'What am I trying to say in my story?' He realized that he wanted to show that on this particular morning, he decided to let his parents sleep in. So even though he was very sleepy and didn't feel like getting out of bed, he did so, and soon had invited his brother,

continued on next page

This Saterday I woke up at 7:17 Am. I roll out of my bunk bed and crauch to the hall when I see that my little brother, Alon was lying in my mom's Extrimely large brownish bed with my dad. Mom must be in the bathrooms I think to myself I crawl into the bed when my mom cames out of the bath room "good morning Ori," She says. She She goes in the bed in the left side next To Alon.
"Alon, do you want to go down stairs?" I ask.
"OK," he says.

Fig. VI-2 Ori's first version of his story

Then I added, "But can I give you one tip?" Waiting for her assent, I said, "The really important part of a story is not always one moment of the story, one small chunk of the story. Sometimes, the really important thing is a relationship or a feeling, not a single episode or event. For example, maybe you want to tell about the evening at Chuck E. Cheese's because you want to show that this was a time when you and your dad felt really close. Or maybe there is a different relationship or a different feeling that you want to spotlight."

"It's Claudia!" Sophie said. "'Cause we gave each other our prizes and that's when we decided to be best friends."

"That was the very night?" I exclaimed. "How did it happen?" I tried to mask my smile, to not show that I found it entertaining to notice how closely this conversation resembled ones I have had with colleagues who've recently announced their engagement. "Who asked whom?" I queried—but didn't linger long before telling Sophie that she definitely knew the big thing in her story!

Sophie decided to write an entry in which she recorded what it was she really wanted to say in her story, and then she set out to make a new timeline, this time being sure to put the events on it that pertained to her friendship with Claudia.

> Why is this idea important to me?
>
> The idea is important to me because it makes me realize that me and Claudia are very good friends and we can trust each other and count on each other to be there for each of us like if I fall back she will always be there to catch me and so will I.

continued from previous page

Alon, downstairs. Listen to Ori's lead, and see if you think he angles his story to show how tired he was." *[Fig. VI-3]*

> Last Saturday, I woke up at 7:17 am. "I'm s-s-s-so tired," I whisper. I snuggle in my warm bed and let my body sink into it. It's 7:20 am. Wow it's early I think to myself as I look sideways to the clock on the wall. 1,2,3! I roll out of bed and land in a big "boom!" "Ouch, that hurts" I say.
>
> I crouch into the hall and stand up when I get there. I decided to check if my brother is awake yet. I walk slowly and open my brother door. No one there. I walk even slower to my mom and dad's room . . .

"A famous poet, Emily Dickinson, once said, 'Tell all the truth but tell it slant.' You will need to decide what truth your story will contain, and you will also need to decide how to slant your story so your truth shines through. Ori did something really smart when he paused to ask, 'What's the big thing I'm trying to show?'"

"Now Ori is going to try starting his Saturday morning story at a different place in his sequence. If any of you want Ori's help thinking about what you want to show in your story, he's agreed to help anyone who needs it."

last saterday I wake up at 7:17 AM "Im S-S-So t-t-tired." I whisper. I snuggle in mywarm bed and let my body Sink into it. It's 7:20 AM, wow its early I think to myself as I look sideways to the Clock on the wall. 1,2,3! I roll out of bed and land in a big "boom!" "ouch, that hurts" I say.
I crouch into the hallway and stand up when I get there. I dicided To check if my brother is awake yet. I walk Slowly and open my brothers door no one I walkeven Slower to my mom and dad's room. It was half way opened so I peeped inside to see if my brother is there. I see that

Fig. VI-3 Ori has tried to angle his new lead to highlight his tiredness.

SHARE

Storytelling with an Angle

Convene the class and remind children of strategies writers use to bring out their meaning. Ask one partner to storytell his or her story in ways that highlight the meaning.

"Writers, please bring your writing notebooks with you to the meeting area. Let's gather." When the class was settled, I said, "Last month we learned to expand the heart of our stories by slowing the action, by giving details, by adding thoughts, and by adding dialogue. These are great strategies not only to expand the important parts of a story but also to bring out what we want to say. Let's practice these strategies right now."

"Right now, take a second to look over your seed idea and also look over the entry you wrote exploring why you want to write this story. Then close your notebooks, and practice telling at least the beginnings of your story to your partner. After you've told the start of your story, see if your partner can guess what it was you were trying to show, bringing out your angle by using actions, details, thoughts, and dialogue, like Ori did earlier." I listened and coached individuals as they practiced.

You'll decide whether storytelling is an important way for your writers to rehearse, and whether your children benefit from the props you provided in the last unit when they storytold using fingers and booklet pages and dots on a timeline to remind them of the march of time. If possible, I'd let those props fall away for most of your children as they can limit as well as support.

HOMEWORK ***Angling Your Writing as You Draft*** Writers, in her memoir *Little by Little,* Jean Little wrote one scene about her first day in a new school. It happened in April, when all the children already knew each other. Jean was struggling because of her poor vision, which made her different from the other children. At the end of the scene she tells us what she wanted to show most of all. She wrote: "I was gradually learning that if you were different, nothing good about you mattered. And I had not really understood, until now, that I was different" (p. 36).

Read the first part of this scene, and notice and mark up ways Jean angled her writing. In fact, every part of the scene brings out her stated intention. Listen.

> "This is Jean Little," my new teacher told the class. She led me to a desk.
>
> "This is Pamela, Jean," she said, smiling at the girl in the desk next to mine. I smiled at her, too.

Pamela's cheeks got pink. She looked away. I thought I knew what was wrong. She was shy. I sat down and waited for lessons to start. I was glad that reading was first.

When it was my turn to read out loud, I held the book up to my nose as usual. The other children giggled. The teacher hushed them. Then she turned to me.

"Are those your reading glasses?" she asked.

I was not sure. I snatched the glasses off and switched. But I still had to hold my book so close that my nose brushed against the page. Everybody stared. Nobody noticed my good reading.

That afternoon when the teacher left the room, Monica pointed at me.

"Look!" she crowed. "She's got black all over her nose!"

I clapped my hand to my face. The class burst into peals of laughter. They only broke off when the child nearest the door hissed, "Shh! She's coming."

After you have learned from Jean Little's craftsmanship, take time to think again about what it is that you most want to show in your story. If you haven't made a timeline of your story, do so now and if you've made one already, try another draft. Be sure your timeline brings out what the story is mainly about. If you are writing about an early morning fishing trip, and you want to show your closeness with your dad, your timeline will feature the things you and your dad did and said and felt. If you really want to show the impatience you felt, just waiting and waiting and waiting for a nibble on the end of your line, then your timeline of events will reflect this."

In this example from Rie, notice how she identifies what it is that makes this small episode matter to her. *[Figs. VI-4 and VI-5]*

I slipped out of my boots and wiggled my toes freely in the air. They were sore from all walking around welcome event. I got on my p-j's and hoppe into my bed. As I was pulling my covers over me my mom walked in to say good night Before she said anything she examed my bed. "Put your wool covers it gets very cold in the night." she said. "Why it's 70 degrees out?" I said. She shook her head and gave me I not going to argue with you look and left. I shuged and closed my eyes.

I woke up 10 minutes later. I looked at my arms they were covered with goosebumps. I felt like the temputure droped 30 degreas. I

Figs. VI-4 Rie's entry

reached down grabed the wool blankets at the end of my bed. As I got comfy I thougt about what my mom had said and why I should listened to her.

Figs. VI-5 Rie page 2

TAILORING YOUR TEACHING One of the most important qualities of good writing is something which people refer to as "voice." Don Murray suggests that voice involves the imprint of the author, the sense that a real person is behind the words. Children are more likely to write with this magical quality if they've first storytold or otherwise voiced their draft.

> Writing and speaking are different but writing, without an understanding of its roots in speech, is nothing. The human voice underlies the entire writing process, and shows itself throughout the life of the writer. It is no accident that children enjoy reading their selections aloud, that professional writers have public readings of their work, or that writing compels us to speak to others, or to voice to ourselves. (Graves 1988, p. 162)

If your students could benefit from oral storytelling in ways which strengthen particular aspects of their writing as they move from seed ideas to drafts . . . you may find it worth the time to provide more storytelling sessions, each time teaching children that writers sometimes keep in mind specific goals. One time, you might teach students that writers sometimes make a point to incorporate dialogue in our storytelling. "Make your characters talk. Say their actual words." Another time, you might teach children that writers sometimes keep in mind what we want listeners to feel. "If you want us to know you were devastated, then tell the story so we know just how devastated you were!"

If your students need more opportunities to rehearse their drafts by storytelling them . . . you might teach children that writers sometimes rehearse for drafting by telling our stories to one person then another. You might begin by saying, "Writers, I know most of you have chosen a seed idea (and some of you have a few possible seed ideas in mind). You've been spending time getting ready to write. Remember that you're going to be writing these stories in ways that will—you hope—get through to your readers, that will make your readers gasp and wince and laugh. So right now, why don't you do what writers do and try telling your stories to people who've never heard them. Aim to make your listeners gasp or laugh or wince." Then pair children with new temporary partners. These temporary partners can provide a fresh audience for each student's seed idea.

Collaborating with Colleagues

The lesson today is one that will require conferring support. If your primary-level colleagues have been using the *Units of Study for Primary Writing* and if they have our DVD called *Big Lessons from Small Writers*, I encourage you to borrow it and watch my conference with Lisa. She is a first grader, writing a story about a sleepover at her friend's house. You'll see that I asked her, "What is this story really about?" and there was a very long pause while she mulled that question over before finally admitting, "I'm not sure." So then I suggested two options, based on what she had already told me about the story. Might she be writing about the fun times that she and her friend had together? Or perhaps she could be wanting to show that sometimes, when you are over at a friend's house, you get a little homesick? Lisa knew right away that she wanted the latter option. So I asked, "Where does that lonesome part start?" I added, "When you got to Romi's house—at the start of the story—page 1—that wasn't really the lonesome part, was it?"

If you study that segment, you will see moves that I make repeatedly as I help children decide what the story really is that they want to tell. You'll see how I help children use their answers to this question to help them rethink their drafts. You'll also see that conferring with a six year old is not all that different from conferring with a ten year old.

After watching the segment, I suggest you try out this conference with your colleagues, helping each other to look again at your own writing and ask, "What am I really trying to say?" I want to tell you a secret that I don't bring out until later with the kids. Usually, there is a timeline to what you are trying to show, just as there is a timeline to the events in the story. That is, usually what a writer wants to show changes across the draft. For example, in my Miss Armstrong story, at the start of the story, I want to show how hopeful I am that I will finally be included in Eliza's group of friends, and then later in that story, I want to show my bitter disappointment when it becomes clear that having a role in the play doesn't give me a role in the popular group of kids. You may realize, too, that there is one thing you want to show at the start of the story you are writing, and another thing at the end of that story.

Try to utterly rewrite your story, bringing out what you want to show. This means that if some detail actually happened in real life, but that detail doesn't convey your point or add to what you are trying to show, you will probably not mention it. You'll also need to take some liberties to angle your story to convey the meaning you select.

This work is not easy, but it is extraordinarily powerful. If you want an added challenge, look at children's literature thinking, "How does this author use every means possible to convey his or her meaning?" Study, for example, Ezra Jack Keats' *Peter's Chair*, and notice how everything in that story works together to support the message that Peter first feels his world is threatened because of the arrival of a little sister.

SESSION VII

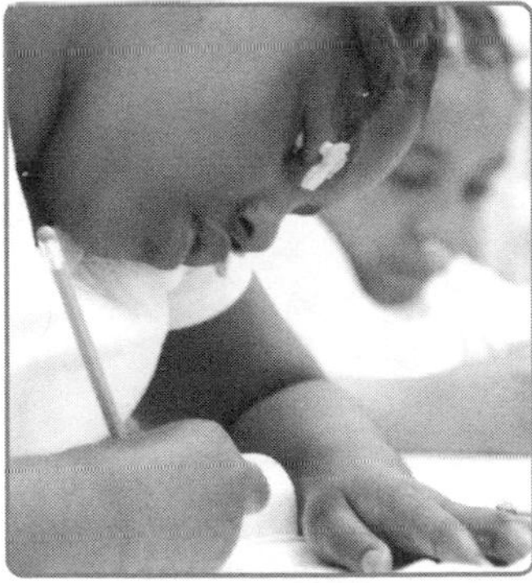

STUDYING AND CREATING LEADS

IN THIS SESSION, YOU'LL HELP STUDENTS LEARN THAT MENTOR TEXTS CAN GUIDE THEM AS THEY DRAFT AND REVISE LEADS.

GETTING READY

- Lead of Yolen's *Owl Moon,* written on chart paper
- Lead for a Small Moment story the whole class experienced, written on chart paper
- Collection of well-crafted narrative picture books very familiar to your students [see CD]
- Copies of chart with three columns: Author's Lead; What the Author Has Done; Our Lead Using the Same Technique
- Monitoring My Writing Process checklist
- Student examples of leads that support intentions of their narratives
- See CD-ROM for resources

In this minilesson, I invite children *to study leads in touchstone texts, learning from the work that other authors have done. The lead to* Owl Moon *can teach us that authors begin a draft thinking, "How can my lead link to the heart of my story?" From the start, readers need to sense what the story is really about.*

Then, too, a close look at Owl Moon *and other published texts can help you and your children pay attention to the grammar and syntax of leads.*

When demonstrating how to study the craft behind Yolen's lead, you can help children notice what adults refer to as a subordinate clause, one that modifies the independent clause that is the heart of the sentence. Although you probably won't try to teach the complex grammar of this structure just yet, children benefit from knowing that when writing narratives, we often begin our sentences with a clause that sets the scene, establishes the time or location, or describes the action. Children tend at first to write simple subject-verb-object sentences: "I rode the merry-go-round." As their skills and experience increase, they learn to begin sentences with subordinate clauses.

- *One sunny morning, I rode the merry-go-round. (States the time)*
- *Inching forward, the merry-go-round started. (Describes the action)*
- *At the top, I looked out. (States the location)*

You'll help writers push beyond the simple subject-verb-object sentences that fill so many of their drafts.

You may wonder why the lead (which is also the topic of Session VII in Unit 1) is worthy of such attention. First, I think that in writing (as in teaching), beginnings are important because they channel what follows. Of course, revising the lead can channel what follows only if children revise their lead prior to writing the narrative; it's less powerful if they return to a completed story and plop an improved lead in place of a preexisting one. I also think it is worthwhile to teach children to revise their leads because working with leads gives us a microcosm in which to teach children the process and payoffs of revision. When suggesting a child write one lead, then another and another, we aren't putting especially high demands on them. Meanwhile, children can get a taste for revision.

MINILESSON

Studying and Creating Leads

CONNECTION

Remind children of the techniques they learned when studying leads in Unit 1.

"Writers, remember that we talked about leads in our last unit? By looking at the work of published authors, you learned some techniques to try. You learned, for example, that it often works to start a narrative by telling a small action, by establishing the setting, or by having a character say something. This time, because we are more experienced as writers, we'll notice even more. Today we're going to look again at the way mentor authors write texts we love."

Name the teaching point. In this case, remind children that by studying the leads in mentor texts, they can learn new techniques.

"Have any of you tried to do a skateboarding trick? Or a skiing trick? Or a new dance step? If so, I bet you've watched someone who can do these things—maybe in real life, maybe on TV—and then you've tried to follow that person's prowess. I'm bringing this up because today I want to remind you that in the same way, writers study other writers whom we admire. This is how we learn moves that we want to use in our writing. Today I want to teach you to expand your options for writing leads by looking closely at how writers whom we admire begin their stories."

TEACHING

Demonstrate a process children can go through as they study the craftsmanship in another author's lead. Highlight the author's technique by contrasting it with what the author could have done.

"When I reach out for an author to study, I reach for one whose writing reminds me of what I'm trying to do, and I reach for an author who has written a text I admire. I've always admired Jane Yolen's lead to *Owl Moon*." I had copied her lead onto chart paper, and now I read it aloud.

COACHING

One of the challenges in this unit is to find ways to raise children's expectations so they tackle narrative writing with a new ambitiousness. By roping in authors as coteachers, I borrow their power and put it behind my teaching.

You may wish to peek ahead to Session XI. In that session, I teach children that narrative writers often plan our stories by thinking of them as story mountains. We sketch a story mountain, and keep in mind that the lead of a story needs to relate to the story's apex. If I was teaching skilled and experienced writers, I might move that session to this place in the unit because in fact, the decision over how to start a story relates to our sense of the story as a whole. I worried, however, that for many children this would be too complex. It is usually preferable to introduce a new and complex idea as a tool for revision, moving it forward in the process during a later cycle of work.

I would normally have returned to the one text that I hope will thread its way through much of this unit. The problem is that the children and I have been studying an excerpt from "Eleven" The start of the excerpt is not actually Cisneros' lead to the essay. In the final unit of this year, children revisit "Eleven," this time noticing the exposition at the start of that text. For now, I chose to study Owl Moon *because it allows me to make the points I want to make and because children know it well.*

It was late one winter night,
long past my bedtime,
when Pa and I went owling.

There was no wind.

The trees stood still
as giant statues.

And the moon was so bright
the sky seemed to shine.

Somewhere behind us
a train whistle blew,
long and low,
like a sad, sad song. (p. 3)

"When I study this lead, the first thing I notice is that even in her first sentence, Yolen has highlighted the narrator's relationship with her father—and the silence of the night, too. I'm pretty sure that for Jane Yolen, this story is really about a silent, wordless closeness she and her dad shared when they went owling. Those elements are present even in her opening lines."

"When I study this lead, I also notice that Jane Yolen isn't hesitant to give us all the vital facts we need to know to understand what's going on in her story. I'm mentioning that Yolen gives us all the vital facts because some people start their stories in ways that are confusing. For example, some authors might start a story like this.":

"Son," my dad said.

"Yes," I answered.

"Come here," my dad said. I walked over to where he lay face down on the grass.

"You read the lead and you think, 'What's happening here?' Granted, creating a puzzle in the first line of a text can sometimes be effective, but I personally prefer leads that answer the reader's questions. In *Owl Moon*, Jane Yolen puts all the vital facts into the start of her story. She tells us *who* is doing *what, where*. She even does this in one single sentence, answering *where* and *when* ('Late one winter night, long past my bedtime'), then *who* ('Pa and I') and *what* ('went owling'). But she doesn't answer these in a boring way. Instead, her chock-full-of-information lead has a 'pull in and listen' tone. You can feel that she's going to tell a story."

There is no one way to describe all the techniques Yolen has used that are worth emulating. I think many people would use more flowery language to name what she has done: She paints a scene, she creates a mood. Those things are true. But I want to highlight a few aspects of her craft that children may not notice but which will make a big difference to their writing. For this reason, I point out that her lead links to her message; this was, after all, the subject of the previous session. I could have proceeded to say that Yolen first paints the background, the big picture, and then zooms in to details, the footsteps on the snow. I decide instead to point out that she starts her story with information because in this class, I found many of the children's stories were confusing and disorienting. In any case, simply saying, "She paints a picture" wouldn't seem helpful enough to me.

You'll notice in all these units of study that the examples we present closely match what the students themselves might produce.

When I weigh the success of a minilesson, I tend to focus on whether it is memorable and replicable. I find that little things can make minilessons more replicable—like the fact that I refer to the well-known terms: who, what, when, where and why.

Debrief by naming the author's craft moves and showing how you could use similar moves in a lead about a class event.

"What I've learned, writers, is that if I want to write like an author, it helps to really study what the author did *exactly*. Let me look more closely at Jane Yolen's sentences. I'm going to try to think, 'How is this different from what I usually do?' When I'm talking or writing in a regular way, I think I tend to say *what I did* first (or what another person did), and only then tell *when* or *where* I—or we—did that thing. I think if *I* had been the one to go owling, I'd say (or write) this. 'I went owling late last night.'"

"Jane Yolen brings a story feeling to her writing partly because she changes the usual order of the sentence. She puts when and where first, then adds a comma and then tells the action. 'It was late one winter night, long past my bedtime, when Pa and I went owling.'"

"If I want to write a lead following Jane Yolen's template (only mine will be about *my* story, not hers), I could try to write a sentence that answers the *who, what, where*, and *when* questions, and one that sequences these in the way that she did."

"So if my story is about how Hermie tried escaping from his cage during today's read-aloud time, I could write the lead this way."

> It was early one Friday morning, just at the start of read-aloud time, when Hermie tried escaping from his cage.

"Of course, tiny specific actions sometimes help, so I could also start the story like this."

> It was early one Friday morning, just as we were settling in for read-aloud, when Katie noticed the empty cage.

"Later today, or whenever you write, some of you may want to emulate Jane Yolen's *Owl Moon* lead."

You may be surprised to see this detailed attention to syntax when students are just on the brink of beginning a first draft. It is true that I believe syntax is more a matter of rehearsal and drafting than of editing. I believe we can launch children in writing with more literary syntax, and that doing this can evoke a quality of writing that can never be achieved through red pen corrections. Then, too, I want children to know that writers love the sounds and textures of language, and pay attention not only to what we say but also to how to convey our content.

Active Engagement

Rally children to study the lead in another published text and to name what that author has done.

"But my bigger point is that, as we learned in our first unit, we can study any author's lead really closely, asking, 'What has this author done that I could try?' I'm going to pass out some other books that all of us know really well. When you get a text, will you and your partner find the lead. Read it once, twice. Read it aloud and then talk together about what your author has done. Has your author written a lead which is similar to the lead of *Owl Moon*? Has your author done something different—and if so, what has the author done? Dissect the sentence like I did when I said Yolen wrote *where* and *when*, and *who* did *what*.

When you pass out books for children to study, I recommend you fill the collection with books which have opening sentences which resemble that which you studied as well as with books which demonstrate another option or two. Classics such as Mike Mulligan and His Steam Shovel, *("Mike Mulligan has a steam shovel, a beautiful red steam shovel.") or McCloskey's* One Morning in Maine, *or MacLachlan's* Sarah Plain and Tall *follow the same pattern as* Owl Moon.

You needn't use these words —*where, when, who, what*—invent your own words for describing exactly what the author has done. If you can, try saying a lead to the Hermie story that would follow the same pattern as the lead you study."

One partnership pored over *My Pig, Amarillo* by Satomi Ichikawa. The lead begins:

> One summer day, my grandpa arrives home with a tiny pig on a leash.
> "Pablito, it's for you," he says. I am so excited. I do not know what to say.

The children decided the story began like *Owl Moon*. The author told when the action happened, then added a comma, then included a simple sentence, telling "who did what." They tried inventing a similar lead to the Hermie story:

> One fall afternoon, my teacher read aloud in the meeting area. "What's that noise?" I whispered. It sounded like Hermie. I was nervous.

Similarly, the children who studied *Smoky Nights* by Eve Bunting saw that the opening sentence told "who did what" and then added a comma, then explained how the action was done:

> Mama and I stand well back from our window, looking down. I'm hiding Jasmine my cat.

The children need not report on their conversation to you. They gain from having the chance to talk about something whether or not you hear and record what they say! If you decide to extend the minilesson by soliciting the class' help in filling out a chart see the CD for advice.

Author's Lead	What the Author Has Done	Our Lead, Using the Same Technique
Mama and I stand well back from our window, looking down. I'm hiding Jasmine, my cat. We don't have lights on though it'salmost dark. People are rioting in the street below. Mama explains about rioting. "It can happen when people get angry . . ." (Smoky Night, by Eve Bunting, p.5)	The first sentence tells who is doing what, and then there is a comma, followed by a tiny explanation of their mainaction. Then the story names the circumstance—the rioting—that happens around the characters.	My classmates and I listened to the story, picturing the scenes in the book. Hermie's cage was empty. Robert pointed out that he'd left a trail of shavings. "We can follow them."
One summer day, my grandpa arrives home with a tiny pig on a leash. "Pablito, it's for you," he says. I am so excited. I do not know what to say. (My Pig, Amarillo, by Satomi Ichikawa, p.5)	The story begins by telling when, then with a main character doing an action in a place, followed by dialogue. Then the narrator expresses her feelings.	One fall afternoon, my teacher read aloud in the meeting area. "What's that noise?" I whispered. It sounded like Hermie. I was nervous. I did not know what to say.

LINK

Rename the teaching point, reminding children that today, and whenever they write, they can let authors become their teachers. Before sending children off, remind them of the strategies on the writing process chart.

"So writers, remember that if you want to do a trick on your skateboard, you watch someone who can do it. You watch really closely, noticing their technique. Perhaps the skateboarder shifts his weight, or leans to one side, or puts his hands out for balance. Whatever he does, you try the same thing."

"Similarly, you learned today that if you want to write a really powerful lead, it helps to carefully study the leads of writers we admire, just like we did for *Owl Moon*. Writers and skateboarders aren't that different from each other! Let's change the wording on our Monitoring My Writing Process chart to match what we now know about leads." On the chart, I quickly wrote "Study published leads."

"So during writing time today and often, you may want to look closely at what an author you admire has done. Let that author become your teacher by paying close attention, studying the craft the author has used."

"If you are admiring a lead, ask, 'Why did it work?' If you are studying anything—the setting, the character development, the question, 'What's this story really about?'—you can pay attention to what the author did pertaining to whatever it is you are studying. Of course, you will want to refer to our Monitoring My Writing Process chart, making sure that you are progressing along in the process of writing your own story." I pointed again to the Monitoring My Writing Process chart as a reminder of all their options. "Let's get started."

We hope that children's learning is cumulative. Because we want children to hold on to what they learned from previous minilessons as they progress, you'll see that we often weave language from early minilessons into our teaching.

You may want to literally count up how many times our link reminds children of the array of optional activities they could pursue during the day, versus how many times the link channels children to do a particular activity right away. I'm quite sure that most of the time, before sending children off, we remind them of their options.

Monitoring My Writing Process	First Piece	Next Piece
Gather entries		
Select and develop one seed idea		
Write an entry about what you are really trying to say.		
Storytell to rehearse for writing		
Read published writing that resembles what you want to write		
Study published leads. Pay attention to what the author did and how the author did it. Let this influence your own writing.		
Draft leads—try action, dialogue, setting		
Make a timeline		
Choose paper, plan story on pages, copy lead		
Write draft with each part on a separate page		
Reread and revise for clarity		
Draft endings—try writing with important ideas and images from the story, and with details that are reminders of the whole		
Revise and edit more now or decide to wait until later, or not to revise		

Writing and Conferring

Getting Ready for Drafting

Today might be a day to help kids confer with each other. I sometimes emphasize this on a day when a particularly long line of kids seems to be following me, looking for assistance, in which case I am apt to ask for all children's attention and tell them there are twenty-nine writing teachers in the classroom, not just one. But I might also choose to teach this lesson now because at this particular juncture in the writing process, it is very important for writers to have listeners.

Most of your children will still be rehearsing for their first drafts. They'll probably be writing in their notebooks, making and revising timelines, trying alternate leads, telling their stories to listeners. As children do this, it's a great thing for them to say aloud the story they plan to write, and to cumulate goals for the draft they'll soon produce.

MID-WORKSHOP TEACHING POINT ***Elaborating on the Important Parts*** "Writers, earlier you learned that a writer needs to decide whether to write in big steps or in tiny steps. Rena just realized that usually we'll slow down and use tiny steps to tell the *important parts* of our stories. Rena began writing about a bike ride. She started inching her way through the story starting with getting a drink on the way to her bike."

> I slowly raise the glass to my lips and settle my mouth on the rim. I tip the cup so that the lemonade pours down my throat. I shiver. I put too much ice in it, and it's over-refreshing. One cube slips down with my last sip.
>
> I feel much cooler now. I know I won't be cool for much longer, though. I am going on a bike ride.

"But then Rena realized the drink didn't matter to her bike trip story! She said to me, 'I stretched out the story of how I gulped down some lemonade, but now I realize I stretched out something that doesn't really matter.'" *[Fig. VII-1]*

continued on next page

If you do decide to help children confer with each other, before you can teach them to do this, you need to decide the kind of help you can imagine kids giving each other. The easiest thing for kids to do is to help each other talk a lot about their subjects. That is, if a child has written about her guinea pig, another child can listen with interest and say, "I didn't even know you had a guinea pig. Tell me more about it."

With coaching, some children can learn to steer the writer, asking, "What's the most important thing you want to say?" or "Can you tell the whole story, and tell it in a way that makes that important?"

In general, I hope that as the year moves along, you'll be able to spend less and less time listening to writers talk about their guinea pig and their sister and their basketball game, and that you'll be able to spend much more time listening to writers talk about their writing strategies and goals and assessments. That is, as you confer, if a child answers your inquiry about what she has been working on as a writer by simply telling you her subject—"I've been writing about my guinea pig"—I hope you'll respond only briefly

I slowly raise the glass to my lips and settle my mouth on the rim. I tip the cup so that the lemonade pours down my throat. I shiver. I put too much ice in it, and its over-refreshing. One cube slips down with the last of my sip.
I feel much cooler now. I know I won't be cool for much longer though. I am going on a bike ride.
We go downstairs, to the basement where our bikes are locked up. My mom takes out the keys and fiddles with her U-lock while I fasten on my bike helmet. I need to adjust the straps on it. It feels too tight. My head must have grown. My mom is ready to go, but she doesn't have to adjust her helmet because her head stopped growing a long time ago.

Fig. VII-1 Rena

to the subject and will, above all, channel the writer to talk about what he or she has been trying to do on the page and the strategies he or she has used to accomplish these goals. So it's a great thing to invite children to take over some of the role of being listeners as writers talk about their subjects.

As you move away from conferences that focus exclusively on content, help children assume the role of being good listeners for each other. Recall that in Session V, I emphasized the experience of talking to someone who listens with such rapt attention that we end up saying and recalling more than we dreamed of saying. This is what children can do in peer conferences.

The jury is out over how to teach children to help each other. Some people start right in with fairly explicit instructions: Look at the writer while he or she reads, tell the writer what the draft made you think and feel, ask the writer open-ended prompts like, "Can you tell me more about this?" or "How did you feel?" or "Can you help me picture it?" or "Start at the beginning, and tell it bit by bit." Other teachers try to instill in children an appreciation for good listeners, and then send kids off to be good writing partners for each other, relying on authentic relationships more than scripts to lift the level of peer conferences.

continued from previous page

"Looking back on the draft, Rena crossed out most of what she'd written, which was so smart of her!" Then I said, "Writers, the most important thing to realize is this: sometimes when we learn something new, we over learn it! When I teach first graders exclamation marks, they add them in all over a draft! And some of you have over-learned what I said about writing in tiny steps, stretching out your story. As Rena said, now she realizes that the main thing in her story was bike riding but she got stuck in the kitchen having a drink of lemonade!"

"You will need to keep in mind that some parts of your story will need to be written quickly, in big steps, and some parts of your story need to be written slowly, in tiny steps. You will know what to skip past and what to stretch out when you know what your story is really about."

"Would each of you look at your writing right now, and put a mark in the margin indicating the really important parts of your story?" After a moment, I said, "These are the parts you'll probably want to write in tiny steps."

SHARE

Learning from Techniques Classmates Have Used

Share the process by which a student has crafted a stronger lead than the one she had.

"Writers, I want to share with you the work that some of you did on leads today. Emily remembered she could start her lead at more than one place in her timeline. Here are two leads that she tried for her story about losing her math homework at a Chinese restaurant." I read aloud the following entries. *[Fig. VII-2]*

Lead #1: "Do I really have to do my homework now?" I asked.

"Yes" answered my mom. Then I started to think of an excuse. "But then how are we going to do it without scissors?"

"I can rip out the cards, now just stop asking." My mom replied. She started to rip out the cards. "It is sooo dim in here!" I said.

Lead #2: The lights were dim as I walked in. I could already smell a whiff of Chinese food. The people were as quiet as ever. I thought, they must like there food.

"Did you notice how one lead starts at the point on the timeline when Emily and her mom were already sitting at the table, and the other starts at the point when they first entered the restaurant? I also want you to notice that Emily created a sense of the setting. She got the idea for doing this from both *Owl Moon* and also from Eve Bunting's *Smokey Nights.* I love the way she came up with her own goals, wrote them in her planning box, and then pursued those goals."

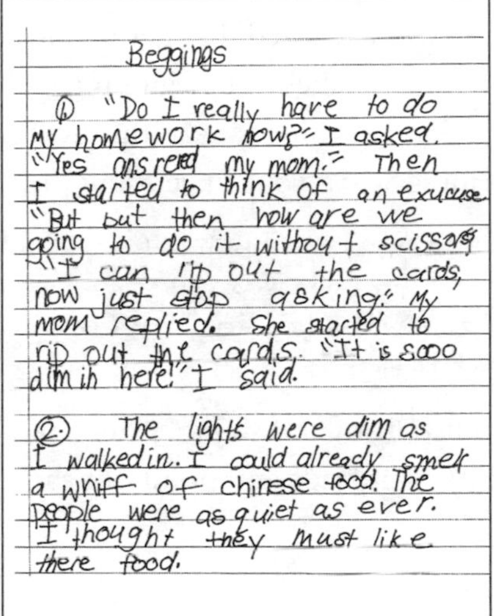

Beggings

① "Do I really hare to do my homework now?" I asked. "Yes ansrered my mom." Then I started to think of an exucuse "But but then how are we going to do it without scissors" "I can rip out the cards, now just stop asking." My mom replied. She started to rip out the cards. "It is sooo dim in here!" I said.

② The lights were dim as I walkedin. I could already smelk a whiff of chinese food. The people were as quiet as ever. I thought they must like there food.

Fig. VII-2 Emily

Share the process of another student who had success using a mentor author's techniques to revise her lead.

"Sophie, you remember, had initially begun her draft this way."

> We walked through the front door of Chuck E. Cheese. The place was packed. We ordered a pizza. It was good.

"But the other day, she realized that her narrative is really a story about she and Claudia, so she tried a new lead. She labeled it 'Beginning Action' but really, she's beginning with action *and* with Claudia. I'm going to read this now and will you list four smart things that Sophie's done. Tell these across your fingers and then get ready to share them." *[Fig. VII-3]*

> We walked into the Chuck E. Cheese. I held Claudia's hand tight, my palm was sweating. I was feeling really happy to be with Claudia. "Hey, Claudia! What game do you want to play?"

"What did you list? Turn and share." After a few minutes, I said, "What smart things have you done? Share your leads and point out each other's smart decisions."

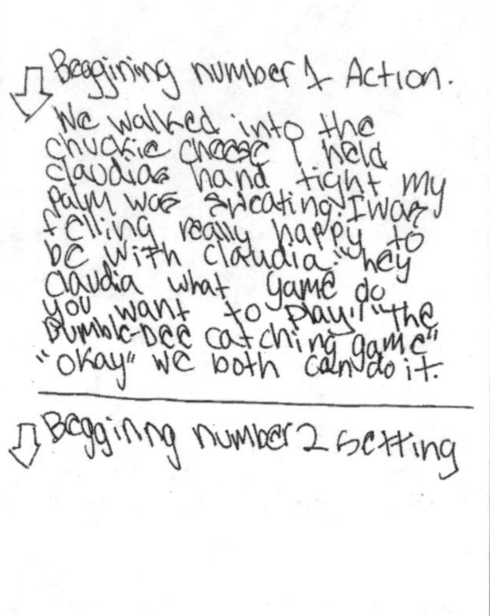

Fig. VII-3 Sophie

HOMEWORK ***Studying and Writing Leads*** Today we studied some leads in stories we know well in order to name the things the author did that made these leads really work well. Tonight your job is to do the same things. Reread the lead in the book you're reading right now and then reread the leads in some books you love. They could be chapter books, short stories, or picture books.

When you reread these leads, do the same work we did in school today. Notice what the author does in the lead and name it on a sticky note. Now, take a look at the leads you've written and revise them using one or some of the things you noticed in published leads. Bring these revised leads to school tomorrow because you'll have a chance to talk to your writing partner about what you did in your lead revisions.

TAILORING YOUR TEACHING

If your students could benefit from studying different kinds of leads to expand their repertoire of possibilities for their own writing . . . you might spend a writing session studying powerful, well-loved leads together with your students and categorizing them. In *Live Writing,* Ralph Fletcher suggests categorizing powerful leads from well-loved books. One category of powerful leads he describes is the Grabber Lead, in which the writer begins deliberately with an element of surprise. Fletcher also discusses Introducing the Narrator leads; the Moody Lead, in which the writer sets the mood or tone of the story; Beginning at the End, in which the writer reveals the ending at the start before unfolding the story; and the Misleading Lead, in which the writer deliberately sets you up for something other than what unfolds. In some strong writing classrooms, teachers and students chart different types of leads with examples from both professional and student writers. After your students know a variety of categories of leads, you can guide them to try out different leads before choosing the one that best fits the overall intentions they have for their stories.

If your students seem so intent on writing titillating or exciting leads that they forget that a lead needs to orient the reader . . . teach them how authors describe actions in ways that answer readers' questions and provide orienting information. You may want to cite the famous lead to *Charlotte's Web,* and you'll also find Takeshi's skilled efforts can be a resource for you in your minilesson. *[Fig. VII-4]*

> I got off the taxi cab with my mom, my brother and me to go drop Faiki off to his piano lesson. When we got off the taxi and the taxi went away, right in front of me was the old deli I used to go to.
>
> "I'm going in the deli, okay?" I asked my mom.. I walked up to the cashier and said. "Hi, do you remember me?" The cashier turned his head and said. "Oh, I remember you, " he said.

Takeshi finally decided to start his story like this.

> "I'm going in the deli, okay?" I asked my mom as I ran up to the deli. "Okay," she said. I was already walking up to the cashier. "Do you remember me?" I said as I stood up to the cashier. He turned his head to look at me. "Oh, hi." he said and I was relieved that he remembered me.

Fig. VII-4 Takeshi

Collaborating with Colleagues

One of our goals in this unit of study is to teach students to make strong reading/writing connections. We want them to realize that mentor texts can teach them everything they need to know about any kind of writing they want to compose. Webster's dictionary defines a mentor as "a close, trusted, and experienced counselor or guide," which perfectly describes the relationships we want our students to have with mentor texts.

You may find yourself tempted to bring great armloads of wonderful literature into your grade-level faculty meetings or study groups. I caution against this, and urge you instead to devote long chunks of time to study a single mentor text closely (and then, perhaps, another one).

For example, you could decide to study Ezra Jack Keats' *Peter's Chair* together. On first glance, this book might appear easy to dismiss. It's written for young children, and can seem to be no big deal. Look again. Members of the Teachers College Reading and Writing Project staff spent perhaps six hours studying just that one book and we were amazed by the craftsmanship. In Session XI, you will help children discover its perfect arc of story structure. But also notice how every part demonstrates Peter's emotional journey. For example, consider the beginning:

> Peter stretched as high as he could.
> There! His tall building was finished.
> CRASH! Down it came. "Shhhh!" called
> his mother. "You'll have to play more
> quietly. Remember, we have a new baby
> in the house." (pp. 7–9)

Peter's world literally crashes down around him.

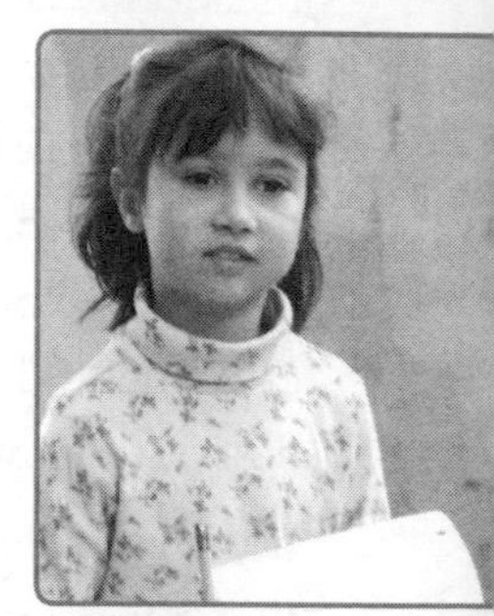

Notice how Keats provides three examples to show Peter's world collapsing: his cradle, his high chair, his crib. These collapses trigger Peter's decision to run away. Likewise, Keats lists three items that Peter packs when he runs away: his blue chair, his toy crocodile, his baby picture. Keats trusts that these few details are enough for the reader to understand the larger picture. Similarly, Keats suggests Peter's emotional change through a series of actions: sitting in his baby chair that is now too small; playing a trick on his mom that she plays along with; eating lunch with his family; and offering to help paint his chair pink. Keats has crafted a story whose seemingly simple elements take the main character—and the reader—on a meaningful emotional journey.

If you know a book really well, you can carry that book with you as you confer, referring to it often. If you want to teach a youngster the importance of precise action words, you can find them in this book. If you want to teach that characters have motivations and they encounter struggle, you can also show this using *Peter's Chair*. If you want to highlight the use of metaphor, you'll find this one book is laden with them. If you want to teach point of view, show-don't-tell, alliteration, answering reader's questions, or a host of other things, you can do so with this one book. When you encounter students who include details that don't support their intentions, you could look together at the details that Keats included (or may have excluded). When a student writes, "We got ready to go," you could teach her to list at least three specific details such as Keats does. And the secret is: you can probably teach qualities of good writing using *any* well-written narrative!

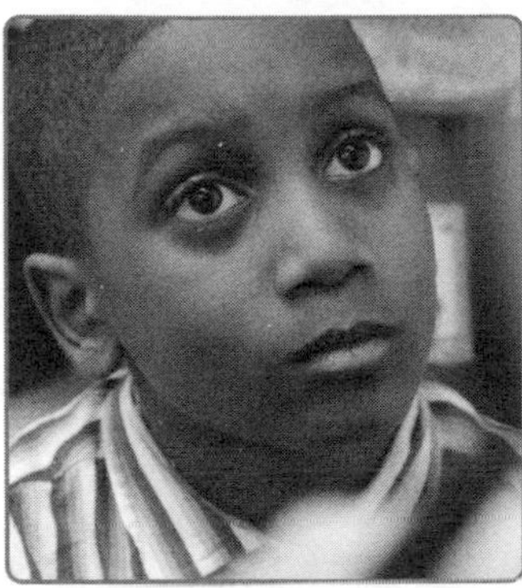

TELLING THE STORY FROM INSIDE IT

IN THIS SESSION, YOU'LL TEACH STUDENTS TO WRITE FROM THE NARRATOR'S POINT OF VIEW.

GETTING READY

- Your own writer's notebook
- Your own story draft, showing a point of view that needs work
- Qualities of Good Personal Narrative Writing chart
- *Homesick*, by Jean Fritz
- Student samples of personal narrative writing showing work of the minilesson, one from a previous year to use before the Share
- See CD-ROM for resources

When I read Ori's writing aloud *during the session on the importance of asking, "What am I really trying to say?" I was drawn to a puzzling detail in his story. He described looking into his parents' room and seeing his mom's "extremely large brownish bed." Later, he also said that he walked down the "brownish stairs." I noticed these details because it was absolutely clear to me that I would never, in a million years, describe my bed or stairs that way. So why had Ori done that? This was the question that led to this minilesson and to the one in Session VII (Revising Leads) in Unit One.*

This minilesson reminds children to write their story through their narrator's eyes. As we taught students in Launching the Writing Workshop, there are details a person in a particular situation would be apt to notice—and details a person in that position would be unlikely to note. If I've just opened my door and sleepily entered the long hallway, I might notice the morning light on the hallway mirror, but I wouldn't attend to the details of the floral pattern on the rug at the end of the hall. I also wouldn't notice mundane details—why would I remark that the floor was brown if it was brown every day? Thinking through the story from inside it, as though it's happening, is what helps us choose which details to include and which to exclude.

Earlier in this series, we encouraged students to write with their full attention on their story, acting out the story in their heads, getting the whole true story down, without concern for whether they were writing well or badly. Now it seems as if we are emphasizing the opposite: asking students to be critical readers of their own writing. The truth is, this is a dichotomy that writers live with. Writers always switch back and forth between writing passionately about a subject, then rereading critically. This unit reflects these two roles that writers must assume; the next few sessions, in particular, emphasize this critical reader role.

Try letting this minilesson lift the level of your writing as well. As you try to make sense of what I say, and apply it to your own writing, make note of your thoughts. You could turn this lesson into a two-day sequence, and on the second day, tell your children how the minilesson affected you and your own writing.

I'm pretty sure your children will come away saying the minilesson you wrote, the one sharing your process, was their favorite!

MINILESSON

Telling the Story from Inside It

CONNECTION

Help children see where they've been and where they're going in their writing process.

"Writers, many of you have written several leads and you've also written entries *about* your seed idea, exploring what it is you want your story to show. Many of you have used Robert Munsch's idea and storytold your story as preparation for writing it."

"If you haven't started your first draft, do that today. Drafting, for a writer, is a lot like sketching is for an artist. Drafts and sketches are fast and tentative and imperfect—but both drafts and sketches can capture the tone and feeling of a subject. Once you get started on your first draft, you'll be lost in your writing like most of us get lost in a good book. Your mind will be on what happened in your story, seeing and hearing and feeling the episode all over again, and you'll try to get it down as fast as you can."

Name your teaching point. In this case, tell children that when writing a personal story, they need to step into the point of view of their narrator.

"As you work on your drafts, I have one bit of advice that I think can set you up to write an especially true story. This is it. You need to put yourself inside the skin of the main character. (The character is you, of course, just you in a different time and place.) Your job as a writer is to tell the story as you see it unfolding, looking through the narrator's eyes."

TEACHING

Tell the story of one time when you wrote a story, staying inside the constraints of your particular perspective.

"I first learned about writing inside a point of view when I was in the middle of washing dishes (in a story) and the phone rang. My arms were deep in the soap suds, so I couldn't answer it. My sister picked up the receiver and I heard her say, 'Hello?' into the phone."

"And then what happened next was that I learned a big lesson. (Remember my advice. I need to put myself, as the storyteller, inside the skin of one person. When I tell this story that means I'm standing at the sink with my arms deep in the dishwater.) I'm still at the sink when my sister picks up the phone. I want to write about the phone call. But my arms are still in the dishwater so the story can't go like this.

COACHING

The truth is that some people write messy, tentative, rapid drafts and some inch along, refining each line as they go. Both ways can work. I tend to talk up the value of fast, tentative drafts because I want children to be game to revise, and I know if they worry about writing a draft perfectly, they sometimes become wed to it.

I believe that when writing, as when reading, we actually can become lost in a story and that doing this yields amazing writing.

When I use the phrase "narrator's point of view" throughout this session and this series, I don't mean it as a way to distinguish the first-person (meaning "I") or third-person (meaning "he" or "she") points of view. Instead, I mean the words more literally: what exactly is in the mind's eye of the narrator at any given time? I use the phrase "narrator's point of view" to help writers understand that if details of the scene aren't in that narrator's perception at that moment, perhaps they don't belong in the writing either!

> My sister picked up the phone. It was my mom telling her that she had been to the doctor.

"I'm at the sink. How would I know whose voice was inside that phone? The story has to unfold as it occurred to me. I'm standing at the sink, my hands in the suds, looking at my sister as she talks on the phone. So the story as I experienced it must sound like this.

> My sister picked up the phone. I heard her say, "What'd he say?" and "Did he give you anything for it?" After she hung up she said, "That was Mom. She's been to the doctor."

I like the visual effect of this minilesson. I can imagine telling this portion of it and I know that within the minilesson, I'll act out how my arms are elbow-deep in sudsy water, and while I still stand there with arms immersed, my sister picks up the phone. And then I can imagine that just by my intonation the children will discern that something has been knocked asunder by the sentence, 'It was my mom telling her that she had been to the doctor.' My intonation and my gestures can make it easy for children to grasp why this story defies reality.

Active Engagement

Set children up to practice telling a story from within the narrator's perspective. Ask them to reread a pretend draft where the point of view needs to be remedied.

"Once you get used to staying inside your own perspective, it's not that hard to watch for instances where, oops, you slip out of it."

"To practice noticing when a story suddenly loses its grounding, listen to my story and decide, 'Is the point of view working?' in which case make a thumbs-up gesture, or 'Did I just lose it?' (show thumbs down)." I pretended to write on my spiral pad, zooming quickly along, and meanwhile voiced this story aloud.

> I stood alongside my bike at the top of the hill. My brother, Alex, and his friend, Brian, waited as I made up my mind. In front of me the road lay like a ribbon. "I'm ready," I thought. I swung my leg up, climbed onto the seat, and pushed on the pedal. [Thumbs up.] Soon I was gently slipping down the road, faster and faster. The world zoomed past me: trees, boulders, woods . . . browns, grays, greens—a blur of color. [Thumbs up.] Then I saw something dart out in front of me. Was it a squirrel? A chipmunk? I swerved to avoid it, lost my balance, and headed into the wild brush on the side of the road. [Thumbs up.] My bike flipped and I went flying. Suddenly I saw nothing. [Thumbs up.] My brother raced down the hill and then they went inside. Brian looked at Alex and wondered if I was alive. [Thumbs down.]

It's always challenging to think, "How can I set things up so children can have a few minutes to practice and apply the concept I've taught?" Part of the challenge is that we want to act as training wheels, enabling children to have success with the concept. In my examples, I deliberately try to use words which make it clear when I'm writing within the first-person point of view, and when I slip out of it. But intonation helps as well.

Ask children to continue saying the story aloud, maintaining the point of view.

"Pretend you are the author. Continue the story from where I leave off. Make it up, based on what you think could have happened, but stay in the point of view of me lying on the ground after the accident."

To get children started, I went back and reread the story before I lost the point of view. "'My bike flipped and I went flying. My arm crashed on a rock with a thump. Suddenly I saw nothing . . .' Okay, take over. Partner 1, begin."

You'll notice that this is a double-decker Active Engagement and you may decide to delete this final portion. I included it because my goal is to set children up to actually do (not to talk about) whatever I've taught.

Link

Rename your teaching point. Send children off to copy their leads and to climb into the skin of their narrator.

"So writers, if you haven't done so already, find your favorite lead. Copy it onto lined paper outside the notebook (or write a new lead on draft paper). You can write on single sheets or fold paper in half to make story booklets, in which case please think about which dot on your timeline will go on each page. Then remember, before you can write, you need to recall the story. And you need to put yourself inside the skin of the person in the story. Are you at the top of the hill, your bike beside you? Or are you at the kitchen sink, up to your elbows in suds? Are you in bed on a cold autumn morning? Wherever you are in the lead of your story, go there mentally before you write. See what's around you, taste it, live it, and as you write, write the step-by-step of what you experience." Then I added this item to our Qualities of Good Personal Narrative Writing chart.

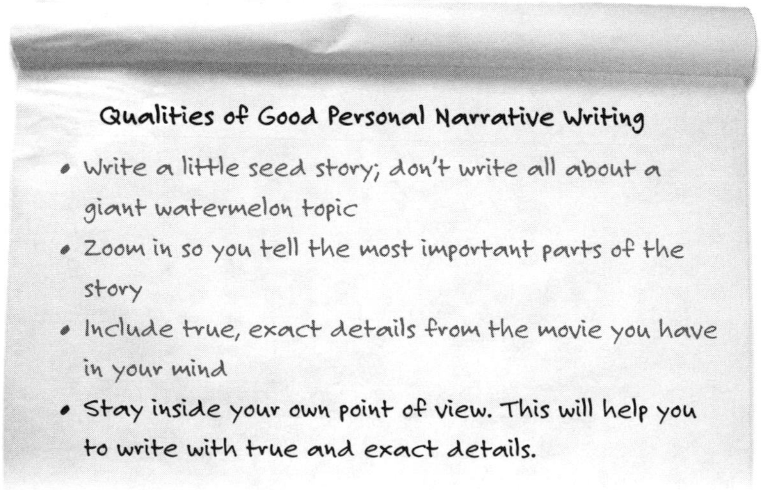

Qualities of Good Personal Narrative Writing

- Write a little seed story; don't write all about a giant watermelon topic
- Zoom in so you tell the most important parts of the story
- Include true, exact details from the movie you have in your mind
- **Stay inside your own point of view. This will help you to write with true and exact details.**

Let's talk about paper. First of all, paper matters. The kind of paper that children use is not inconsequential. You'll notice that most of the writing that I include in this book has been written on single sheets of notebook paper. Some are pages from within writer's notebooks and others (the rough drafts and final drafts) are loose pages which writers store in their folders. I don't have many examples of children writing in booklets, and yet I continually mention them.

This is why. In just the past few months, my colleagues and I have come to believe that many writers, and especially those who struggle, benefit from writing narratives across pages in little booklets. The booklets only work, however, if the writer first allocates one step of the story to page one (one dot of the timeline), one step to page two, and so forth. This means that the pages are not apt to be full, leaving space for revision.

Writing and Conferring

Reenacting Events

As you confer with children, you'll find that by studying their work and trying to understand their understandings of writing, you become much smarter as a teacher. I suggest you pay special attention to children's use of details and try to articulate what you ascertain. My observations tell me that when teachers encourage children to add descriptions, especially to write with sensory details, the resulting text often doesn't ring true unless the details are those that the narrator would notice from his or her vantage point. So I sometimes think that even if the goal is for writers to write with detail, the one strategy that can best produce those details is for writers to make movies in their minds, reenacting the events as they write about them.

But it is important for children to remember that, as James Merrill said, "The words that come first are anybody's words. You need to make them your own." If a child wrote, "I walked up the walk and inside the front door. I had a snack. Then I went to my bedroom." you might say, "Your story could tell about walking inside *anybody's* front door. Listen to how Jean Fritz, in her memoir *Homesick,* describes walking inside *her* house."

> I flung open the iron gate and threw myself through the front door.
>
> "I'm home!" I yelled.
>
> Then I remembered that it was Tuesday, the day my mother taught English at the Y.M.C.A. where my father was the director.
>
> I stood in the hall, trying to catch my breath, and as always I began to feel small. It was a huge hall with ceilings so high it was as if they would have nothing to do with people. Certainly not with a mere child, not with me—the only child in the house. Once I asked my best friend, Andrea, if the hall made her feel little too. She said no. She was going to be a dancer and she loved space. She did a high kick to show how grand it was to have room. (p. 13)

MID-WORKSHOP TEACHING POINT ***Noticing if the Details Ring True*** "Writers, when you are writing from inside the skin of a character (you), remember that the details you see and include in your draft will be the details that the character notices *in the moment of the story*. Do your details ring true? For example, last year, one of my students, a boy named Andy, wrote about sitting down at the lunch table. Think about the real, true details you focus on when you sit at the lunch table and then think about Andy's piece. Does it seem to you these are the details he truly noticed when he sat at that table?" *[Fig. VIII-1]*

> I carried my tray full of food from the lunch line. I went over and put my tray on the yellow metal table. I pulled the red metal chair in as I sat beside the table.

"I don't think that during his lunch, Andy really paid attention to the metal or to the color of tables and chairs in his cafeteria, do you? I think he was trying to add sensory details because he knows writers do that, but he'd forgotten that the sensory details need to be *true ones* that he noticed from the narrator's point of view. Talk with your partner about your own writing so far today."

I carried my tray full of food from the lunch line. I went over and put my tray on the yellow metal table. I pulled the red metal chair in as I set beside the table. Everyone was sharing snack. William had cupcakes and I wanted some. Thomas shared some popcorn with me. He put it on my tray. "Thanks, Thomas," I said.

Fig. VIII-1 Andy

I might show this excerpt to a child in a conference, saying, "Do you see how Jean Fritz describes that hallway in a way that reveals not only the hallway, but also reveals her as a person? If your first draft said, 'I walked up the walk and inside the front door. I had a snack. Then I went to my bedroom' and you wanted to revise this to show yourself—your point of view, your kitchen—what might you write? Would you say, 'I walked into our kitchen and opened the refrigerator to see if Mom had made the casserole for tonight's dinner'? Would you say, 'I sifted though a pile of mail but it was all bills to my mom, and this time they had threatening labels: "Third bill,"' and so on. What might you say to show yourself entering your kitchen?"

Then I'd look for a few places in the child's draft where he or she could apply this same concept and help the child get started.

"Francesca's draft describes the day her cat died. I might cite this in a conference, instead of referencing a text by a published author. The power of this writing comes, I think, because Francesca put herself back into the story moment, losing herself in that moment as she wrote. I might say to a child, "Try, as you listen, to be there: to stand in Francesca's shoes, to see through her eyes, to feel right along with her. I think you'll see that her details about her cat ring true because she wrote this draft, keeping her attention focused on the true story of what really happened "

> It was a Sunday, a strange Sunday. I knew that something was going to happen. Sam was walking weakly, as usual, but worse than other days. I went to play with my friend Lucy. When I came home, Sam was barely walking but still alive.
>
> Camilla (my little sister) picked Sam up and put her on a soft white chair. Everyone was looking at her, even Lucy. I knew she was probably going to die so I cried. My Dad started making tea to calm us down but it did not help. What would it be like without Sam? "It will be really quiet," I started thinking. I looked at Sam, with her little white paws and her cute tail. She was almost dead. She took three breaths of air. On the last one, I was looking at a dead cat. The room was silent. Too silent. I could feel Sam's spirit floating up to heaven. I don't know why but I had a big feeling that today was her 19th birthday. I looked at the candles. They were still burning like Sam's spirit was still alive and here. It was a good feeling.

SHARE

Using Details from the Moment

Share an example of a child's writing that includes details from inside the story.

"Writers, I want you to think about how you might describe a brand-new house that you just moved into. You *could* write something like this: 'There are three bedrooms along the hall. Each is about the same size. There is also a dining room.' But *anyone* could see those things. A stranger to the house or a real estate agent might describe it that way. In a really good story, characters (and you are the main character in your story) let the reader see the world as the character saw the world in the moment of the story."

"I think Kim Yung does this really well. The way she writes about the new house—the one she's just moved into—lets me feel as if I am seeing that new house through her eyes. It's almost like she's got a video camera, and as she goes from room to room, we go from room to room with her. Remember what rooms look like when there is no furniture in them yet—when they contain just carpet and sun? Listen to how Kim Yung writes about her new house." *[Fig. VIII-2]*

> After looking through this never-ending house, I went to my room that I chose and sat down on the furry carpet. The sun shined through all the windows until it reached the soft carpet. It was nice and warm when you stepped on it. It made you want to stay in that spot. I was going to like this house. It had everything. I would rise up every morning with a happy and bright smile. I would like that feeling. I would go downstairs and eat a healthy breakfast. Life would be the greatest in this house.

"Sensory details work in a story when they are the details that the character (that's you) really, truly notices in the moment of the story. Kim Yung's details about her new house ring true. Remember Felix's story about his grandfather's funeral? In the story he wrote about when he realized it was his grandfather in the coffin. He wrote, 'I grabbed my grandma's hand tight. I felt her bones.' He wrote that as he tried to reconcile himself to the fact that his grandfather had died, he looked down and found that he was staring at the new shoes on his feet that his grandfather had bought for him. These details let us, his readers, see through Felix's eyes."

After looking through this never
ending house I went in my room
I chose and sat down on the
furry carpet.
The sun shined through all the
windows until it reathed the
soft carpet. It was nice and
warm once when it was stepped
on. It felt nice. It made you
want to stay in that spot.
It felt like it was made
to be a bed.
I was going to love this house.
It had everything. I would rise
up every morning with a happy
and bright smile. I would like
that feeling. I would go downstairs
and eat a nice healthy breakfast
life would be the greatest
in this house. I would take nice
walks along the gray streets. I

Fig. VIII-2 Kim Yung

If your students could use another example of writing from inside the story, inside the moment, inside the narrator's mind, bring them back to Francesca's piece about the death of her cat. Francesca writes second by second about the last bits of life of her cat, never once pulling away or offering descriptions outside of that intense focus on her beloved pet.

Children could also take out Felix's piece and study this same aspect of writing in-depth, to emulate. [Launching the Writing Workshop, Fig. VIII-1]

Ask children to reread their drafts and note, and perhaps revise, their use of details.

"Right now, would you reread your own writing and look at your details. Which ring true, as if you have lived through this event? Which don't seem like they are really true to what you saw, felt, or noticed that day? Talk with your partner; see if you can revise more details to make them ring true."

HOMEWORK ***Rereading While Visualizing the Story*** Remember in reading today, we tried to make pictures in our minds as we read. Remember how I read about the girl who walked step-by-step up to the school, then pulled open the big front door? Remember how I stopped at that point, and asked you to tell your partner exactly what you were picturing? You all pictured the girl pulling back the handle and drawing the door open. The details the author gave us about the steps up to the door, and the heaviness of the door really drew us to make those pictures. Some of you hadn't pictured the school itself. You said, 'It doesn't say what the school looks like,' and I told you that readers nevertheless draw on all the schools we've ever been to, using all we know to mentally paint pictures in our minds. Today you have learned that both readers *and* writers need to make movies in our minds. As you reread your drafts, are you able to mentally paint pictures in your mind of your story world? Where are those pictures strong in your draft? Where do they need work? Use that lens to guide your important revision work.

TAILORING YOUR TEACHING

If your students are able to write, staying in the moment . . . they may be ready to try writing from slightly more difficult-to-enter moments. When we write a personal narrative, often we tell a story of a childhood experience. It's helpful, in writing these experiences, to try to time-travel back to the age we are in the story. As an adult, Sandra Cisneros may not compare that old red sweater, with its sleeves all stretched out, to a jump rope—but that's the way Rachel, the eleven-year-old narrator of "Eleven," sees that sweater. And chances are that as an adult, Sandra can think of many smells that are far worse than cottage cheese, but that's the smell that Rachel experiences, since she is eleven.

It is not always true that when the narrator of a text is five or eight or ten, he or she uses the language and the metaphors that are suitable for his or her age, but it's helpful, in writing these experiences, to try to time-travel back to the age we are in the story.

If your students are able to write in a way that maintains the narrator's point of view consistently . . . you might want to stretch them to include the narrator's state of mind. Suggest that what writers see in an event can reveal their state of mind or emotions at that time and that a writer's state of mind or emotions can become part of the narrative.

For example, I could look at my dog, snoozing in the corner, and see the burls and snarls in her fur. Alternatively, I can look at the same snoozing dog and see the gentle rhythmic rise and fall of her ribs, and I could notice her eyes, flickering underneath her eyelids as she dreams. These two different views of the dog reveal a difference in the writer, not in the dog, who sleeps through it all! A writing teacher once said, "We do not see with our eyes or hear with our ears but with our beliefs."

Another way to approach this is to use a whole-class shared experience. Again, you could use the story of the bus that broke down on a field trip: the narrator's state of mind could be relief that she's off the bus because she feels nauseous or dread because she has to use the bathroom and just wants to get back to school.

This idea of using a narrator's state of mind will most likely be a challenging nuance to teach young writers, but it can work if we mine our class for an example of student work in which a clear state of mind is revealed.

You could turn to a student's piece and ask him what his state of mind or emotions were in the moment the writing is about. Put the piece on an overhead and then ask students to turn and talk about how a different state of mind would change the piece.

For active engagement, ask the students to think about their state of mind in their story and to find places where they show it. If they can't find any places where they reveal their state of mind, they may decide to revise the piece to better reflect it.

Remember, this is a high-level strategy and may not be an appropriate lesson for the whole class. You could gather small groups of writers who are ready for it.

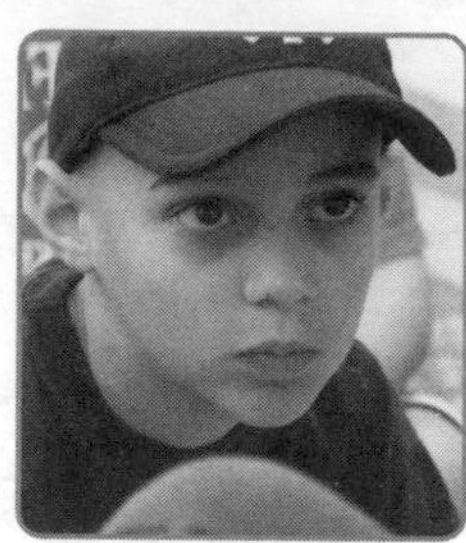

Assessment

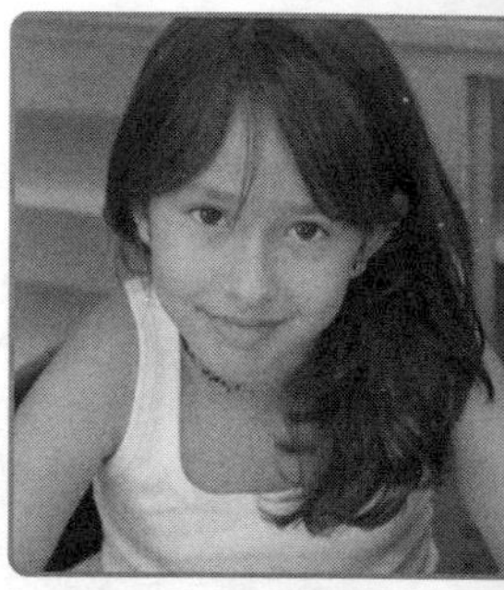

While your children are working within a narrative frame, you'll want to give special attention to their abilities to handle the elements of narrative writing. Look, for example, at their abilities to handle the passage of time. You may notice that at first, some children are so worried about conveying a sequence of events that they rely exclusively on the transition words *first, second, third* or *first, then, next.* The resulting writing is odd, but you'll want to keep in mind that this writer is merely trying to do as you've taught and to show a sequence of events.

Invite children to study how Sandra Cisneros shows the passage of time. Cisneros often shows that as one action is ending, a second one has started, usually with the one causing the other. In this paragraph, for example, three events fit together like tongue-and-groove joints in woodworking.

> Maybe because I'm skinny, maybe because she doesn't like me, that stupid Sylvia Saldívar says, "I think it belongs to Rachel." An ugly sweater like that, all raggedy and old, but Mrs. Price believes her. Mrs. Price takes the sweater and puts it right on my desk, but when I open my mouth nothing comes out. (Cisneros 1991, p. 7)

Cisneros doesn't say, "After that Mrs. Price puts the sweater on my desk. Next I open my mouth." The passage of time is implied; in this instance one event causes the next. Between these sentences, Cisneros could have written the connective *and* but readers supply that transition for her. Children can study this paragraph and try to emulate this way to sequence events in their own writing.

Sometimes Cisneros wants to shift between telling what happens externally and telling what Rachel is thinking and feeling. She has cues that she uses to switch between describing an action and revealing a thought or feeling.

> I don't know why but all of a sudden I'm feeling . . . and I try to remember . . . In my head I'm thinking . . . This is when I wish . . . That's when everything I've been holding in . . . I wish . . . but I wish . . . I wish . . . because today I want . . .

Children can take this set of phrases and tuck it in the back of their notebooks to help them manage these transitions. Again, like tongue-and-groove joints, Cisneros blends dialogue with description, action, and Rachel's thoughts, often within the same paragraph. You could consider again, with your children, the Sylvia Saldívar paragraph above using subtle cues to help the reader follow along. Also, like many writers, Cisneros doesn't always say outright who's speaking. The speaker is implied based on the flow of dialogue. Children can try this too.

> "Rachel," Mrs. Price says. She says it like she's getting mad. "You put that sweater on right now and no more nonsense."
>
> "But it's not—"
>
> "Now!" Mrs. Price says. (p. 8)

You may want to sort your children's writing into piles based on their use of conventions related to narrative writing. It's likely you'll see a group that could use some support in each of these areas where the writer needs to cue the reader to a shift of some sort, be it a shift in sequence, a shift between external and internal events or a shift in speaker. Assessing your children's understanding and control of various transitions in writing will help you plan some quick, helpful teaching to various small groups.

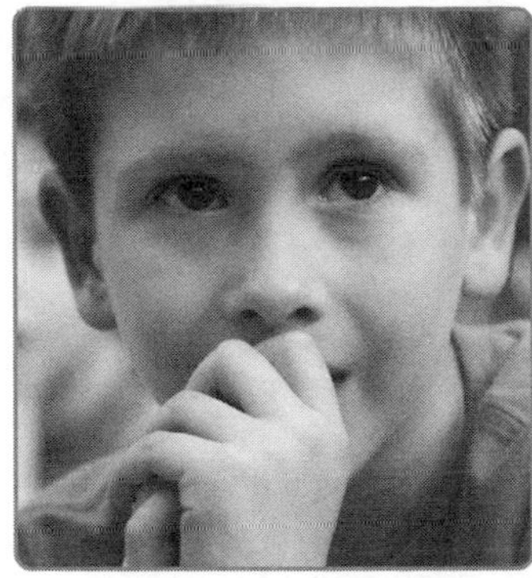

BRINGING FORTH THE INTERNAL STORY

IN THIS SESSION, YOU WILL TEACH STUDENTS THAT WRITERS CAN STRENGTHEN OUR PERSONAL NARRATIVES BY BRINGING FORTH THE DEEP CONNECTION BETWEEN EXTERNAL ACTIONS AND INTERNAL RESPONSES.

GETTING READY

- Student anecdote that can be used to introduce importance of internal events
- Red-sweater scene from Sandra Cisneros' "Eleven," written on chart paper
- Passage from Chapter 11 of *Olive's Ocean*, by Kevin Henkes, one copy for each partnership
- Qualities of Good Personal Narrative chart
- Student examples of revising to bring out the internal story based on overall intentions
- See CD-ROM for resources

I recently observed a teacher lead a very nice minilesson. *She said to her class, "Yesterday you learned that you can improve your stories by making your characters speak," and she reminded the students how they'd added a line of dialogue into a little class story about flying a kite. "Today," the teacher said, "I want to teach you that you can also improve your story by writing not just the external story, but also the internal story." And she showed the class that she could add a line in which she looks up at the kite and thinks that she loves to fly kites.*

> I loosened the string on my kite. "Fly, fly," I whispered. I thought about how much I liked flying kites.

That line was added to the story, and all the children dispersed to insert lines of thought into their own narratives.

That teacher was right to teach children that writers shift between recording an action, transcribing a bit of dialogue, and conveying a thought. But as I reflected on this lesson, I realized that in the teaching of writing, most lessons can be taught either as little tricks that writers can do easily, or as gigantic truths that underpin our entire understanding of life. I ended up writing a keynote speech about that minilesson, and in my speech I argued that sometimes, in our efforts to lure children to try a technique, we convey, "This is easy. It's no big deal!" And that is both true and not true—because bringing out the internal story can be a very big deal indeed.

When we teach children to record not only the event but also their thoughts during the event, we are teaching them that in the end, their lives are not just what happens to them, but also their responses to what happens. Another child could fly that same kite, loosen that same string, whisper those same words of encouragement, and have entirely different thoughts.

For this reason, each one of us is ultimately the author of our own lives. We do not always control what happens to us, but we control our response to what happens.

In this session, I try to help children understand that it is not a small thing to develop the internal story. I try to give them a few specific tools for doing this well.

MINILESSON

Bringing Forth the Internal Story

CONNECTION

Tell a student anecdote to illustrate the writing challenge many children may be facing by this time in the unit.

"I've been talking with many of you about the importance of focusing your stories. But some of you worry that if you focus your story too much, it'll be too short. Caleb, for example, wanted to tell about going to a sports store with his dad to buy a baseball mitt and then riding his bike to his friend's house and playing a game with the mitt. I said, 'Caleb, it seems to me that you have two or three different small moments, different scenes in this story. Is there one that is particularly important?'"

"Caleb answered that above all, he wanted to write about going into the store to pick out his mitt, but he worried about narrowing the story down to just that. 'Won't it be awfully short?' he asked."

Name your teaching point. In this case, tell writers that our lives are not just what happens to us. They are our response to what happens to us.

"What I said to Caleb and what I want to teach all of you is this. Our stories are not just what happens; they are also our response to what happens. I used to worry that real writers had richer lives than me, and a great writer named Roethke said to me (actually he wrote this, but I put his quote on my bulletin board and I pretend he said it just to me), 'Lucy,' he said. 'It is an illusion that writers live more significant lives than non-writers. Writers are just more in the habit of finding the significance that is there in their lives.'"

"These are hugely important words for me. It means that I can write about any moment in my life—a ride on the Ferris wheel, a time when my dad picked me up from the basketball game, a few minutes after school with some classmates when they told me my dress looked antique enough to be a costume in the Civil War play—and I can make that moment carry the biggest truths of my life. You can do the same."

"Specifically, I want to teach you that if I'm going to write not only what happens but also my response to what happens, then much of the story will be the internal story, and not just the external one."

"In a story, I can run, spin, climb, clamor, dig, holler—but I can also yearn, fantasize,

COACHING

You'll notice that today's minilesson picks up a point which was taught in yesterday's mid-workshop teaching point, and will be woven into our instruction across the year. Qualities of good writing are easy to name but challenging to pull off!

The picturebook, Roxaboxen *by Alice McLerran has always seemed to me to be a metaphor for writing. A few children play on a desert hill. There is not much there—just some broken crates, cacti, sand. But then one girl, Marion, finds a rusty tin box and declares it to be treasure. And it is. Inside the box there are smooth black stones. The girls use them to frame roads, and soon they have build themselves a kingdom of Roxaboxen. This is why I write. To take the rusty tin boxes of my life, to declare them to be treasures, and to make something of them—and of myself.*

I've learned that three examples—from Keats and Rylant, or any number of master writers—are enough to illustrate a point. Notice that I reference stories both from previous units and our present unit that are now part of the lexicon of the class community.

remember, regret, worry, imagine. Often a character's internal life is as rich and as poignant as her external life. If you think about it, in the entry that I wrote a couple of weeks ago, nothing much happens: 'The teacher says some of us are to stay after school, I gather my books and sit with the kids, one girl makes a list of costumes people will need, and she records that I already have my costume.' Though nothing much happened *externally* in that story, *internally* I've traveled a roller coaster of hope and heartbreak."

I will want to help children know that they can convey the internal story not only with the words 'I thought,' but also with 'I pretended,' 'I worried,' 'I remembered,' 'I wanted to say,' 'I noticed,' and a dozen other such phrases.

I liken the emotional journey of my story to a roller coaster ride. Metaphors are one way to pack a punch.

Teaching

Return to the class mentor text (in this case, "Eleven") to study the balance of external and internal story.

"When I pause in the middle of a draft to reread my writing, I sometimes say to myself, 'Let me reread and pay attention to whether I've told the internal as well as the external story.' And when I make a planning box for the writing work I'm going to be doing in the day ahead, I sometimes say to myself, 'Today, I want to be sure to tell the internal story.'"

"And I sometimes study mentor texts, thinking, 'How has this author written the story of what she was thinking and feeling?' I ask, 'What has she done that I could do also?'"

I pointed to our chart-paper copy of the red-sweater scene in "Eleven." Then I said, "Watch me as I study what Cisneros has done, and try to extrapolate lessons that can help me. Hmm. One thing I notice is that she seems to seesaw back and forth between writing what happens and writing what she's thinking. For example, the phrase "Not mine, not mine, not mine" conveys an internal thought, but this passage, " but Mrs. Price has already turned to page thirty-two, and math problem number four (p. 8)" is external—it's what happens."

The minilesson is predominantly an oral form. As my colleagues and I work across the New York City public schools, we often need to provide modifications and supports for our English Language Learners and for other students who need more than just the oral mode of learning. Throughout these units, notice the supports we provide, such as charts, student copies of texts, clear and consistent language that we chart and reference, use of gestures, use of demonstration texts. Here I return to our class copy of "Eleven" (Cisneros 1991, p. 8) and provide support for key concepts through the use of gestures.

> I move the red sweater to the corner of my desk with my ruler. I move my pencil and books and eraser as far away from it as possible. I even move my chair a little to the right. [external gesture]
>
> Not mine, not mine, not mine. [internal gesture]
>
> In my head I'm thinking how long till lunchtime, how long till I can take the red sweater and throw it over the schoolyard fence, or leave it hanging on a parking meter, or bunch it up into a little ball and toss it in the alley. [internal gesture]
>
> Except when math period ends Mrs. Price says loud and in front of everybody, "Now, Rachel . . . " [external gesture]

As I read each of these passages aloud, I tapped the side of my head as a gesture to emphasize internal section of the text and showed open hands as a gesture for external sections.

"My writing teacher, Don Murray, once told me that if you want to have a character in the kitchen, thinking about something and getting more and more angry and worried, you might as well have that character chopping carrots. Then your writing could go like this."

> "Where is he?" I thought, looking out the door to see if my son's car was in the driveway yet. Nothing. "Dang it all," I thought, getting the giant cleaver and the cutting board out. I lay a carrot on the board. "Why's he late?" Chop, chop, chop, the little slices piled up. "I said to come straight home," I remembered, lining another carrot up under the giant blade. Chop, chop. I went to the door again, but still no car. "This is the last time," I thought reaching for a head of lettuce. Slamming it onto the counter, I turned to see if I'd broken the stem, the heart, I always called it. Then I glanced at the clock.

I try to teach writers that usually the internal story needs to be carried by an external story. If the writer wants to sit on a stool in the kitchen and experience a whole sequence of thoughts and feelings, in between each new thought or feeling, the character will need to slice a carrot or turn down the teakettle, even if the actions exist only to support the internal story.

Active Engagement

Provide a brief scene from another mentor text and ask students to study the balance of external and internal stories.

"You'll see examples when you read. I recently read a chapter book called *Olive's Ocean*, by Kevin Henkes. One small chapter in this book tells how the main character, Martha, was standing outside the airport (she was going to her grandma's at the beach), with her mom, dad, and brother, Vince, waiting for the shuttle bus to take them to the car rental place, and then she was jostled while boarding the bus. That's all that happened *on the outside* in this chapter. But meanwhile, things were happening *inside* of Olive. Listen to part of this chapter. She begins by describing the glittery feeling she has when she is en route to summer vacation at the beach with her grandmother, whom she calls Godbee. Partners, look at the copy I gave you now. Later, I'm going to ask you to tell your partner the external and then the internal events of this story."

> They were outside, at the airport, waiting for the shuttle bus to take them to the car-rental lot. Martha thought she smelled the ocean already and was immediately excited. She breathed deeply, letting the feeling sink in. They would be at Godbee's shortly, right on the water, and every molecule, every atom, knew it.
>
> She called the feeling the glittery feeling, and she always experienced it when they were this close, when they were at this part of their trip to Godbee's.
>
> The glittery feeling. She'd named it because it felt to her as if her skin and everything beneath it briefly became shiny and jumpy and

Olive's Ocean *is a beautiful novel but the content of some chapters makes it a better choice for middle school children. The chapter I share is fine for elementary school children!*

This choice of texts to illustrate the teaching point is time-consuming, but crucial. Several factors make this scene from Olive's Ocean *a strong choice. First, notice its brevity. In a minilesson, unless it's a familiar text like "Eleven," you don't have time to both introduce and teach from a new, longer text. Second, notice the balance between external and internal, and how most of the scene occurs internally, which reinforces the focus of this minilesson. Third, notice how the main character, Martha, like Rachel in "Eleven," connects with a group of fourth-graders. I try to choose texts with a keen awareness of my audience.*

bubbly, as if glitter materialized inside her, then rose quickly through the layers of tissue that comprised her, momentarily sparkling all over the surface of her skin before dissipating into the air.

Martha closed her eyes and let her arms drift slightly upward. She couldn't help herself. A small joyful squeak escaped from her throat.

"What do you think you are? A bird?" It was Vince.

Her arms fell.

"The bus is here," said her father. "Grab everything and hurry."

Her mother accidentally bumped her with a suitcase as they jockeyed for a place on the curb among the crowd. "Move, honey," she said.

The glittery feeling was gone.

"Writers, will you tell your partner the sequence of external events that happened in this story." I listened while children talked. "Many of you said, 'Not much happened. A girl is jostled while getting on the bus. That's it!' But now, follow along in your copy while I read the story again, and this time tell your partner the *internal* events or feelings, or thoughts that occur in this story." I reread the text, and again children talked.

"So you see that the only external thing that happens in this episode is a girl is jostled while getting on the bus. But meanwhile, she has gone through a whole sequence of internal changes. You can learn from what Kevin Henkes has done!"

LINK

Remind students to reread and revise their drafts, bringing out the internal story, and to rely on mentor texts for support.

"Writers sometimes talk about rereading drafts with particular lenses to make the drafts stronger, and there are many lenses that writers use. For example, we could reread our drafts noticing word choice, or clarity, or our use of dialogue. We could reread noticing especially our use of punctuation."

"Writers, as you go off to work today, you may decide to reread your drafts, and to do so in a manner which allows you to notice the internal story. You may ask yourselves, "Did I provide a balance of internal and external? Did I seesaw back and forth between writing what happens, and writing what I'm thinking? Alternatively, you can draw on anything you've learned in order to write or revise your draft, making it the best it can be."

As students went off to work, I added this revision strategy to our Qualities of Good Personal Narrative Writing chart.

Again, notice the supports I try to provide to meet the needs of all students in the class. It helps that, during this active engagement, I have students work with their partners and provide them with copies of this text. This facilitates their ability to both read and analyze it. But also notice that I read aloud the text, twice. I want to provide a fluent rendition of this text so the children can hear its tone, its coherence, and can better attend to the challenging textual analysis that is the aim of this activity.

Just as we see the world differently when we view it through different colored lenses, we can look at a draft and attend to different aspects of it. The metaphor stays consistent with the word revision itself, which literally means "to look again." It's a metaphor that I return to often.

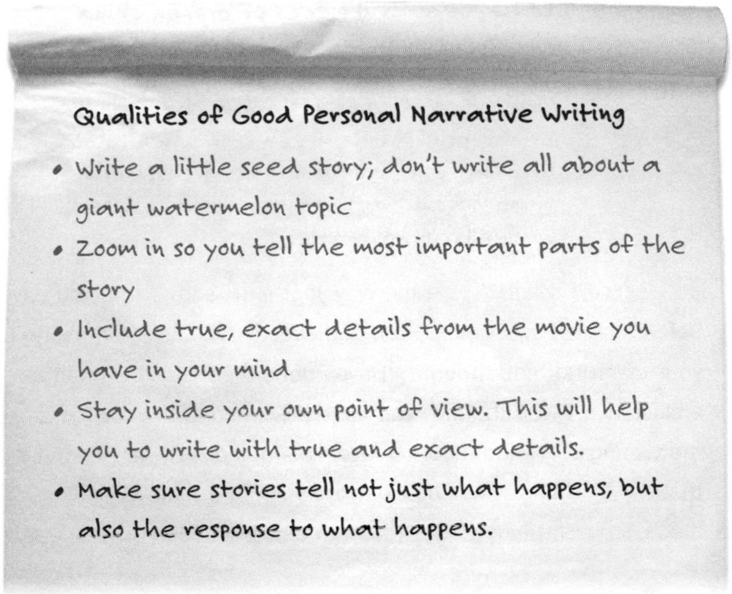

Qualities of Good Personal Narrative Writing

- Write a little seed story; don't write all about a giant watermelon topic
- Zoom in so you tell the most important parts of the story
- Include true, exact details from the movie you have in your mind
- Stay inside your own point of view. This will help you to write with true and exact details.
- **Make sure stories tell not just what happens, but also the response to what happens.**

WRITING AND CONFERRING

Uncovering Internal Details by Reenacting the Story

I pulled my chair up next to Becca. She'd written an entry about cotton candy, then moved on to an entry about beach combing. "What are you working on as a writer?" I asked.

"Well, I figured out what I really wanted to show. I found a really nice piece of sea glass. And I wrote a little about it—details about it being lime green, and how I held it up to my eye. But it is still pretty short," she said. "So I was gonna think, 'What else do I want to show?' and tell about the cool rides." I looked over her piece: *[Fig. IX-1]*

> Combing the beach, sifting the sand. We are looking and digging carefully for seaglass and shells. I am a scientist digging up the past at an archeological site. I am a pirate searching for buried treasure. But so far, all I've found is smashed Corona bottles, and crushed beer cans, while Mabel kept running over to me, beautiful pieces of broken china and big, pretty shells. All of a sudden, something incredible happened—I found a nice piece of seaglass, for a change!!! It was bright, bright, lime green and when I held it up to my eye it was a grass-green world that looked back at me. Happily I sipped water from my bottle.

"Becca," I said, "I love the way your entry shows that you have already done so much work with it. Even before I pulled up my chair, you had already switched from being a writer to being a reader, and you reread your own draft and thought, 'Have I done the things I wanted to do?' I love that on our own, you boxed in a place which you thought was especially important, your focus. And I also love that you thought through the writing challenge that you face. Lots of kids just say, 'I don't know what to do next,' but you figured out that the hard part is writing extensively about a topic as small as a piece of sea glass. It's not doing anything much, so it isn't easy to describe it in detail, is it?"

MID-WORKSHOP TEACHING POINT **_Working with Partners on the Internal Story_** "Writers, give me your eyes and your attention." I waited for complete attention, as students finished their sentences. "Juliet is writing about a toy sculpture that she admired in a store window near her apartment. Not much action happens, sort of like the glittery feeling scene in *Olive's Ocean*. But Juliet has worked hard on bringing out the internal story. Listen to how she seesaws between writing what happens and what that makes her think and feel, like Cisneros does in 'Eleven'."

continued on next page

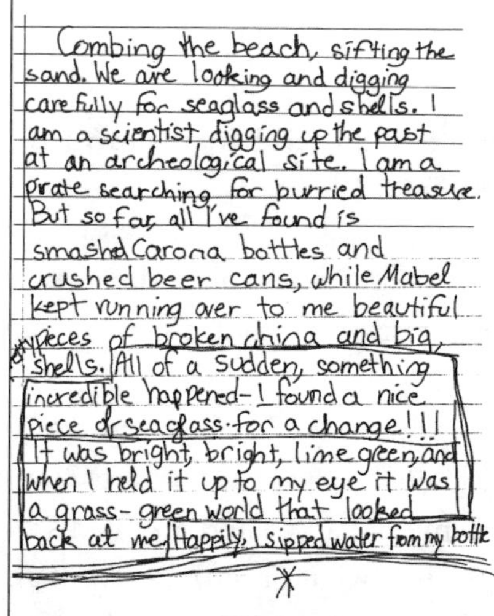

Combing the beach, sifting the sand. We are looking and digging carefully for seaglass and shells. I am a scientist digging up the past at an archeological site. I am a pirate searching for burried treasure. But so far, all I've found is smashed Corona bottles and crushed beer cans, while Mabel kept running over to me beautiful pieces of broken china and big shells. All of a sudden, something incredible happened—I found a nice piece of seaglass for a change!!! It was bright, bright, lime green, and when I held it up to my eye it was a grass-green world that looked back at me. Happily, I sipped water from my bottle.

Fig. IX-1 Becca

"I love the way you are taking charge of your own writing. It really feels like you are your own job captain. Congratulations." Becca beamed, pleased that I had noticed.

Then I said, "You are right to think, 'My story is a bit short,' because it is, but the answer doesn't need to be to move on and tell about the rides. Because if you did that, then when you asked yourself, 'What am I really trying to say in my story?' you'd have to answer, 'Well, I say this one thing and then I say this other thing—and your message would get all blurry. So instead, you can either make this sea glass story bigger, or move on and find something else that you'd like to highlight. I'll help you do either one of those. Which makes more sense to you?"

She answered, "The sea glass?" with intonation that suggested she wasn't too sure.

So I said to her, "Let's pretend it is right here on the floor. You see it. You reach down and pick it up." Then I gestured, "Do that now." I picked up a similar piece of imaginary sea glass. "Hold it. Turn it over in your hand. What are you thinking?"

Becca said, "I feel lucky. I can't believe I just found pretty sea glass for a change."

"What does it remind you of?" I watched as she began writing a new passage with plans to insert it in her original piece. *[Figs. IX-3 and IX-4]*

> I am slowly walking along the beach, looking for a beautiful shell or rare piece of sea glass. But so far, I haven't had much luck; and all I've found is crushed soda cans and broken Corona bottles. Then, I step on something cool among the sticky, hot sand. I walk past it; then realize that it might have been seaglass. I walk back to where I thought it was. I feel around with my foot. I hit it again. I look down at the piece of something that I have just stepped on. I pick it up. I can't believe that I have just found a pretty piece of sea glass for a change. I decide to examine it, just in case it's a phoney piece of plastic.

continued from previous page

Juliet read aloud: *[Fig. IX-2]*

> One afternoon, I stepped off the bus, like usual. I said hello to my mom, like usual. I looked at the store window to see the sculpture, like usual. But . . . where was the sculpture? OH NO!!
>
> Maybe I had seen it wrong, I thought. I decided to look one more time.
>
> OH NO!! Where was my favorite sculpture from the store window? Where was it? There was an empty space in the store window, where the sculpture used to be. Like a building getting knocked down, and becoming a vacant lot.

"Did you notice how Juliet showed her thinking by asking questions in her head? She also repeated "like usual" to show the routine of these actions. We could feel Juliet's disappointment in not seeing that sculpture anymore."

"Right now, get together with your writing partner. Share a section of your draft where you worked on bringing out the internal story, as Sandra Cisneros or Kevin Henkes did, as Juliet did. Ask your partner if the feelings you tried conveying in that part come through. Then return to your work plans. Okay, get started."

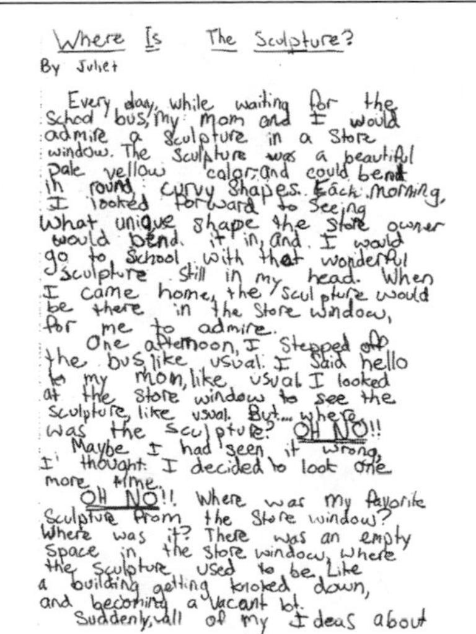

Where Is The Sculpture?
By Juliet

Every day, while waiting for the School bus, my mom and I would admire a sculpture in a Store window. The Sculpture was a beautiful pale yellow color, and could bend in round curvy Shapes. Each morning, I looked forward to seeing what unique shape the store owner would bend it in, and I would go to School with that wonderful sculpture still in my head. When I came home, the sculpture would be there in the Store window, for me to admire.

One afternoon, I Stepped off the bus like usual. I Said hello to my mom, like usual. I looked at the Store window to see the sculpture, like usual. But... where was the sculpture? OH NO!!

Maybe I had seen it wrong, I thought. I decided to look one more time.

OH NO!! Where was my favorite sculpture from the Store window? Where was it? There was an empty space in the store window, where the sculpture used to be. Like a building getting knoked down, and becoming a vacant lot.

Suddenly, all of my Ideas about

Fig. IX-2 Juliet

I run my fingers over the cool, smooth surface like a pond in January. I enclose it in my sweaty palm. It feels like I am holding a flat sheet of ice. I hold it up to my eye, to make sure that it is transparent like sea glass is, and a limey sort-of fluorescent green world is looking back at me.

Definitely sea glass, I decide. I hold the grassy, neon green triangle up to my chest, and call, "Mabel, look what I found!!!!!" I can't believe that I finally found a nice piece of sea glass. So what if Mabel has found 2 pieces of china along the shoreline?

"Becca," I said. "After this, when you want to write the internal story, remember it helps to reenact whatever it is you are describing, because sometimes when you act things out, you think up more to say."

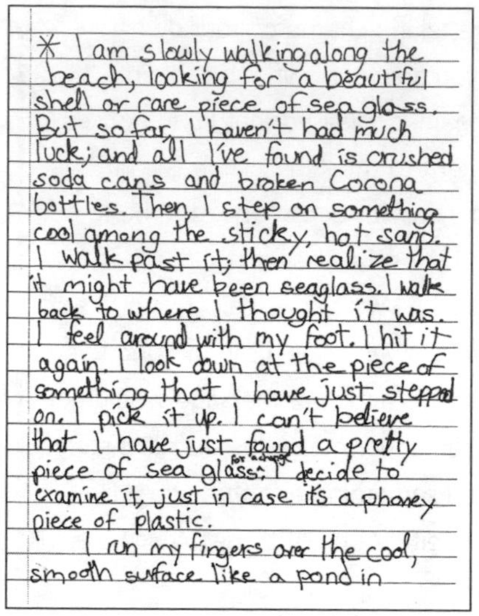

* I am slowly walking along the beach, looking for a beautiful shell or rare piece of sea glass. But so far, I haven't had much luck; and all I've found is crushed soda cans and broken Corona bottles. Then, I step on something cool among the sticky, hot sand. I walk past it; then realize that it might have been seaglass. I walk back to where I thought it was. I feel around with my foot. I hit it again. I look down at the piece of something that I have just stepped on. I pick it up. I can't believe that I have just found a pretty piece of sea glass for a change. I decide to examine it, just in case it's a phoney piece of plastic.

I run my fingers over the cool, smooth surface like a pond in

Fig. IX-3 Page 1 of Becca's revised story

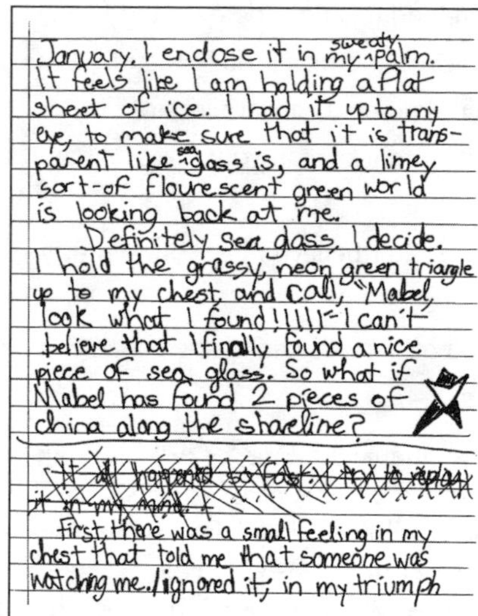

January. I enclose it in my sweaty palm. It feels like I am holding a flat sheet of ice. I hold it up to my eye, to make sure that it is transparent like sea glass is, and a limey sort-of flourescent green world is looking back at me.

Definitely sea glass, I decide. I hold the grassy, neon green triangle up to my chest, and call, "Mabel, look what I found!!!!!" I can't believe that I finally found a nice piece of sea glass. So what if Mabel has found 2 pieces of china along the shoreline?

First, there was a small feeling in my chest that told me that someone was watching me. I ignored it; in my triumph

Fig. IX-4 Page 2 of Becca's revised story

SHARE

Listening to the Internal Story

Ask children to meet with partners and to share their writing before they added the internal story, and after they added it.

I listened in as Joey and Felix shared their writing with each other. I'd heard Joey's original entry earlier in the unit: *[Fig. IX-5]*

> Jumping in the pond really late at night
>
> Me and John were going to jump in the pond really late at night. I just could not. John kept on encouraging me to do it. He said, "You can do it, come on. Nothing is going to happen."
> I had to do it. I jumped. I closed my eyes and tried to think of good things. Splash. "I did it!" I yelled.
> John ran up to me and said, "Great job. You did it! You're the best."

"Joey," I said, "It is clear you brought out the internal angle so much more by showing more actions and details, by including more dialogue. But I also love the way you paid special attention to the external story—the actions—as well!" *[Figs. IX-6, IX-7, and IX-8]*

> I was terrified. I never was going to do it. I just could not. I was totally scared. I was thinking in my head about jumping in the pond and feeling the water touching me. The ice cold water. It was not pretty. I was trying to think of good things like beautiful skys and seawaters. But it did not work. John went over to me and said to me that its ok, really, knothing is going to happen to you. Then he said "Here, why don't I show you? Then you can do it." I saw John walk up to the dock with full confidence in his eyes. He lifted his feet and flew in the air. I saw a big smile across his face and his mouth wide open screaming his guts out. Then his foot went under. It only made a tiny splash but then his knee started to go under and I was really amazed because he still had that wide open smile all the way across his face. He was great. Then the splash was greater each

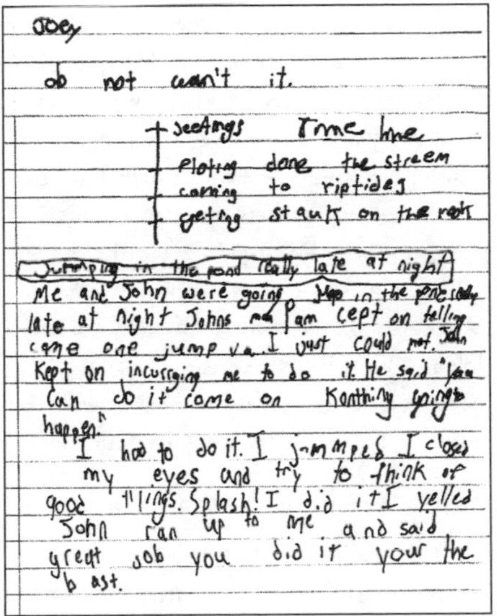

Fig. IX-5 Joey's original entry

Fig. IX-6 Joey, page 1

time his body went down more into the pond. Then his whole body was down under the water. It kind of reminded me of the time me and John went canoeing, white water class 2. The riptides turned white because of the strong current. When John jumped in the water/pond the water turned white. Then he spurted out of the water like a cork. He swam over. He climbed up the ladder and stood on the dock. He said "Its your turn." Then I walked to the end of the dock bent my knees and I jumped in the air. I opened my eyes and actually felt kind of fun. Then I screamed. My feet went in, then my knees and my waist. I was almost in shock because I thought it would be the worst moment of my life. I guess I was wrong. My head went under. I smiled under water and then flew out of the water. I saw John. Then he started clapping his hands. I really felt good because John really comforted me and also he thought I did good and I really liked that.

"It's clear that Joey was reliving that moment as he wrote this draft—seeing it, feeling it, hearing it—which helped him not only to include actions, details, and dialogue that rang true, but also to weave in his thoughts and feelings that bring out his angle."

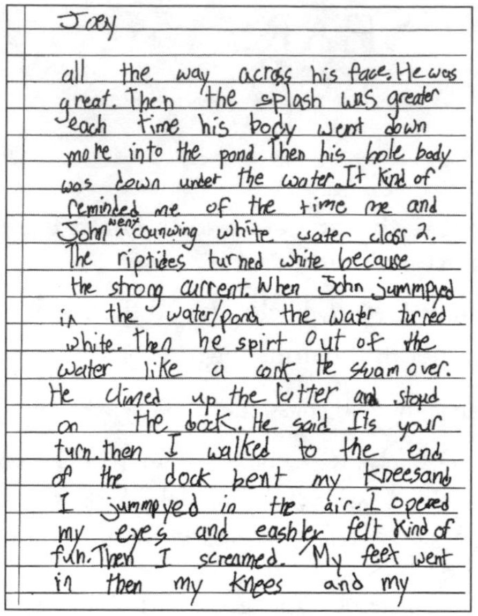

HOMEWORK ***Writing the Internal Story*** Today at the start of our lesson I suggested that our lives are made up of not only what happens to us but also our responses to what happens to us.

As writers, this means that we pause in our actions and ask, "What was I thinking?" We offer our readers clues to reveal our thoughts and feelings. This is especially true in the heart of our stories.

Tonight for homework, your job is to reread your draft and find the heart of your story. Reread that part as if you're using a stop-action camera. For each chunk of action, ask, "What was I thinking/feeling?" Check that you give clues that reveal your thoughts and feelings. If you haven't included clues that reveal your thoughts and feelings in the heart of your story, you will want to add some tonight.

Joey

all the way across his face. He was great. Then the splash was greater each time his body went down more into the pond. Then his hole body was down under the water. It kind of reminded me of the time me and John went canoeing white water class 2. The riptides turned white because the strong current. When John jummped in the water/pond the watr turned white. Then he spirt out of the water like a cork. He swam over. He clined up the latter and stoud on the dock. He said Its your turn. then I walked to the end of the dock bent my kneesand I jummpyed in the air. I opened my eyes and eashley felt kind of fun. Then I screamed. My feet went in then my knees and my

Fig. IX-7 Joey, page 2

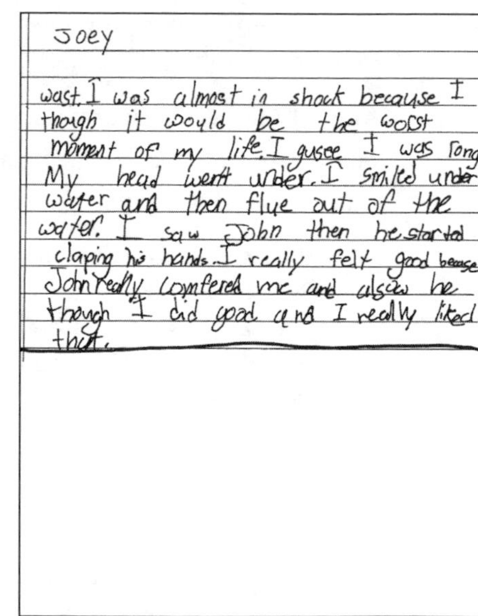

Joey

wast. I was almost in shock because I though it would be the worst moment of my life. I gusee I was rong. My head went under. I smiled under water and then flue out of the water. I saw John then he started claping his hands. I really felt good beause John really compfered me and alsow he though I did good and I really liked that.

Fig. IX-8 Joey, page 3

TAILORING YOUR TEACHING

If your students have difficulty finding places in their pieces to include the internal story . . . you might tell them that writers add the internal story into the most important parts of our pieces. This will be more manageable than sweeping through their whole piece to find places to include internal thoughts. Remind them of the storytelling work they did when they were developing their story ideas. Remind them how they tried to make their readers (or listeners) have strong reactions, how they made them gasp and laugh and cry. Now, ask your writers to storytell the important parts again, this time interspersing phrases that begin "I thought," "I noticed," "I remembered," "I pretended," "I wanted," and so on. They can do this oral storytelling work with their partners and then go back to their pieces to include the internal story. Make sure to remind them they can always storytell the important bits of their story with the internal story added to try to strengthen their writing.

If your students are writing stories with tiny actions that move through time, but still need help showing how each action reveals the internal story . . . teach them that each action is attached to a feeling and that writers choose action words that fit the feelings they want to convey. Each action can be a tiny window into the character's feelings. Often, students add in internal thought. Of course, this works in many cases. But it can often be more powerful to show students how the actions that they choose for their characters to make can reveal a great depth of feeling.

You might show them an excerpt from your writing that first states what the character is thinking. You might say, "Writers, you know that one way to show what's going on inside a character is to add the words that the character is thinking in his head. Here's a part of an entry from my notebook where I am on the boardwalk at Coney Island and I am really frightened to go on the Cyclone. I'm telling the reader how I'm feeling through my thoughts."

> I walked along the boardwalk. I don't want to go on the Cyclone, I thought. Why do I need to go?

But I can make my feelings much more powerful by showing them through the actions I take and don't take. For example:

> I stood frozen on the boardwalk, my feet refusing to take one more step toward the Cyclone. I squeezed my sister's hand tightly, tugged on her arm and turned to walk back to the car. But I was unable to escape as my sister dragged me in the direction of the screaming people.

Mechanics

As I've pointed out earlier in this series, a very common issue to see in children's writing is that it is swamped with dialogue and there's little else there. This may seem at first to be a problem children are having with the mechanics of integrating dialogue into their pieces, but the problem is often a bit more intricate than that. Oftentimes, it helps children to learn that writers aim to create a working balance of strong pictures and strong sounds in their writing.

When conferring, I often carry the familiar children's book *Yo! Yes?* by Chris Raschka. I use the book to point out to children that there are two elements that make up this story. There is dialogue, and there are pictures. On every two-page spread, there are a few words—these are the exact words the characters are saying. That dialogue is crucial to the story. However, every two-page spread also holds illustrations, and those illustrations add equally crucial information to the reader's understanding of what is happening. As writers, there is a lot we can learn from this book.

When we include direct dialogue in a story, this adds tremendously to the story. But Raschka's book wouldn't make sense if it was only dialogue: "Yo! Yes? Hey! Who?"—the book's first four pages—make no sense without the pictures which convey who is talking, how that person acts, the intonation in the voice . . . .

When I confer with a child who has written chunks of text which read as a sound track only, I point out that the child's draft resembles Raschka's book without the pictures—and as such, it does not yet make sense. Raschka filled in the missing information with pictures, but the writers with whom I confer need to do this with words. Every chunk of dialogue needs a written image, created by words which reveal who is talking, what action that person makes or what intonation the person uses.

ADDING SCENES FROM THE PAST AND FUTURE

IN THIS SESSION, YOU'LL TEACH STUDENTS THAT WRITERS USE SCENES FROM THE PAST OR FUTURE TO BRING OUT THE INTERNAL STORY AND ADD POWER TO THEIR NARRATIVES.

GETTING READY

- Passage from "Papa Who Wakes Up Tired in the Dark," by Sandra Cisneros, written on chart paper
- Timeline of "Papa Who Wakes Up Tired in the Dark," written on chart paper
- Student examples of narratives that show moving back and forth in time
- Whole-class Small Moment story written on chart paper (you might reuse the class story from Session VII)
- See CD-ROM for resources

***When we write, we take the booming rich, nuanced, chaos** of life itself and we simplify and channel and shoehorn all that into a single line of print that unrolls across the page. When we write curriculum, we work in similar ways. We take the vastness, richness and complexity of all our dreams and worries, all our disciplinary knowledge and practical know-how and somehow we cut and craft, select and simplify, until our plans and hopes are set onto the page in what is temporarily, at least, a best-going-draft.*

In order to write a line or to create a curriculum, we make choices along the way that temporarily compromise the multi-layered, multi-faceted nature of what we want to say as teachers and as writers. And so early in the year, when we sense that many children are accustomed to writing in such an unrestrained, unstructured manner that they record anything tangentially related to the last word they've written into their pages, this series of books suggested teaching children that stories proceed chronologically, with a character doing one thing and then the next in a step-by-step fashion. But of course, that was over-simplifying, and today we open the door, wander outside, and let children peer at the sky. Today we teach children that in the midst of their tightly controlled sequential narratives, they—the main character—can blast through barriers of time and space by the simple miraculous act of remembering, or of fantasizing.

MINILESSON

Adding Scenes from the Past and Future

CONNECTION

Invite children to recall a fantasy story in which the character suddenly steps into another world. Explain that time travel can happen similarly in personal narratives when the narrator remembers the past or envisions tomorrow.

"Most of you have read or seen the film version of *The Lion, the Witch and the Wardrobe*. You'll remember that in the midst of a hide-and-seek game, Lucy hears her brother's footsteps coming and slips into a wardrobe, a closet. It's full of coats. She pushes towards the back of the closet, rustling in through the soft coats, and suddenly something cold brushes against her arm—a tree bough, covered with snow. Lucy looks down and she sees she is standing in snow. Ahead, a lamp gleams golden and from afar she hears the sound of approaching sleigh bells. She's in another world."

"When you and I write, we put one foot in front of the next. We are playing hide-and-go-seek. We hear someone approaching, worry that we'll be found, and slip into the closet. One thing—the sound of footsteps—leads to another."

"And sometimes in the sequence of these actions and reactions, we take a step that transports us to another world. In the stories we are writing this month, we aren't transported to a magical kingdom—but in just as magical a fashion, we may well burrow into a coat closet and find ourselves startled by the brush of a tree bough, by something from another time or place, something that signifies that suddenly we are in another space in the world of yesterday, or of tomorrow.

Name the teaching point. Specifically, tell children that in a personal narrative, characters can time travel—by remembering or by envisioning tomorrow.

"Today I want to teach you that characters in personal narratives sometimes travel through time and place. We do this by remembering and by fantasizing."

TEACHING

Share examples by both professional and student writers that show writing about both imagined future events and remembered past events.

"Let me show you an example of a writer who wrote a story of something that actually involved just about five minutes of real time. In this story, the narrator thinks *ahead*,

COACHING

This is, of course, an elaborate way to teach children that they can break out of the confines of sequential time when they write narratives. My detour will be suitable for some classes of children but it could confuse others. Use your professional judgement, then, to revise this session (and every one) so that it will work well for your children. As you weigh your choices, it may help you to know that the reason I rope The Lion, the Witch and the Wardrobe, *into this lesson is that I want children to realize that there can be a very concrete, physical, embodied quality to the memories and fantasies which we tuck into a personal narrative.*

imagining what will happen in the future. (In others stories, the narrator may think *backward*, recalling what happened years ago.) You'll see in this story we're going to study, that the narrator still moves step-by-step through time—but her mind jumps into the future, and for a little bit of the story she imagines a scenario that has not yet actually happened. Then she returns (like children in Narnia return) to the very real sequence of events."

"This example, written by Sandra Cisneros, is a text you have already studied: 'Papa Who Wakes Up Tired in the Dark.' Listen," I said and I pointed to the chart paper as I read aloud.

> Your abuelito is dead, Papa says early one morning in my room. *Está muerto*, and then as if he just heard the news himself, crumples like a coat and cries, my brave Papa cries. I have never seen my Papa cry and don't know what to do.
>
> I knew he will have to go away, that he will take a plane to Mexico, all the uncles and aunts will be there, and they will have a black and white photo taken in front of the tomb with flowers shaped like spears in a white vase because this is how they send the dead away in that country.
>
> Because I am the oldest, my father has told me first, and now it is my turn to tell the others. I will have to explain why we can't play. I will have to tell them to be quiet today.
>
> My Papa, his thick hands and thick shoes, who wakes up tired in the dark, who combs his hair with water, drinks his coffee, and is gone before we wake, today is sitting on my bed.
>
> And I think if my own Papa died what would I do. I hold my Papa in my arms. I hold and hold and hold him. (Cisneros 1989, p. 56)

"When I want to study a text so as to learn from what the author has done I don't just read it once or twice. I reread, reread, reread. I turn it inside out and study how it was made. So watch me do that," I said.

"I'm going to reread it with special glasses," I said, "with special lenses. I could notice Cisneros' word choice because it is beautiful, or the way she uses tiny details to make the character of Papa come to life. But I'm going to give myself the job of rereading this and paying attention to the timeline of events, watching for when Cisneros moves from telling about the sequence of events in her bedroom that morning to telling about another time and place."

The text I show as a model only gestures towards what I've described. You and your colleagues will surely be able to find texts which are more clear examples. Look through any Calvin and Hobbes *books and you'll see countless examples of how, in the midst of an all-too-real sequence of events, Calvin is suddenly transported into his own little Narnia, returning to the reality of his life in time for the next event. In truth, this is exactly what happens in Sendak's beautiful story* Where the Wild Things Are. *I didn't reference that text because I don't want to fan the flames of fantasy writing—not just yet, anyhow—although of course fantasizing is very much a part of all our comings and goings.*

I've studied this beautiful text for years, admiring so many aspects of Cisneros' craft that I won't mention in this particular minilesson. I won't mention the way her text begins with dialogue, and the dialogue—written in Spanish—reveals the character of Papa. I won't admire the way this narrative begins not with the narrator doing an action, but with the abrupt intrusion of her Papa's words, and the narrator's dawning realization of what happens. There's more, too; the alliteration of harsh sounds as Papa crumples like a coat and cries, the repetition of 'cries' as the narrator takes in the fact that here, before her very eyes, her brave Papa is crying (she's never seen him cry before). I say none of this for now, but my respect for the craftsmanship shines through my reading of this text, and for sure I carry it with me so the text can help me launch a thousand ships as I confer.

I reread, and at the start of the second paragraph I said, "Here, I can tell she's traveling in her mind, thinking of what will happen later today, tomorrow. It's as if she has a second timeline inserted into the first." I showed them the following timeline.

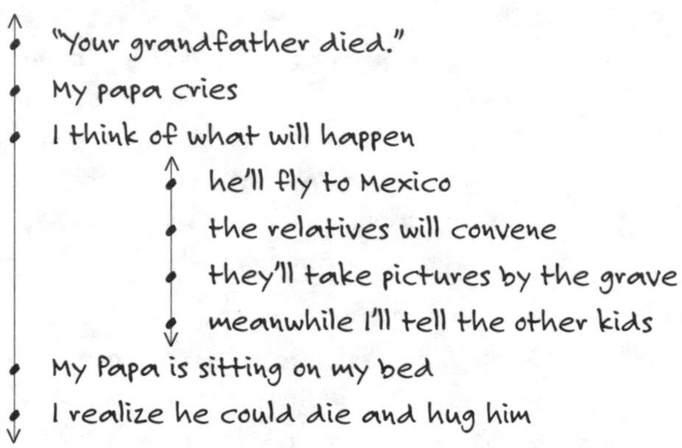

"Your grandfather died."
My papa cries
I think of what will happen
he'll fly to Mexico
the relatives will convene
they'll take pictures by the grave
meanwhile I'll tell the other kids
My Papa is sitting on my bed
I realize he could die and hug him

Then, looking back on the timeline of actual events, I said, "Do you see that the actual events only involve a few minutes?"

"But meanwhile, in the second paragraph, the narrator pictures what will happen soon, that her father will go to the funeral in Mexico, and she imagines sharing the news with her siblings. These events happen only in the narrator's mind."

Active Engagement

With a whole-class exercise text, practice jumping forward or backward in time.

"So writers, I'm hoping you realize that you can decide, in the sequence of your narrative, that you want to leave the physical sequence of events on a timeline and tell the story of another time and place—one you imagine, that might happen in the future, or one you recall, that happened in the past. When you do this, as when C.S. Lewis wrote *The Lion, the Witch and the Wardrobe*, something very concrete and specific will happen and suddenly you'll be transported to another time and place."

"Let's try it. Remember Gregory's story, "Al is Dead" which we studied earlier this year? As you'll recall, Gregory had written a story about the day his dad told him that his fish Al was dead. I'm going to read you Gregory's revised story about when he saw his fish lying in the trash. Partner 2, pretend you wrote the story, that Al was your fish, you got him and six others at a pet store, with a bag of turquoise sand and all . . . I'm going to set you up to time travel. Write in the air how you might add on to Gregory's story." Then I read and dictated the following story:

> Dead. Ever since I had fish, I had Al: the best algae-eater in the world. Once I heard he was dead, I did not cry. I just was still. Then I asked, "Where is he?" My dad said, "In the trash." I asked to see him.
>
> I walked over to the trash can, stepped on the pedal and the lid opened. I looked in and saw wet paper towels, orange peels, and a pile of coffee grounds. Lying on top of the coffee grounds was my golden fish Al. I picked him up and flicked off the coffee grounds that had stuck to him. "Al," I said, "What happened?"
>
> I remembered back to the day I'd gotten him. My dad and I pushed open the door to Carver's Pet Store. I walked over to the fish tanks, and started eyeing them . . . (take it from there, Partner Two).

For a minute, only, partner 2 wrote in the air the words he or she might say. Then, before the child could get lost in the pet store, I spoke up, and pointing to Gregory's draft, I read the remaining section of it:

> I looked at Al, lying dead in my hands. For a second I thought, then I said, "We can give him a funeral." My dad looked doubtful for a minute but I picked him up and said, "He was special." Then I cried. Al was gone.

LINK

Remind children that as writers, they need to draw on their entire repertoire of strategies to accomplish whatever it is they want to do.

"Writers, whenever you are writing a narrative, remember that you have the option of having your narrator or main character either imagine a future event or recall a past event. Today, you have lots of options. You could check for true and honest details in your writing, study mentor texts for powerful leads, or bring out the internal as well as the external story. You could make sure that you angled your writing to show your intentions or that you wrote the heart of your story in a step-by-step way." As I spoke, I pointed to our class charts, including the Qualities of Good Personal Narrative Writing chart, as references. "Most of all, you want readers to dream the dream of your story. So as you reread, stop and ask, 'Is this what I really wanted to show? Is this what's most true and honest about my story?' Let the lens of truth be your guide for revision. Let's get started."

Often in a unit of study, the minilessons you teach early on introduce children to some goals and strategies that are essential to the work of the unit, and the teaching you do later in the unit is more of an option children may or may not draw upon. That is surely the case in this instance.

Writing and Conferring

Revising with Scenes from the Past

I pulled my chair alongside Joey, who was working with an enormous sense of industry. "What are you working on?" I asked.

"I'm doing time travel," he answered, his face flushed with excitement. "'Cause when John dove in the water and it was all wave-y, I had already put that thought about when we were canoeing in Class II rapids. So now I wrote about what we did when we were canoeing and I'm gonna make myself think of that," he said, showing me that he'd inserted a code into the swimming story: *[Fig. X-1]*

> Then the splash was greater each time his body went down more into the pond. Then his whole body was down under the water. It kind of reminded me of the time me and John went canoeing white water class 2.*

This was the section Joey planned to insert into the swimming story: *[Fig. X-2]*

> We got pulled in by a riptide. We paddled as hard as we could. It was getting us even closer and closer to the big rock. We tried the draw, that didn't work. We tried the back paddle, that didn't work. We tried the J-stroke, that didn't work. Suddenly we hit the rock.

MID-WORKSHOP TEACHING POINT ***Using Flashback to Convey the Main Feeling*** "Writers, what I'm noticing as I confer with you is that many of you are finding that when you want to build up the feeling that you had in a story, to really make readers feel what you were feeling, it helps to tuck just a tiny bit of time travel into your draft. For example, Becca has been writing about when she stayed for a week at her friend Clarissa's house, and suddenly experienced a pang of homesickness and worry. In her first version of her narrative, she just *told* about that. She wrote:

> "I do this every year," and I smiled to myself, thinking it would be a wonderful time. I looked down the hill at the rest of the Catskills and thought, "This is a beautiful house." But then in the night I felt a rush of pain in my stomach. Tears built up in my eyes, until they paused at the brim of my lower eyelids, then the tears suddenly flowed down my cheeks like small rivers. "I don't know what to do . . . I miss my family . . . I need them!" I sobbed. Then I imagined them in a car accident and cried even more.

continued on next page

Fig. X-1 Joey's entry shows a code

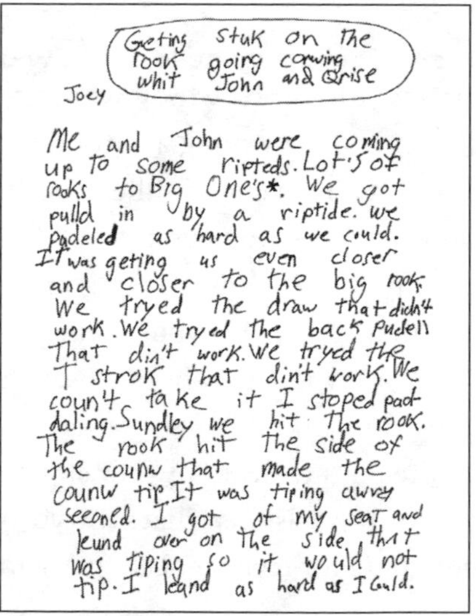

Geting stuk on the rook whit going John coming and Crise

Joey

Me and John were coming up to some ripteds. Lot's of rooks to Big One's*. We got pulld in by a riptide. we padeled as hard as we could. It was geting us even closer and closer to the big rook. We tryed the draw that didn't work. We tryed the back pudell That din't work. We tryed the J strok that din't work. We coun't take it I stoped padling. Sundley we hit the rook. The rook hit the side of the counu that made the counu tip. It was tiping awey seconds. I got of my seat and leand over on the side that was tiping so it would not tip. I leand as hard as I culd.

Fig. X-2 Joey's insertion text

I looked over what Joey had done and thought, "Now what?" He'd done exactly what I'd taught, and done it with great excitement—yet his revisions were in all likelihood going to detract from the story, distracting the reader away from the main idea which was Joey's appreciation for his friend's mentorship. I scrolled through my options. Clearly what I'd like best to do is to teach Joey that when a writer moves from one sequential story to a secondary one, that secondary story needs to enhance the story's main message. Joey could have written the paddling story so that it illustrated that yet again, while paddling together, John had been willing to go first and had paved the way for Joey. But it wasn't clear to me that any such thing had happened during the paddling story. And more to the point, Joey had just a very short while to bring his story to completion. It was far and away his longest story ever and his proudest accomplishment.

continued from previous page

"Becca decided she could actually go into her mind and tell about what she imagined could happen to her parents, so she wrote this."

> A terrible feeling came over me and took control of my mind. Words appeared in my mind and turned into worries. I saw my dad driving the car and my mom beside him. I saw a deer jump in the road. I saw the car bang into the rail and flip over. "What If My Parents Get Into a Car Accident!" I thought.

"Then Becca returned to the sequence of her story events, writing this."

> I was shaking. And my insides didn't know what to do. I called my mom and she told me that it's okay, that I should calm down . . .

"She's finishing the story now. I think Becca can teach all of us that one way to build up the main feeling that we want to convey in a story is to consider detailing what exactly we remember, or worry will happen, or hope for . . ."

"Joey," I said. "Can I shake your hand? Congratulations. You've just done exactly what authors do. You told the story of one moment, and it sparked the memory of a second, related story. I love that you didn't summarize this secondary story, the one you'll insert, but that you instead told it step by step. Congratulations!" I moved on, noticing that another day I had a pointer that I'd want to share with the class—and with Joey.

Share

Showing Significance through Adding Scenes from the Past or Future

Share an example of a student's writing that shows moving to a new scene at a new time, making sure that it strengthens the writer's overall intent.

"Writers, many of you are moving backward and forward in time, and your pieces are becoming richer as a result. Caleb's first draft went like this." *[Fig. X-3]*

> I looked up. Shelves upon shelves of mitts stared back down at me. The air conditioner made me feel like a snowstorm was forming in my intestine. I had tried on more than ten mitts and was about to give up. Finally I found one. It was perfect.

"But then Caleb thought, 'What am I trying to show in my story?' and he wrote a note to himself, 'I want the reader to know that my mitt is special to me.' He again wrote about shopping at Sports Authority, but this time he shifted between telling about shopping and telling about what he imagines himself doing with the glove in the future. He moves forward in time. Listen." As I read aloud, I emphasized the parts that revealed Caleb's intentions by shifting to an imagined future. *[Fig. X-4]*

> I pulled the soft, leathery mitt from the shelf. I slid it onto my left hand. I imagined myself fielding thousands of grounders and swiftly throwing them to the first baseman. I imagined myself leaping over the centerfield fence and watching the white streak land in it, the mitt. I slid if off, held it in my hands and started turning the mitt around, reading all the labels: "Mizono, max flex, 12.5 inches." Then I slipped it on again and the tingling sensation started again. I imagined me, tagging a runner at the plate. I imagined the headlines of a sports section in 2020, "Madison's fielding scorches fans."

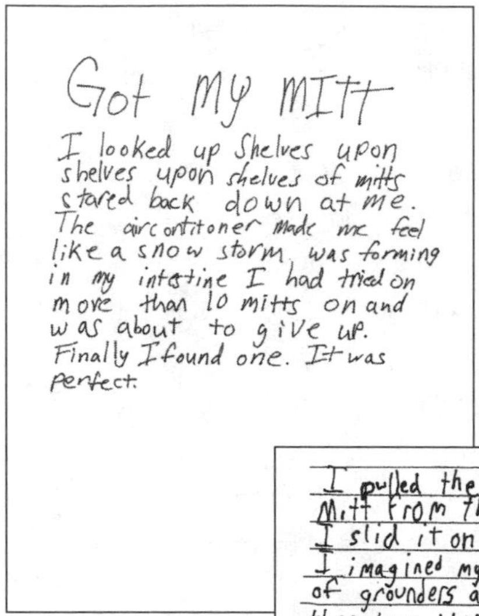

Got My MITT

I looked up Shelves upon shelves upon shelves of mitts stared back down at me. The air condtitoner made me feel like a snow storm was forming in my intestine I had tried on more than 10 mitts on and was about to give up. Finally I found one. It was perfect.

Fig. X-3 The start of Caleb's draft

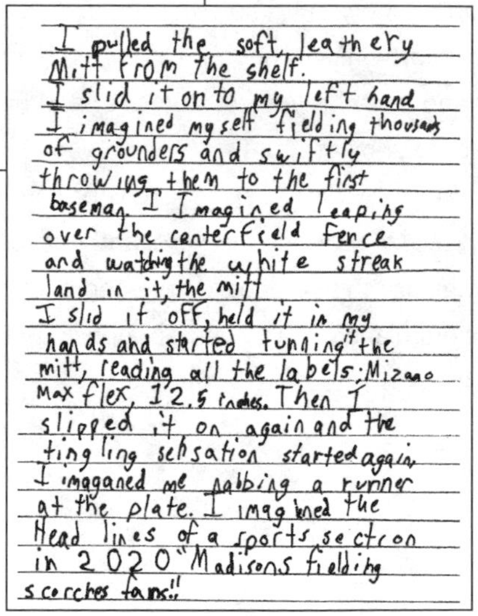

I pulled the soft, leathery Mitt from the shelf. I slid it on to my left hand I imagined my self fielding thousands of grounders and swiftly throwing them to the first baseman. I Imagined leaping over the centerfield fence and watching the white streak land in it, the mitt. I slid it off, held it in my hands and started tunning the mitt, reading all the labels: Mizano Max flex, 12.5 inches. Then I slipped it on again and the tingling sensation started again. I imaganed me tabbing a runner at the plate. I imagined the Head lines of a sports section in 2020 "Madisons fielding scorches fans!!

Fig. X-4 Caleb rewrote the middle of his draft so now he leaps forward in time.

HOMEWORK ***Using Past Memories to Emphasize Meaning*** Tonight, please work some more on adding a scene from the past or future to emphasize the significant part of your writing. Here's an example from Juliana to again show you what I mean.

Juliana is writing about meeting her dad, Chris, for the first time at a restaurant. But, she interrupts the story with this memory to emphasize how much this meeting matters to her. *[Fig. X-5]*

> I remember that when I was in pre-school, I asked my mom if I had a daddy. She said "No, not everyone has one." She reminded me that Alexandre in my class didn't have a daddy and that her own daddy died when she was a teenager.
>
> Then when I was in kindergarten my friend asked how come I didn't have a father. "I just don't," I said. He said I had to have a father, everyone had one. I went home and told my mom that Joseph said there was no such thing as not having a father. She said that Joseph was right. Everyone had a father because a mother couldn't make a baby all by herself. But not everyone had a daddy. A daddy was someone who stayed with them and took care of them. My father was a man named Chris who lived in South Africa. He helped make the baby but did not want to be a daddy. Our family was just me and her with no daddy.

Juliana uses *I remember* as a starting point for her flashback, and this flashback leads up to and gives importance to the story that she is writing. Try that tonight.

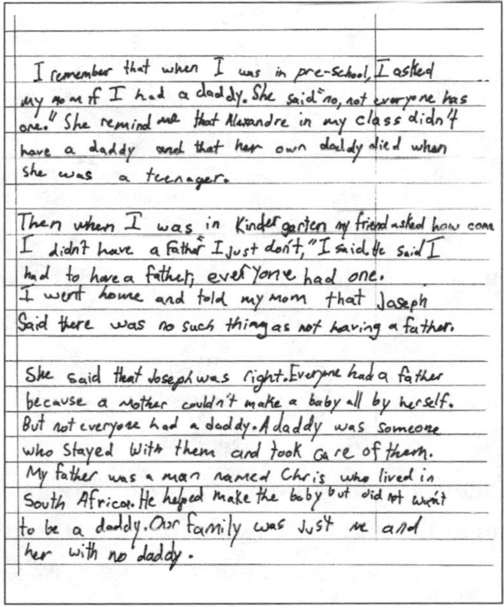

I remember that when I was in pre-School, I asked my mom if I had a daddy. She said "no, not everyone has one." She remind me that Alexandre in my class didn't have a daddy and that her own daddy died when she was a teenager.

Then when I was in Kindergarten my friend asked how come I didn't have a father "I just don't," I said. He said I had to have a father; everyone had one.
I went home and told my mom that Joseph Said there was no such thing as not having a father.

She said that Joseph was right. Everyone had a father because a mother couldn't make a baby all by herself. But not everyone had a daddy. A daddy was someone who Stayed With them and took care of them. My father was a man named Chris who lived in South Africa. He helped make the baby but did not want to be a daddy. Our family was just me and her with no daddy.

Fig. X-5 Juliana

TAILORING YOUR TEACHING

If your students would benefit from studying the words and phrases a mentor author uses to move back and forward through time . . . select some text passages to analyze, and then have students select one (or more) of these passages to use as mentor texts as they add scenes from the past and the future into their own pieces.

For example, in *Stevie*, by John Steptoe, once Stevie leaves to live with his mother and father again, Robert starts to remember all the fun they used to have together. The text includes passages like these:

> I remember the time I ate the last piece of cake in the breadbox and blamed it on him.
>
> We used to play Cowboys and Indians on the stoop.
>
> I remember when I was doin' my homework I used to teach him what I had learned. He could write his name pretty good for his age.
>
> I remember the time we played boogie man and we hid under the covers with Daddy's flashlight.
>
> And that time we was playin' in the dark under the bushes and we found these two dead rats and one was brown and one was black.
>
> And him and me and my friends used to cook mickies or marshmallows in the park.
>
> We used to have good times together.

Ask your students to study the words and phrases John Steptoe uses to insert these memories into his story. Your students will surely notice how Steptoe uses phrases like, "I remember," "We used to," "That time we," and so on. Developing a list of these words and phrases that authors use to move back in time will help your students figure out how to insert their own memories into their pieces.

If your students seem to plop scenes from the past or future into their narratives, and if this movement through time tends to distract from the big idea of their stories rather than reinforce it . . . you could use the same passages from Stevie listed above; however, this time your lens is how they each show the big idea of Robert's regret that *Stevie* left. Begin by suggesting that when writers add backward and forward movement to their stories, they do it for a purpose. Authors try to heighten the big idea of their story, and often it helps to add some scenes from the past or future to make the big idea clearer to the reader. In other words, they ask themselves, "What am I really trying to say here?" and add past and future scenes in order to strengthen the overall meaning of their pieces.

For Active Engagement, return to a piece of writing that is familiar to the class but that doesn't have any future or past scenes included. (It could be one of your entries, a whole-class text, or a student piece.) Have your students consider where and how to add past or future scenes to make the overall meaning of the piece shine through.

If your children studied this unit in a previous year . . . you'll want to cite a different mentor text and to create a new sort of active engagement. You might return to the example of a class event, such as when the class hamster got loose. You might say something like,

"Let's write a story about the other day when Hermie escaped from his cage during our read-aloud. Here is a draft of the start of that story." You could point to the story on chart paper. "Let's pretend we wanted to show that Hermie has escaped before, and that we get worried whenever this happens. Where could we think backwards, recalling what happened before, or think ahead, imagining what might happen in the future? Let's try to embed these jumps in time right into the middle of the narrative." Then you could take a moment to read the draft aloud.

> One fall afternoon, my teacher read aloud in the meeting area. "What's that noise?" I whispered to my partner. It sounded like Hermie. I looked over at his cage. Hermie was standing on top of his exercise wheel, pushing open the corner of the lid to his cage with his nose. Then I saw the brick. Someone forgot to put it back on top of the lid. I was nervous. I did not know what to say.
>
> When I looked again, Hermie was gone. I noticed the lid was pushed open, and I knew that Hermie escaped again.
>
> A moment later, I heard scraping sounds under the radiator. I saw Hermie poke his head out. He was in the same hiding spot as last time. Should I raise my hand and tell the teacher? Interrupt the read-aloud or wait until we finished? How were we going to catch him this time?

"Work with your partner on this. Get started."

Collaborating with Colleagues

As your children near the editing phase of the writing process, their attention will need to turn to the smaller and smaller details of their writing. To prepare yourself for this, you too may want to study the smaller choices writers make.

Writers learn to value the true word, the word that actively leaps to mind in the moment. You can teach children that writers reach not for the ornate or the impressive word, but for the true word, the precise word. It is unlikely that we'd see our canine ambulating with its nostrils declined toward the earth. We might, on the other hand, see our beagle running, its nose to the ground, chasing a scent. Point out to children that the sections of stories that seem beautiful often are not fancy ones. For example, I love Rylant's description of sleeping in a house full of relatives in *The Relatives Came*. She writes, "It was hard going to sleep with all that new breathing in the house." There's not a fancy word or a bit of figurative language in the sentence, but it's one of my favorite examples of descriptive writing. Part of its power is Rylant's choice to use that one word, *breathing*, usually a verb, as a noun.

With colleagues, study the careful word choices, the true words that authors use in mentor texts, particularly nouns and verbs. Strunk and White, in *The Elements of Style*, state: "It is nouns and verbs, not their assistants, that give to good writing its toughness and color" (p. 72). Carefully chosen nouns allow writers to be specific. So, instead of, "I grabbed a bag for the trip," it's more accurate to say, "I grabbed a *suitcase* for the trip." Instead of, "I packed my things," it's more accurate to list, "I packed my *shorts, T-shirts, and tennis racket*." If I want to show that I packed for a big trip, and the suitcase was heavy, instead of, "I took the suitcase off the bed and put it on the floor," it's more revealing to write, "I *wrestled* the suitcase to the floor."

For example, notice the beautiful choice of words in *Salt Hands*, by Jane Chelsea Aragon. Consider the following excerpt:

> I went to the door. It was dark. It was still. The night air was warm.
>
> I didn't want to frighten the deer, so quietly I went in and sprinkled some salt into my hands.
>
> I tiptoed outside and stepped toward him silently. He looked at me. His eyes were big and brown. He watched me for a long time.
>
> I knelt on the grass. The deer flicked his white tail back and forth. I sang a song to him softly, while he nibbled on fallen pears.
>
> He shook his head and twitched his ears. He was listening to my song.
>
> He moved closer to me cautiously. I whispered my song. Then slowly, I held out my hands.

Notice the careful choice of verbs: *tiptoed, stepped, knelt, flicked, sang, nibbled, twitched, whispered*. Notice the simple and true choice of nouns: *salt, eyes, grass, tail, pears, head, ears, song, hands*. Or the sparse, careful use of adverbs and adjectives that convey the author's intentions of silent communion: *quietly I went in . . . stepped toward him silently . . . his white tail . . . sang a song to him softly . . . fallen pears . . . moved closer to me cautiously . . . Then slowly, I held out my hands.*

Then bring this awareness to your students. For a Mid-Workshop Teaching Point, or other teaching opportunity in the writing workshop, you might try angling some common situations by working the nouns and verbs. For example, you could start with the common sentence, "I walked into the room." Show how you might change *walked* to *snuck* if you wanted to show that you were there without permission. Then you might change *room* to the *kitchen* to make that more accurate. Students could try changing *walked* and *room* for other specific scenarios as practice for careful word choice, especially for nouns and verbs.

IN THIS SESSION, YOU WILL TEACH STUDENTS THAT ONE POWERFUL WAY TO REVISE THEIR NARRATIVES IS TO BRING OUT THE STORY STRUCTURE.

GETTING READY

- *Peter's Chair*, by Ezra Jack Keats, and *Shortcut*, by Donald Crews; be sure students are familiar with both
- How Stories Tend to Go, drawn on chart paper
- Your own example of using story structure to tell a common, everyday event
- Story mountain for *Peter's Chair*, sketched on chart paper
- See CD-ROM for resources

BRINGING FORTH THE STORY ARC

In Session XI of Unit 1, we introduced timelines *as a construct to support students' planning and revision. In this session, we introduce students to a similar but more complex structure: a story arc.*

As teachers of reading and writing, we are keenly aware of the underlying structures in the genres we encounter. It is for this reason that my colleagues and I emphasize the format, the architecture, of a minilesson. We know that by uncovering the form of minilessons, "the way minilessons tend to go," we let you in on the genre's secrets. An awareness of a genre's form allows writers to compose in that form. This is true for any human endeavor. Music has its minuets, waltzes, and sonatas; law has its hearings, plea bargains, and trials. Mastery requires an awareness and application of forms.

In this lesson we introduce students to story arcs as a way of describing the pattern stories usually follow. In a very rough sense, narratives usually have some description of the situation, then something happens, and then there are some results. Another way of describing "the way stories tend to go" is to say that stories revolve around a character who yearns for or reaches towards something, who encounters trouble, and who as a result, finds new resources within himself or herself or the world . . . and changes in the process.

In this minilesson, we analyze very simple texts. But don't be fooled by these texts' simplicity. Some people maintain that it's the mark of genius to make the complex seem simple. This is true for these stories. My colleagues and I have used Peter's Chair *for countless craft lessons. Look at this text closely, and you will notice that Keats has no wasted words; every word forwards Peter's emotional journey through the story. After guiding students to perceive story structure, we show them how this newfound awareness gives them power to revise their narrative drafts.*

This session, then, invites substantive revisions, suggesting that just as the sculptor finds a lion emerging out of his block of marble and works the material to bring forth his vision, so, too, writers can sometimes see a story arc hidden within the details of a rough draft, and work with his or her material to bring forth that design. It's a wonderfully complex, rich way to revise—one which has everything to do with vision as well as re-vision.

MINILESSON

Bringing Forth the Story Arc

CONNECTION

Let your students know that revision begins with seeing possibilities in drafts that at first we think are finished.

"Some of you have been coming to me saying, 'I'm done.' That's a great feeling, isn't it? To reach the end of a draft! When I get to the end of a draft, I sit back and enjoy being done. I take time to clean up my writing folder. I get a drink of water . . . and then I get back to work!"

"As I told you earlier this year, writers have a saying: 'When you're done, you've just begun.' Once we've reached the end of a draft, we're in a very special place because now we can make our best work even better. I know you are thinking that your drafts are already pretty good—as good as your final pieces from Unit 1, that's for sure—and you are right. And over the next few days, you'll have a chance to take the best that you can do so far . . . and make your best, better. That's how learning goes."

"The word *revision* comes from the word *vision*. It literally means to look again. Today I want to teach you one way to revise (to resee) your writing."

Name your teaching point. Specifically, tell children that they can revise their drafts by bringing out the story structure.

"Today I want to teach you that, just as our writing workshops usually follow one general plan or format, so, too, stories usually follow one plan or format; they both have a 'way they usually go.' Writers know how stories usually go, and when we write stories, our stories tend to follow the same general plan. One way to revise our writing is to bring out the story structure that is probably hiding underneath our personal narratives."

TEACHING

Analyze aloud the story structure of a well-known story, such as Ezra Jack Keats' *Peter's Chair.*

"Writers, by now you have come to realize that our writing workshops usually begin with a minilesson, then there is work time, then we meet to share. You can count on that.

COACHING

I want children to embrace the concept of revision and to anticipate major, significant changes. The message is that revision is not a time to tweak and polish. It instead offers a chance to reinvent, to reimagine. I want children to approach their revision work with zeal and resourcefulness.

This session will work best if your students already know the text you'll refer to later in the session. I refer to Keats' Peter's Chair *but any simple story with a traditional story arc will suffice. Williams'* Knufflebunny *is perfect. The red sweater excerpt from "Eleven" in Cisneros'* Woman Hollering Creek and Other Stories *is not suitable.*

Pause for just a second to realize how many words related to the teaching of writing are linked to sight: point of view, focus, zooming in, vision, lenses, perspective . . . but the greatest of these is re-vision.

When planning this unit, I went back and forth over the question of whether to teach this lesson on story structure as part of planning, just before children begin their drafts, or as part of revision. For me, a sense of structure is one of several magnetic poles exerting a force on my content from the very start. For this reason, I was tempted to make this Session VI. But, on the other hand, I worried that children might let their sense of story and their attentiveness to form overpower everything else so that writing a narrative became filling in a format rather than dreaming the dream of an event. So this session is here, at this late point in the sequence of the unit, and probably it will be most influential for your stronger students, allowing others to gain time for continuing with trajectories you set earlier.

You know how writing workshops usually go. In a similar way, stories, like writing workshops, have a pattern, a way that they usually go. Most stories begin by introducing the *main character* and usually that main character has hopes or desires. Then, the main character's hopes or desires usually lead to that main character getting into some sort of a *problem* or *trouble* or *tension*. Finally, *things happen* related to that problem, and the story ends in a *resolution*."

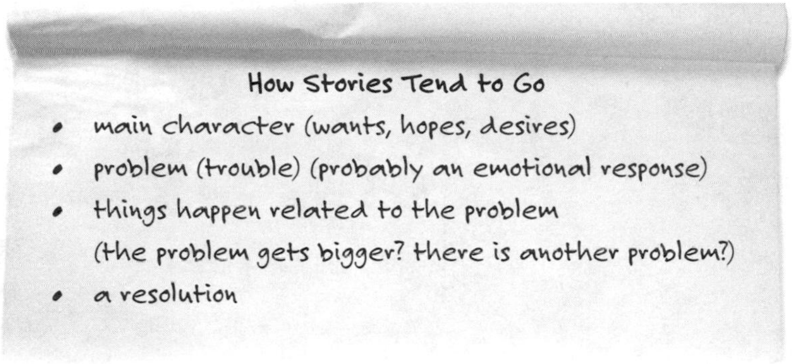

How Stories Tend to Go

- main character (wants, hopes, desires)
- problem (trouble) (probably an emotional response)
- things happen related to the problem
  (the problem gets bigger? there is another problem?)
- a resolution

"So let me show you what I mean by showing you the *story arc* as I see it in Ezra Jack Keats' *Peter's Chair*." I read the story as if to myself, almost murmuring, skipping irrelevant passages to keep the rendition quick.

> Peter stretched as high as he could . . .

"Yup, there is the character and he's physically reaching for something—he already wants something. I guess he's wanting to make a tall tower. He may have deeper wants, too."

> "Shhh. Remember we have a new baby."

"Yup, there is the problem! His tower falls down and all that his parents worry about is waking the baby." Then I added, in an aside, "Do you notice that the story never really comes right out and says that Peter has a problem? It just shows it: Peter has to tiptoe around because of his sister. His parents aren't paying attention to him, they are paying attention to his sister's needs."

> "That's my cradle. They painted it pink!"

"More stuff is happening about the problem—and again, the story doesn't really come right out and *say* it is a problem for Peter that his parents are taking his stuff and painting it

Notice my emphasis on the predictable nature of the writing workshop. Here I build on students' growing awareness of the structures of both their daily life and of stories they read.

We will, of course, revisit this content in the unit on writing short fiction. But it is fascinating to realize that our personal narratives work best if they are not just true chronicles of a life experience, but if they are also shaped like a story. Consider the implication of this in relation to the narratives you've been writing.

Of course, not all stories go like this. Starting with this common, simple structure, however, can help children craft their narratives into pieces of writing that feel like stories, pieces that have a touch of suspense, or that have, at the very least, an unfolding of interrelated events.

Donald Murray has suggested that the secret of all dramatic writing (as he calls this sort of narrative) is the quality that can be summed up in the adage "show don't tell." This is simple to say and enormously complex to put in action.

pink for his little sister, but we can figure that out. So let me keep reading and you see if the ending of this story follows the plan for most stories."

> Peter picked up the chair and ran to his room . . . "Let's run away, Willie," he said.

"The story is winding up, isn't it? Peter is upset enough that he's taking action. He took that chair and ran away because he didn't want his chair painted pink too! I think he's trying to get his parents' attention in a drastic way! I think this is the heart of the story, the problem Peter is facing has gotten so bad that Peter wants to run away with Willie. Let's read on":

> But he couldn't fit in the chair. He was too big!

"You know what? I'm sensing a turning point to the problem, a resolution, which is how stories go. I bet that Peter is starting to realize that he's too big for his baby things." Skipping past other details which add to the sense of resolution, I read from the ending:

> Then Peter says, "Daddy, let's paint the little chair pink for Susie."

"That definitely shows resolution: Not only does Peter rejoin the family, but it seems that he's learning to accept Susie. He is offering to paint his little chair pink! Ezra Jack Keats doesn't come out and say that the problem is resolved, but we're able to figure it out."

"Writers," I said, taking hold of a marker pen and drawing a mountainlike arc across chart paper, "here's an easy way to see the story structure in *Peter's Chair.* We'll call it a *story mountain* because of its shape. The main character, Peter, *wants* his family to be the way it was: just him and his mom and dad." I locate this in a dot at the base of the story mountain, and continue making dots, as on a timeline. "*But then* there's a new baby, Susie, in the house. Things happen to Peter that make the problem get worse." As I spoke, I moved up the incline of the story mountain, marking key moments. "*And so finally,* he and Willie run away: Peter can't take it anymore." Then I pointed to the top of the story mountain. "Then comes the resolution, starting with Peter finding he no longer fits in his old chair and including Peter's mom inviting him in for lunch. In the end [and I pointed to the last portion of the story mountain], Peter helps his dad to paint his blue chair pink for Susie."

Active Engagement

Retell *Shortcut*, using voice intonation to help children perceive the story's structure.

"Let me retell the story of *Shortcut* to you. Please listen and in a minute I'm going to ask you to talk with your partner about whether this book has the same structure as *Peter's Chair.*

Sometimes I help children realize that writers don't show-not-tell all parts of our stories, but we do use this adage to develop the heart of a story.

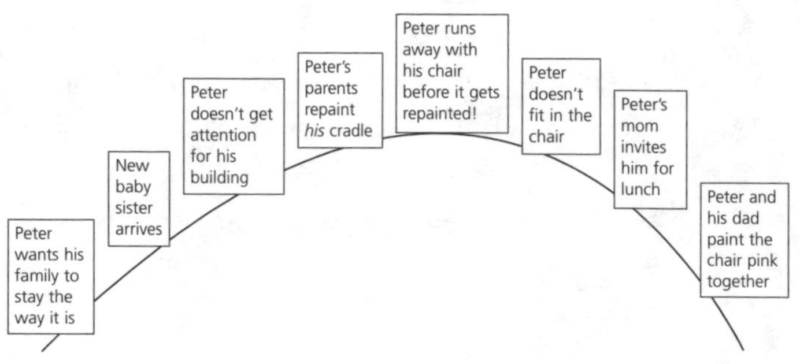

The big difference between a timeline and a story mountain is that in the latter, one section of the story is given prominence. We can refer to that one section as "the heart of a story" or as the rising action and climax or as the peak of the story—and the way this teaching is evolving, we'll end up using all of these terms despite the fact that this means we're using mixed metaphor. If children are confused, the confluence of different terminology probably won't be the main cause for that confusion. Instead, the hard part will be applying what they learn about Peter's Chair *to their own drafts.*

Remember how stories tend to go," and I pointed again to the story arc. "So in *Shortcut*, the children take the shortcut home and a train comes clackity clacking down the track, bearing down upon them. They holler, they run, they leap out of the way. Then they hear the train, clickety clacking away from them. Walking home, they resolve not to tell anyone . . . and never to take the shortcut again. Turn and talk to your partner. See if you can plot *Shortcut* on the same structure as *Peter's Chair.* Be sure to explain your thinking. Ready? Begin."

If you feel that the students need another example, you could add: "Writers, do you see that all these stories have a structure that is the same as the one in The Little Engine That Could? *Remember from when you were little, that story of a train that makes it over the mountain, carrying toys and treats to all the good little girls and boys? It starts up the mountain, but the load is heavy, the train is small, so it chugs along, going, 'I think I can, I think I can, I think I can,' until finally—Hurray! Toot toot! It's on its way to all the good little boys and girls."*

LINK

Remind children that stories, like the writing workshop, follow a form. Help writers realize that a knowledge of story structure can help them re-vision their work and decide upon their next steps.

"So writers, always remember that stories, like the writing workshop itself, have a way-they-usually-go. Knowing the way-things-usually-go helps a person to be more planful. Because I know that I'll only have thirty or forty minutes to confer during writing time, I can look over my plans for a day and realize I'll never get around to all the one-to-one conferences I hope to hold, and so I can revise my plans with the constraints of the workshop in mind. I can, for example, decide to hold a small group strategy lesson rather than to try conferring with eight of you individually."

"In the same way, writers, because you know how stories usually go, you can look over what you've written so far and revise what you've done and what you plan to do next, keeping in mind that your personal narrative will probably be stronger if you bring out the elements of story that are buried in it."

"You will need to look at whether your story is still more like a timeline, with one event leading to the next, each of equal size and importance. If that's the case, you'll want to be sure to figure out what your story is really about and what you can do to show that. Turning a timeline into a story mountain is the same process as building up the heart of your story. Remember how Peter's feeling builds as one thing after another happens, and he feels worse and worse? If you haven't built up the incline in your story, take the key section and stretch it out. If knowing how stories go gives you other ideas for revision . . . do those now! This is your chance. Off you go."

Writing and Conferring

Developing Elements of Story

I pulled my chair alongside Sirah. I knew, even before I began the conference, that Sirah was well on her way to writing an effective piece of writing, and looked forward to helping her make a good story into a great one.

"Sirah," I said, "I'm wondering how you decided which parts of this event to include in your writing?"

Sirah answered, "Well, I was telling the story the way it happened. I went to the hotel to go swimming and I was playing in the pool when a hurricane hit. Then, we thought the hurricane was gone, so we all went in the pool, but then it came back so we all went home."

"So, you remembered the way the story happened from the beginning to the end and that's the way you wrote it?"

Sirah nodded. "Yep. The whole story was not even one hour so it's focused."

"That's smart of you, Sirah. I'm glad you are thinking about keeping it focused and you are right that one way writers focus is by limiting the amount of time that passes."

Then I said, "But Sirah, I'm going to give you another very important tip that will help you to focus your writing. Another way we check that our story is focused is we check to make sure that all parts of the story relate to the story mountain. And for you, the peak of your mountain is . . . "

Sirah interjected, "When the hurricane hit."

I nodded. "So, that's at the peak of your mountain. If you want to be sure your writing is focused, you need to think how all the other parts of your story relate to this part," I said, sketching her story mountain. "So, for example, you started your story when you arrived at the hotel for your swimming lesson. Could you think of a point in time that is more closely related to when the hurricane hit? You can still be enjoying yourself and having fun. But you want your starting place to begin to lead the reader to the most important part of your story."

Sirah replied, "Well, my cousin and I were on the beach collecting shells. We had a whole bucket. This is where I first had a feeling that the hurricane was coming."

MID-WORKSHOP TEACHING POINT **_Developing Story Mountains_** "Writers, many of you are struggling a bit with your story mountains and that's as it should be. You're wise to go through several drafts of a story mountain—it is lots more efficient than writing several drafts of a story! Let me remind you of a few pointers."

"Remember that your story will probably contain only two or three small moments, two or three vignettes that perhaps each occupy about twenty minutes. To pull this off, remember that you don't need to start the story at the start of the action. If you are writing about a ski trip, you needn't start it with the drive! You could start it with the moment when you slide off the ski lift at the crest of the mountain. Usually, it helps to start the story close to the trouble, to the rising action, when you can see the story's mountain peak rising ahead of you."

continued on next page

"Okay, so you might start it when you were on the beach and you had a feeling that a hurricane was coming?" As I spoke, I graphed what Sirah said on a story mountain. Then I said, "Sirah, do you see that one way, then, to be sure your story is focused is to check that your beginning and your ending relates to the main part (the peak) of your story? You've done that for your lead; try it now with your ending. You have everybody leaving and going home at the end. But, just like your beginning, you want your ending to be related to the most important part of your story. Don't leave and go home! Think of other possible endings that stay close to the heart of the story."

continued from previous page

"Be sure that you ask, 'What's my story really about?' and be sure that your answer to that question translates into your story mountain. If Rie's story is really about how her father helps her feel safe when they're surfing in big waves, she's not going to want to start her story with a description of eating lunch at the beach sitting under a colorful umbrella, even if that is what she did before she went surfing in the waves. If her story will end up being that she was very scared and her father made her feel safe, her lead needs to at least hint at those scared feelings. So she can only have herself eating lunch at the start of the story if her father disrupts the lunch to cajole her into the waves."

"That leads to my third point. You may need to invent some actions to show what you are feeling. If you want to show that you are afraid to go out in the thundering surf, then you can make your father plead with you to go out. You can have him grab your hand and say, 'Come on, scaredy-cat.' Every single bit of the story need not be exactly true."

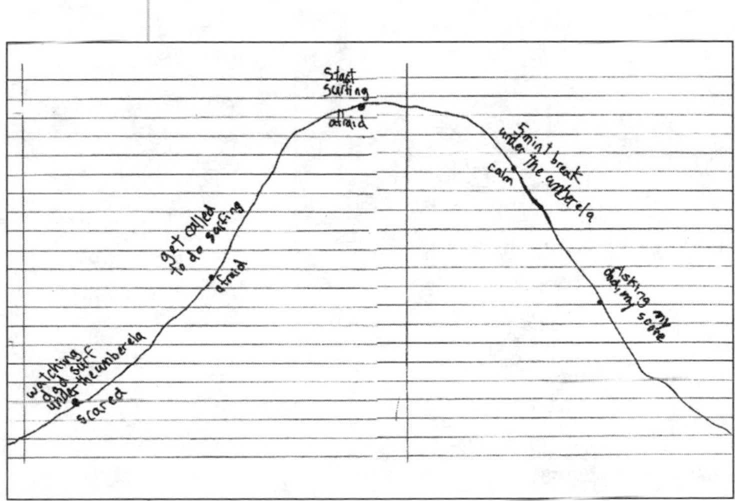

Fig XI-1 Rie's story mountain

SHARE

Mapping Internal and External Story Arcs

Show children a story arc drawn in "mountain" form. Show another story arc for the same story, this time for the character's internal changes.

"Oh my gosh writers, I've got to stop all of you because the work I am seeing right now is so drop-dead amazing I can't stand it! Holy-moly. I go from desk to desk, from writer to writer and I feel like I'm on some sort of magic carpet because one moment, I'm walking with Takeshi into a delicatessen, seeing the very same man behind the counter who was there five years ago, and the next minute I'm with Sirah, living through a hurricane. You are building up the important parts of your stories in such powerful ways that I feel as if I need to hold my hat or I'll be swept away by your words!"

"Listen to Sirah as she reads to you just the story mountain where trouble grows. Remember her story starts with her gathering shells when she was on the beach near her home in Senegal. She'd been taking swimming lessons at the hotel, when she saw a dark cloud coming. She worried it was a hurricane but no one believed her. Then—listen. See if you think she has what writers call rising action! *[Figs. XI-3, XI-4, and XI-5]*

Sirah's story is a spectacular illustration of rising action, but my worry is that children will feel as if they need high winds to flatten buildings and raise roofs in order to create the increasing tension, the drama, of an effective story. I might, therefore, decide to instead share a story such as the one Sophie wrote. She brought out story tension by showing that she had butterflies in her stomach as she rehearsed for the moment when she'd ask Claudia to be her best friend.

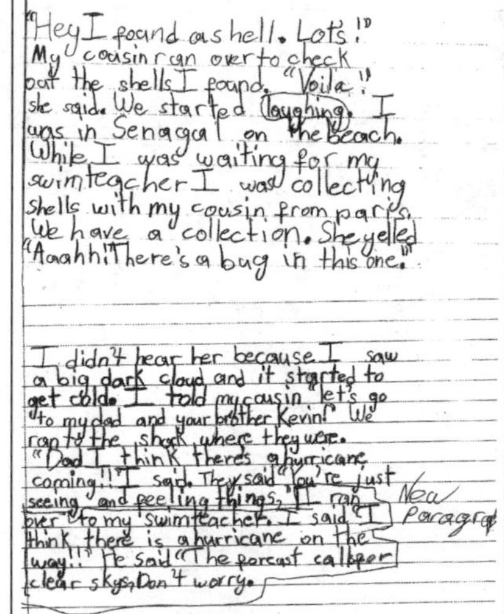

"Hey I found a shell. Lots!" My cousin ran over to check out the shells I found. "Voila!" she said. We started laughing. I was in Senagal on the beach. While I was waiting for my swimteacher I was collecting shells with my cousin from paris. We have a collection. She yelled "Aaahh! There's a bug in this one."

I didn't hear her because I saw a big dark cloud and it started to get cold. I told my cousin "let's go to my dad and your brother Kevin!" We ran to the shack where they were. "Dad I think there's a hurricane coming!!" I said. They said "You're just seeing and peeling things," I ran over to my swimteacher. I said "I think there is a hurricane on the way!!" He said "The forcast called for clear skys, Don't worry.

New Paragraph

Fig. XI-3 Sirah, page 1

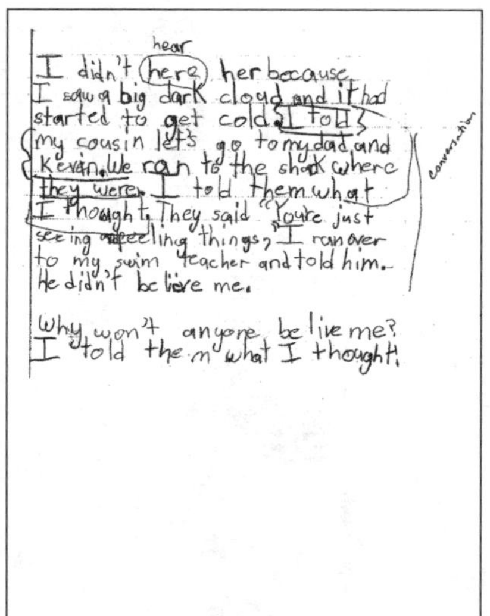

I didn't here (hear) her because I saw a big dark cloud and it had started to get cold. I told my cousin let's go to my dad and Kevin. We ran to the shack where they were. I told them what I thought. They said "You're just seeing ~~and~~ feeling things," I ran over to my swim teacher and told him. He didn't believe me.

Why won't anyone believe me? I told them what I thought!

conversation

Fig. XI-4 Sirah, page 2

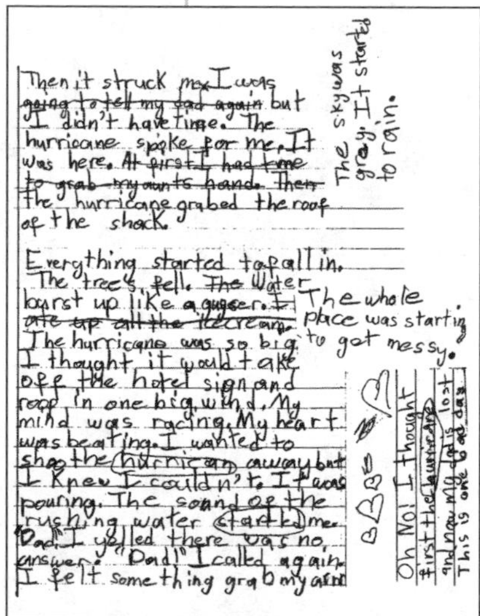

Then it struck me. I was ~~going to tell my dad again~~ but I didn't have time. The hurricane spoke for me. It was here. ~~At first I had time to grab my aunts hand. Then~~ the hurricane grabed the roof of the shack.

The sky was gray. It started to rain.

Everything started to fall in. The tree's fell. ~~The Water~~ burst up like a guyser. ~~I ate up all the icecream.~~ The whole place was starting to get messy. The hurricane was so big I thought it would take off the hotel sign and roof in one big wind. My mind was racing. My heart was beating. I wanted to shoo the hurrican away but I knew I couldn't. It was pouring. The sound of the rushing water startled me. "Dad," I yelled there was no answer. "Dad!" I called again. I felt something grab my arm

Oh No! I thought first the hurricane and now my dad is lost This is one bad day

Fig. XI-5 Sirah, page 3

HOMEWORK ***Planning Revision with Story Arcs*** Earlier today, when we looked at the story mountain of *Peter's Chair*, I noticed that Keats built gradually toward the heart of the story. He showed a few events that made the trouble seem worse, before it resolved, and that helps build Peter's feelings of jealousy, exclusion, and anger.

Right now, think back on the story mountain that you imagined for your own narratives, and compare it to the story mountain for *Peter's Chair*. What's missing from yours? What final revision could you do that would bolster the structure of your own narratives? Your time for making changes is almost up, so work fast and furiously.

TAILORING YOUR TEACHING

If your students are hesitant to revise, perhaps because they are not sure what parts of their stories could benefit from revision . . . you may want to teach them that a big part of revising is having a strong sense of audience as you reread your writing. Show your students how writers actually envision particular readers as they revise. Teach them to reread with this strong sense of audience in mind by asking questions like these:

- What parts will the reader enjoy? Where does the writing sound good and give a clear picture of what was happening?
- Are there any places where the reader might get confused? Where do I lose focus?
- Have I left out actions, details, and dialogue the reader needs in order to follow my story?
- Where might I include more thoughts and feelings to make my intentions clear to the reader?

Using your own narrative draft, demonstrate how you jot notes in the margins or underline or circle parts that help you revise for your audience. For active engagement, students could practice this careful reading and rereading with their own drafts, or with a whole-class narrative draft on chart paper (or projected on overhead transparency).

Assessment

You are nearing the conclusion of your second unit of study, and of this round of work with narrative writing. Soon you and your children will move to the brave new world of essay writing. Before you do that, take a bit of time to review the journey that you and your children have traveled thus far, and to reflect on their growth.

When you think about your children's growth, remember that the word *evaluation* includes in it the word *value*. Reflect for a moment on what you are really after as a teacher, on what the values are that led you into this profession in the first place. Then look at your children's growth (and your own) towards those things you choose to value.

Consider, for example, the progress your children as a group and individuals in specific have made toward composing writerly lives for themselves. It wasn't long ago when you were preoccupied with teaching your children strategies for generating ideas for writing, and with helping children realize their lives are worth writing about. Has your class as a whole come to understand that topics for writing are everywhere? Which children continue to need help generating topics for writing? Which choose small topics but struggle to bring out the significance in those topics? Which choose gigantic topics and have trouble trusting that "the smaller you write, the bigger you write?"

In thinking about your children's writing lives, consider their initiative as writers, and their investment in their own writing. Which of your children seem to have caught the writing bug, coming to you with stories of writing while at home, on the playground, at a sleepover?

In a similar fashion, you will want to consider children's progress towards your other values. For example, I care very much that children develop increasing independence as the year progresses. I'll want to consider children as a group and as individuals, weighing the extent to which they've developed independence. How likely is it that I'll teach a minilesson on one strategy, and a writer decides to work, instead, towards a whole different goal? How often does a particular child initiate revision? Reach to make a reading-writing connection on his or her own? Then, too, which children can sustain work for long periods of time without needing me to carry them along?

Today's a good day for assessment—and not just the sort of assessment that comes from looking at written products.

IN THIS SESSION, YOU WILL TEACH CHILDREN THAT WRITERS DON'T JUST END STORIES, WE RESOLVE PROBLEMS, LEARN LESSONS, AND MAKE CHANGES TO END THEM EFFECTIVELY.

GETTING READY

- Your ongoing writing with several possible endings
- See CD-ROM for resources

ENDING STORIES

One of the extraordinary things about the teaching of writing *is this: almost any lesson we could possibly teach is equally applicable to a six-year-old and a sixty-year-old. The challenges of writing well are enduring ones.*

Whether writers are six or sixty, the challenge to end a story well is an important one. Abby Oxenhorn, a kindergarten teacher who co-authored the Small Moments *book in* Units of Study Primary Writing: A Yearlong Curriculum, *found she finally resorted to laying down the law for her youngsters. "You are not allowed to end your story 'and then we went to bed!'" she said. Five-year-old Emma responded by ending her story about a ride on the ferris wheel by saying, "and we lived happily ever after." Soon that ending, too, was on the off-limits list. Of course, Abby and I were secretly thrilled that even these littlest writers knew that stories need something special at the end.*

In this session, you'll help children consider ways to end their stories. You may not need to lay down the law as Abby did, saying, "No fair ending your story with 'then we went to bed' or 'we lived happily ever after"... but you will need to decide how to nudge children to take on the challenge to write a good ending as an invitation to fashion a new insight, develop a new thought, resolve an issue, or learn a lesson. Because although you may not have a chance just now to teach this to your children, the truth is that when we consider ways to end our stories, we are also inventing ways to resolve our problems. This is life work, at its richest!

Minilesson

Ending Stories

Connection

Remind children that they've learned to consider personal narratives as stories.

"Writers, yesterday we thought about *Peter's Chair* and about our own stories, too, as stories which are structured like story mountains. Whenever you write a personal narrative, remember that you can get a lot of power by using story structure—the structure we saw in *Peter's Chair* and in *Shortcut*, too. A friend of mine describes the structure that one finds in most stories this way: 'Somebody wanted . . . but then . . . and so, finally . . .' This structure makes people read stories on the edge of our seats, wondering how the problem will turn out!"

Name your teaching point. Specifically, tell children you'll teach them how to write the resolution to their stories.

"Today, I want to help you wrestle with just one part of your story arc, and that's the part represented by the words 'and so, finally . . . .' Today, I want to remind you that writers don't just *end* our stories, we resolve our problems, we change our feelings, we learn our lesson."

Teaching

Tell children that writers draft possible endings, and do so by asking ourselves a series of questions meant to elicit the story's real meaning.

"What I want to tell you today is that just as writers often take time to draft and revise different leads for our stories, so, too, we need to draft and revise alternate endings. But when we think about how we'll end our stories, we don't think so much about whether we'll end our stories with dialogue or with a small action or with a thought. Instead, we think this: What is my story really, really about? What was I wanting or struggling to achieve or reaching towards in my story? How does that story end? And what is it I want to say to my readers about this struggle, this journey?"

"For example, let me pull out the story I began writing earlier in this unit. I'm going to read it over now and see if I can ask myself those questions and begin considering possible endings. It will be harder to figure out an ending to my story about Eliza insulting me, because there wasn't a happy ending or a resolution in my life . . . not that I can remember,

Coaching

Crafting resolutions, whether in writing or in life, is no small task. Learning a lesson, realizing the nature of life, making a change, or finding meaning in the events around us is tough! To write well about it, we need to have experienced it with awareness. Celebrate your students doing the best they can at this!

In this minilesson, I am going to use my own writing to demonstrate how I go about considering and drafting alternate endings. I could instead have decided to use a mentor text. "Papa Who Wakes Up Tired in the Dark" would have been a good choice. If I wanted to use this text, I'd need to imagine what Sandra Cisneros probably did in order to arrive at her ending. I might, for example, tell children that she may have considered ending her story, "I ran off to tell my sister that our abuelito had died." Then I could say, "But she probably thought, 'Wait, this isn't really a story about the narrator and her sister,' leading her back towards the ending she arrives at.

anyhow. I do have a somebody, namely me, who wants to be liked by the popular kids in my class. But then, things get in the way, there is trouble. They make fun of my clothes. They still don't accept me. And so, finally . . . Huh, you know what I am noticing? There isn't any resolution in my story. The story essentially goes like this."

> Lucy got a part in the play. She hoped that would help her gain acceptance by the in-group. It didn't help.

"And the story is left hanging, isn't it? To make the story better, I need to figure out how to bring the story to some resolution. But I need to remember what my story is really about—which is my longing to be popular—and I need to think, 'What action could I put at the end of my story that goes with the real message of my story?'"

Picking up a marker pen, I wrote on chart paper:

> That incident happened more than forty years ago, but I still remember it. And now I try to help children grow up understanding that popularity isn't the only thing that matters.

Rereading that ending, I said, "Sometimes I do that. I stand way back from the actual event and look at it from a distance." Then I picked up my marker pen and tried another ending:

> "I think your dress is fine. It's not antique at all," Emma said, shooting an angry look at Eliza.
>
> Then I said to Emma, "Do you want to meet after school and figure out our costumes?" Eliza made a big huffy noise and turned away.

"In a similar way, I hope that thinking of story structure might help you form a vision for how you can revise your endings."

Active Engagement

Ask children to think of making the same sort of "mountains" for their own narratives.

"So, let's try it. Take out your drafts, and imagine the story mountain structure for your own narratives. Use that story mountain to help you revise your endings. Ask yourself, 'What is my story really, really about? What was I wanting or struggling to achieve or reaching towards in my story? How does that story end? And what is it I want to say to my readers about this struggle, this journey?' Now look through your draft for the journey. What are the emotions that you, the main character, are feeling in the beginning? Do they

If you wonder whether this might be too sophisticated for your children to really grasp, you are probably right . . . but children learn by the seriousness with which we address them, by the earnesty in our voices. They certainly will not master the content of today's teaching . . . but it's okay that some days suggest a horizon.

It may be that your students would benefit from another example. You can add other examples from your own writing to this minilesson or you could use an example of a student's writing.

build toward the heart of your story? Do your emotions start to change at the turning point? Do you reach a different emotional state by the end?"

"Okay. Turn and talk to your partner about how you can imagine revising your ending to show the heart of your story—to reinforce what your story is really, really about."

Link

Assure writers that you understand the tendancy to slap any ol' ending onto a completed story, but rally children to invest themselves in drafting endings that convey what they want to say.

"Writers, if you are like me, then you probably are accustomed to ending your stories any ol' way. I know that I'm usually tired by the time I reach my ending, and so I just slap something down on the page. But when I revise, I look closely at my ending, because I know that it is what readers will read last. It's what they'll carry with them. Today, I hope you learned that our endings need to link back to the top of our story mountain. Our endings, like our beginnings, need to help convey what it is we most want to say. Today is your last day to work . . . so let's not waste a minute!"

We walked into the Chuckie cheese. I held Claudia's hand tight. My palm was sweating. I was feeling really happy to be with Claudia. "Hey Claudia what game do you want to play?" "The Bumble bee catching game!" "Okay" We both ran to the game. While we were playing we were laughing and having a great time together. "Claudia I am having such a great time with you today!" "Me to Sophie." When we were done playing I walked closer to Claudia, waiting for the right moment to ask her. I was so nervous! I didn't know what she was going to say! I took a deep breath, and said it! "Claudia I have something to ask you." "Ya Sophie" "Well I wanted to

Fig. XII-1 Sophie

know if you wanted to be my best friend and, I'll be yours?" I hugged her she hugged me back. I still felt like I had butterflys in my stomach. "Claudia" "Ya Sophie" "Your the best" "Thanks Sophie" "Are you ready to go get our prize yet?" "Ya. I'm ready lets go." We walked over to the register. When we got there the wall was full with prizes. "Hey Sophie what prize do you want?" "I don't know yet. What do you want?" "Well" "The teddy bear" we said at the same time. "Excuse me" I asked. "Can we please have two teddy bears"

Fig. XII-2 Sophie

"Coming right up" The lady behind the counter said. She handed us the two teddy bears. "There so cute" I said. We hugged our two matching teddy bears. "Hey Claudia" "ya Sophie" "now theese teddy bears can mark our friend ship forever" "forever" Claudia said. While we went home we had our two new matching teddy bears marking our friendship on our laps. "Claudia you are the best friend anybody could have in the whole world"

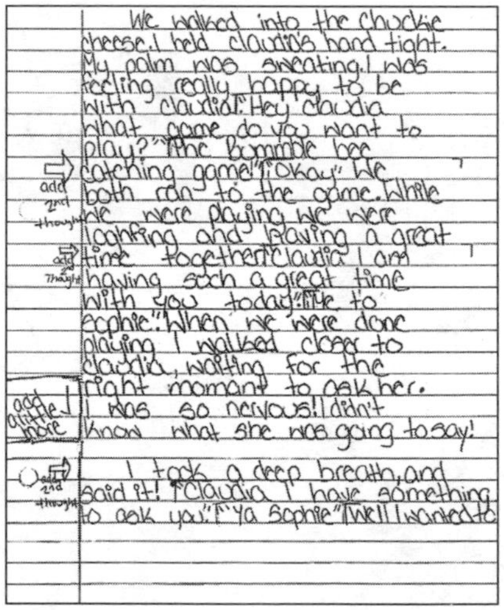

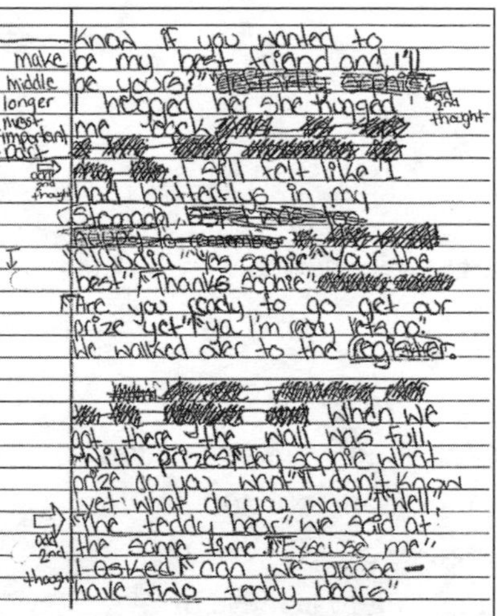

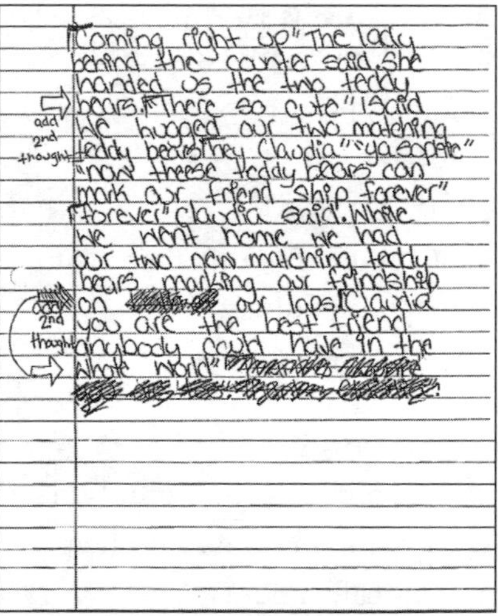

Fig. XII-3 Sophie

Writing and Conferring

Using Story Mountains to Improve Our Narratives

I watched Sophie make the finishing touches on her story mountain. She looked up and said, "I can't decide whether to start with driving to Chuck E. Cheese, or with when we're there, 'cause I want to have a beginning part before we, you know, say we'll be best friends."

"That's a wise question. I love that you aren't just thinking about what would make a catchy beginning—you are thinking about how the beginning will set readers up for the middle," I said.

"But Sophie, my hunch is that your story could work starting either place in the sequence of actions, but that the really crucial question to ask yourself is this: what is the internal story you want to tell at the beginning? You've graphed the events, the external story, but not the internal storyline. You've written the external events on your story mountain. Can you think (at least for the start of it) what your internal feelings are and graph those?"

Sophie pulled close to her draft and added the words, "feeling happy to be with Claudia," and "feeling even more happy" onto her story mountain.

MID-WORKSHOP TEACHING POINT ***Focusing Story Endings*** "Writers, can I have your eyes? Rie is stuck on an ending. Can you see if you could help her? Remember Rie's story? She's writing about how she let her dad convince her to go surfing this summer even though she didn't want to and she was so happy that she did, because she realized afterwards that she could do anything. The most important point in her story is when she's actually up on her board—surfin'."

"Let's say that Rie is going to end her story where she walks out of the water with her dad to have some lunch. In her first draft, the story ends with her thinking about the mac n' cheese that she's going to eat soon . . . but Rie realizes that feels like a whole new story. She knows it will throw her writing out of focus."

"Who can help Rie write an ending? So far she's written: 'My dad and I walked out of the water. "I've got mac 'n' cheese, guys!" my mom yelled from under the umbrella.' Can anyone help?" Soon Rie had a plethora of suggestions, and I sent all the children back to help themselves, as they helped Rie.

"I love your sense that the feelings grow, that they become more intense! That's just what happens when a story picks up its pace," I said." But I'm wondering how the story will work if it goes like this: 'I was happy to be with Claudia. I was even happier, I was the happiest. Then we said yes, we were happy.' When we read novels during the reading workshop and we talk about characters, we often talk about characters struggling and overcoming struggles. Or at least we talk about a character going through some kind of change." Then I said, "Can I leave you for a bit to think more about your story? My question for you as a writer is this: Was it all just happy, happier, happiest? And even if it was all just one growing feeling of happy, could you maybe tweak the truth so there was some change of feelings, some development? Could you make a story mountain so it showed changing feelings, paralleling the changing sequence of events?"

Later that morning, Sophie told me she decided to start by telling that at first she'd been scared Claudia wouldn't want to commit to the friendship, and that just before she popped the question, Sophie's happiness had been tinged with anxiety. With all this in mind, she set out to begin another draft. *[Fig. XII-4]*

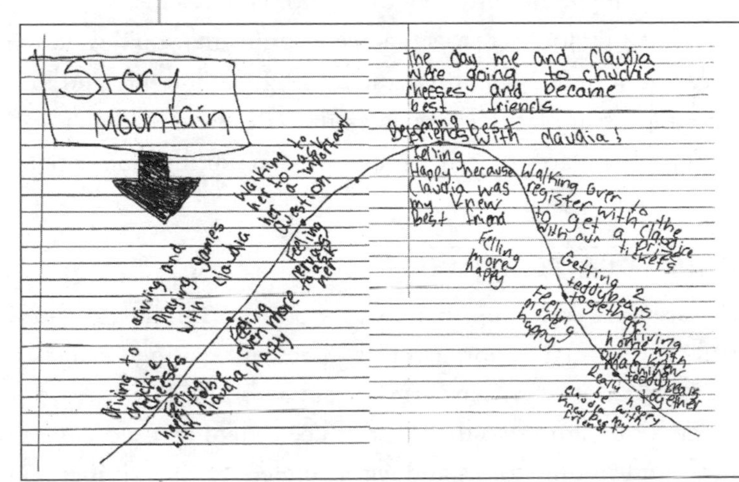

Fig XII-4 Sophie's story mountain

Share

Partners as Editors

Ask children to share drafts with their partners, who will function as editors.

"Writers, tomorrow we'll work on editing your drafts, and in the blink of an eye, your parents will be here and we'll read these stories out into the world. So during today's share, it's really important that you swap papers with each other, and spend some time functioning as editors."

"Exchange your writing with your partner. Readers, please read the draft as if you are a stranger to it. You won't be double checking for perfect spelling because this is still a rough draft. But double-check for sense, for clarity. If there are places where you are confused, leave a sticky note, explain the confusion, and perhaps suggest a way to clarify the draft. If you see small sections that could easily be spruced up, tell that to the writer too. Now is not the time to suggest a whole new draft . . . but it is the time to lend a hand."

HOMEWORK ***Reading Aloud for Clarity*** Writers, tomorrow we'll begin editing your pieces and recopying them into final drafts. Tonight, read what you've written for clarity, for sense. If your partner found places that were confusing, you'll want to clarify them.

Then read your draft again, this time reading it aloud. Pretend that you have a circle of people listening. Hear places where you stumble, where you can't read the draft really well. Those are probably places that merit revision and editing. So revise tonight to make sure the draft sings.

TAILORING YOUR TEACHING

If your children are revisiting this unit for a second time and you want to vary the minilesson . . . you might approach this work with endings as a lesson on focus. You could say, for example, "Writers, we've spent a good bit of time thinking about how and where to begin our stories so that we can keep them focused. We've thought a lot about what's important in our stories and we've angled our beginnings so that they are focused towards this point."

Then you could elaborate, "The way we choose to end our stories is equally important. We need to end on a point that will keep stories in focus. The end is the last point that our readers will remember. We want them to remember what's most important to us!" Shifting, you could say, "Today I'm going to teach you that writers decide where to end their stories by asking themselves: 'How does this ending connect back to what's most important in my story?' We think about the final action that will happen in our stories as well as the final thoughts that our characters have and we look to see if these fit with the most important point of our story. This helps to keep our stories focused!"

In the teaching component, you'd want to use your own story as an exemplar. Mary Chiarella said to her class, "I'm going to show you what I mean by using my story. You remember, it's the one that I'm not at all proud of. The one about 'the time I told Maria Guadagno that she couldn't hang out with my group of friends anymore.'" Then Mary reviewed the main points of her story:

- I'm sitting with my new friends happy to be part of a crowd
- Ann Margaret tells me that I need to go and tell Maria that she can't be part of our crowd anymore and I'm feeling bad about it, but relieved that I'm not the one being kicked out
- Then, I walk across the field with my new friends feeling fierce and powerful to be part of the group
- I tell Maria that she can't be part of our group anymore and I'm feeling powerful because I have all my friends around me—this is the most important scene, because it shows how I would have done anything, even something completely dreadful, to be popular!
- Then we walk away and I turn back and see Maria crying. For a moment, I'm feeling sad for her.
- But then my friends call me over to play dodge ball and I run away feeling happy that they want me to be part of their game.

Mary said, "The last action in my story is when I go off to play with my new friends. But, I need to make that fit with the most important part of my story—the part where I treat Maria horribly." Thinking aloud, she said, "So, let's see. I need to end with actions that somehow connect back to the most important part. I also need to ask myself: What's the last thought that my character, that's me, will have? It needs to have something to do with Maria. I'm going to hold the most important part in my mind while I envision this last point in my story. Maybe it can go something like . . . " and she tried one ending:

> "Hey Mare, come on and play kickball with us!" I continued to follow my friends to the playground. But something didn't feel right. What had I done? How could I treat someone so badly? I should go to her, tell her how sorry I am, ask her to come play with us.
>
> "Hey Mare, we can't start without you!" my new friends called again.

Pausing, Mary said to the kids, "Now I'm also trying to show that I would do anything to be popular, even treat another person badly." Looking back at the chart paper, she said, "I think I'll end with—'I'd been waiting to hear that for so long. When will I get this chance again? I wondered. I turned on my heels and ran to the playground.'"

Debriefing, Mary said, "Writers, did you see how I decided where to end by thinking about the most important point in my story and how the last actions and thoughts fit with what's most important? If I had ended by just running off and playing with my new friends thinking about how much I love dodge ball, it would feel like the ending belonged to another story! It would bring my writing out of focus!" You could, in a similar way, use your story to teach children that when we work on endings, we bring out our focus.

Assessment

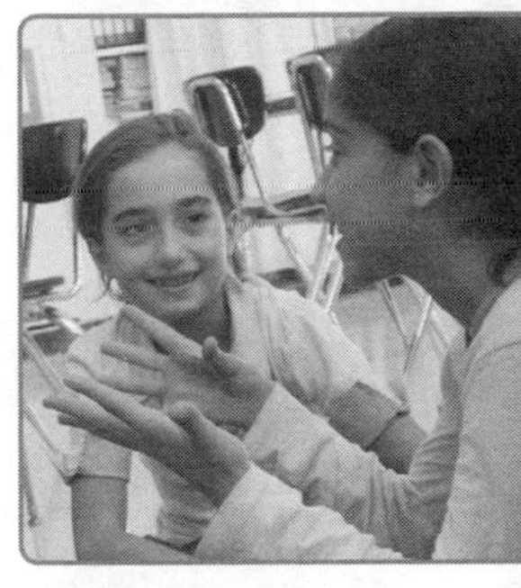

You and your students are approaching the end of the second unit of study and your students' work with personal narrative writing. In this unit of study, your students learned more about working through the stages of the writing process, about crafting writing that engages and affects readers, and about using the conventions of written language with higher levels of accuracy and fluency than ever before. Although you and your students will soon move on to another genre, essay writing, the lessons learned in the personal narrative unit are foundational to all the writing work that follows—across the year and throughout your students' lives.

Because this second unit of study provides opportunities for students to deepen their understanding of personal narrative writing, one way you might assess your students' writing is by comparing the drafts of students' published personal narratives from the first unit of study with their drafts from this unit of study. As you compare the two pieces of writing, you'll be able to note changes in their understandings of the genre and of the writing process.

In this unit, your students have also learned two extremely important skills that will serve them well in writing workshop and beyond. First, you taught your students how to be resourceful learners who bring all they've learned before and apply it to new and more challenging situations. They know how to use class charts, and they understand that the strategy they learned during last Tuesday's minilesson might be applicable in their work tomorrow. Another important thing your students know is that they can use their favorite authors as mentors to guide them as writers. They've learned how to read like writers, noticing the things authors do that make a piece of writing compelling. These two grand ideas, bringing everything you know to the table and mentoring yourself to an expert in order to become stronger at something, are life skills that your students will be able to apply to their writing, their art, their relationships, their athletics . . . and so on.

Another kind of assessment you might consider takes these two grand ideas into consideration. You could give your students copies of their published pieces from the launching unit and ask them to revise these pieces. You might think about setting up their work by saying something like, "Writers, you've had another few weeks to learn more and more about writing strong personal narratives, so I'm going to give you a chance to show what you know. I'm going to give each of you a copy of the personal narrative you published in the first unit of study. I want you to reread it with this question in mind, "Knowing what I know now about writing, how would I change this piece to make it stronger?" The students would write their revisions right on the copy of the piece of writing. This will give you invaluable insight into what your students have brought away after two units of study on personal narrative. If you have a student who only edits for punctuation, you may consider spending more time working on revision strategies with that child down the road. If you have a student who revises to elaborate more on the heart of the story, you know he's grown an understanding about the structure of personal narratives.

SESSION XIII

EDITING:

THE POWER OF COMMAS

IN THIS SESSION, YOU WILL SET STUDENTS UP TO LEARN ABOUT PUNCTUATION, COMMAS IN PARTICULAR, FROM WRITING THEY ADMIRE. THEN YOU WILL ASK STUDENTS TO TRY USING COMMAS IN THE WAY THEY'VE SEEN THEM USED, IN ORDER TO MAKE THEIR WRITING MORE EXACT.

GETTING READY

- Copies of three familiar texts containing commas (one set per partnership)
- A chart on the blackboard or chart paper with three columns, labeled "Examples of Commas in Mentor Text, What Does the Comma Do?, and Using the Comma in My Own Writing"
- Prepare for Share by reading celebration in the next session
- See CD-ROM for resources

We all resist doing what we're told. *Even if the truth is sound advice, good counsel, and the right thing to do, it's still irksome. Following rules too often and too carefully chafes.*

It's simply not enough, then, for our students to see editing as simply a matter of following the rules of English grammar at every turn. In this session, we aim to present editing as an adventure, potentially full of exploration, discovery, and invention.

As I discussed in A Guide to the Writing Workshop, *the book that opens this series of units, there are four methods for conveying a teaching point that we use over and over again in our minilessons: demonstration, telling and offering an example, guided practice, and inquiry. Of course, we also use combinations of these methods. The majority of minilessons we've laid out in this series so far have used the first three methods. In this session, we use the inquiry method of exploring a teaching point.*

To use the inquiry method, we set up a situation in which children can explore a problem. In this case, we'll set the stage for kids to ask and try to answer the question, "How can commas help us in our writing?" Of course, this same basic minilesson can be used to help children start exploring any punctuation mark or any grammatical structure or any aspect of language. Just as children studied powerful published texts to think about techniques for writing leads, so too can they study mentor texts to think about techniques for using commas—or any other meaning-making mark. Then, once they've determined some uses and effects of the comma, they can try doing the same thing in their own writing.

Two wonderful books that you can turn to for more about teaching conventional English grammar, including punctuation, are A Fresh Approach to Teaching Punctuation, *by Janet Angelillo, and* The Power of Grammar, *by Mary Ehrenworth and Vicki Vinton.*

MINILESSON

Editing: The Power of Commas

CONNECTION

Remind children they will be cycling through the writing process again and again, each time learning new strategies for creating better writing.

"So writers, many of you are now satisfied with the big shape of your stories. You've made sure the important parts are developed, you've crafted your stories so that they contain a story arc—a story mountain—and now you are ready to turn your attention to the detailed changes you could make, the final editing you could do to polish your story. Every time you go through the writing process, every time you make a piece of writing, you'll go through these steps, and you'll have an opportunity to learn new ways to make your writing stronger."

Name the teaching point. In this case, tell children that one way to learn how to use punctuation marks is to study their use in published works.

"What writers know is that every single punctuation mark that exists in the world—now what are some punctuation marks? Right, periods, commas, quotation marks, dashes—every single punctuation mark has hidden power. As a writer, you are allowed to use any punctuation mark you want, but if you want it to bring its hidden power to your own writing, and not just sit there doing nothing on the page, then you have to know that punctuation mark's secrets. And they all have secrets!"

"Whenever you want to learn a punctuation mark's secret, when you are ready to add its power to your writing, what you have to do is study that mark. You have to scrutinize it, examine it, study it with both your eyes and your whole mind to figure out what it does. Today, what I want to teach you is this: You can figure out any punctuation mark's secrets by studying it in great writing."

TEACHING

Explain that just as children learned to write strong leads from studying mentor texts, so too can they learn to use commas powerfully.

"A little while ago, you studied leads in published writing to see what the author did and then you tried those same things in your own leads, remember? Well, I told you then and I'll tell you now that you can use that same technique for learning just about anything about writing. We can do the same with punctuation marks! First, we'll study the

COACHING

One way you can tailor the level of difficulty of this minilesson is by compiling sets of examples of comma usage of varying levels of complexity. You might, for example, select examples of commas separating items in list. On the other hand, you might select a set of unconventional comma uses, or omissions, as in the opening passages of Toni Morrison's The Bluest Eye.

punctuation mark. What would the writing be like without it? What message does the mark send to readers about the words? Does the mark change the sound or speed of the words?"

"Then, after we've figured out some of the secrets of commas, some of what their power is to change and frame words, we'll put commas into our own writing, both things we've already written and things we've yet to write, and we'll try to bring that same power to our own writing."

When you use the inquiry method to teach, you'll find that you always have the option to angle your teaching toward improving children's methods of inquiry or toward ensuring that children understand and can use the information they've derived. In this minilesson, I try to do both, but I emphasize the process of learning from mentor authors over the content of how to use commas. You may tip the balance in the other direction for your students.

ACTIVE ENGAGEMENT

Set children up to explore the punctuation mark with their partners.

"Okay, to study a punctuation mark, you'll need to read aloud parts of a text with the mark in them, and think about it and talk about it. Remember, some of the questions you and your partner can think about are: What would the writing be like without it? What message does the mark send to readers about the words? Does the mark change the sound or speed of the words? Here are three books you all know well for you to examine. Now take some time to copy this chart into your notebook and then with your partner fill in the first two columns, which are similar to the ones we used when we studied leads. Leave the last column blank for now:"

Examples of Commas	What Does the Comma Do?	Using the Comma in My Writing

As children studied the texts, I listened in and began compiling a list on chart paper of comma uses that children had discovered. After a bit, I stopped them.

"So children, let me stop you now, even though I know you haven't finished. The comma has many different powers, doesn't it? You are finding some of them; I heard you.

Now take some time to use a comma in your own writing (you can look back for a place in your notebook)." I gave them a few moments and then gathered their eyes. "This is some of what you said, and how you filled in your chart."

Examples of Commas	What Does the Comma Do?	Using the Comma in My Writing
"For one minute, three minutes,maybe even a hundred minutes, we stared at one another" (Owl Moon)	"Commas make you think about what goes in between other things happening."	(James) I saw three, seven, a million mitts piled on the shelves.
"If you go owling, you have to be quiet, that's what Pa always says." (Owl Moon)	"Commas mean 'stop' but not all the way."	(Olivia) I hated her, but she was still my sister.
"A farm dog answered the train, and then a second dog joined in." (Owl Moon)	"Commas mean that's one part of it, but there's another part coming up."	(Hanna) There was pink frosting, rainbow candles, and a plastic ballerina with a silver skirt.

"Will you turn to your partner again and talk about how these discoveries about commas are the same or different from what the two of you discovered about commas?"

LINK

Remind children of what they learned, both specifically and generally.

After a short time to talk, I signaled for children to turn back to me. "Is there anything absolutely pressing that you mentioned with your partners? No? Okay, then, today in your writing work, and from now on when you are writing, do two things: You need to try to make commas use their full power, not just sit there; you also need to keep noticing commas in the writing all around you—in your own writing, in your friend's writing, in your favorite books, on your milk carton at lunch, everywhere! Keep learning about the power of commas so that you can put it all in your own writing when the time comes for you to edit. So remember, we learned today that you can always, as a writer, study the work of an author you admire, and learn ways to make your own writing better! Go ahead and get started."

When you teach children by giving them materials to explore and learn from instead of simply waiting for them to find what you've told them to find, you won't know exactly what they are going to come up with. This means that you have to trust their intelligence and powers of observation to lead them to conclusions about what they are studying. You will have to decide for yourself how far to let children lead the study. If they come up with a hypothesis about the functions of commas that you know from experience will prove to be false or undependable, you have a choice to make. Will you ask them to test their hypothesis until they discover for themselves that it won't hold? Will you point to an example that will show them that it won't hold so that they can test it quickly? Will you take the rule and treat it as correct until the class discovers the error? Each teaching path has its purposes, and you will have to choose the one you believe will be best for your class.

In this Active Engagement, I have highlighted discoveries from three sets of partners that will serve the class well although the "rules" are not yet honed to perfection. That will come. The other discoveries by other partnerships are still in the air, but by highlighting these three and offering children a chance to talk about how their observations relate to these, I hope our class knowledge will be consolidated. If any invented rules conflict with these statements, they are likely to come to light here, and we can decide as a class which to follow.

Writing and Conferring

Studying Commas by Studying Mentor Authors

Today's session has been about commas, but in the larger sense, it has been about teaching children that they can learn from authors if they study the writing they admire with a writing question in mind. If you decide to confer to support today's minilesson, you can either support children in learning from mentor texts, or you can help them use commas with greater skill. Of course, one path does not necessarily exclude the other, but it may help you confer with greater clarity if you decide which is your primary goal in each conference. Which lesson will give the child a leg up at this moment in his writing development?

You may want to confer with several examples of comma uses from mentor texts at your fingertips. You could lay out a sentence and together puzzle over the comma use it demonstrates. Working through the process of discovery with the child and then helping him apply that discovery to his own writing is the same as giving the child another active engagement part of the minilesson.

If the child has shown you that he knows how to learn from mentor texts and is now trying to apply that learning, to be more correct and pointed in his use of commas, then you will want to research his understanding of comma use by asking him questions and studying that use in his own writing. Alongside the child, you could ask two questions of his writing. (Limiting yourself to two questions makes it more likely the child will internalize and ask himself the same questions.)

- Is there a place (or another place) in this sentence where a comma's power would help?
- How is this comma affecting this sentence?

If a child seems able to put commas into her writing after it is written, the next step can be to help her compose her drafts with commas, inserting them as she goes. If she already does that, the next step can be to help her write her notebook entries with commas. The more automatic comma use is for the writer, in other words, the earlier in the writing process she is able to use commas, and the more fully she can utilize their power. This concept of helping children use language and grammar automatically, earlier and earlier in the writing process, so that they can reap its full power, is true for all conventions of our language—grammar, punctuation, vocabulary—all of our syntactic structures. We can create only what we can imagine, and learning the relationships and possibilities offered by grammar educates our imaginations.

MID-WORKSHOP TEACHING POINT ***Discovering Uses for Commas*** "Can you all stop for a minute? I want to tell you what Raji learned just now. He was studying the commas around him and he noticed another power they have. He said, 'They go around words, to say "I'm gonna say more about it."' Do you know what he means? Here's the example he gave from his book."

> To make words seem off to the side
>
> Example: It was cherry-flavored, my favorite

"That's another power for commas that you can use if you need to in your own writing. Remember, if you want to know ways to get power out of every mark on your page, you can study great writing. I'll add this observation to our list for powers of the comma! Okay, you may get back to your writing."

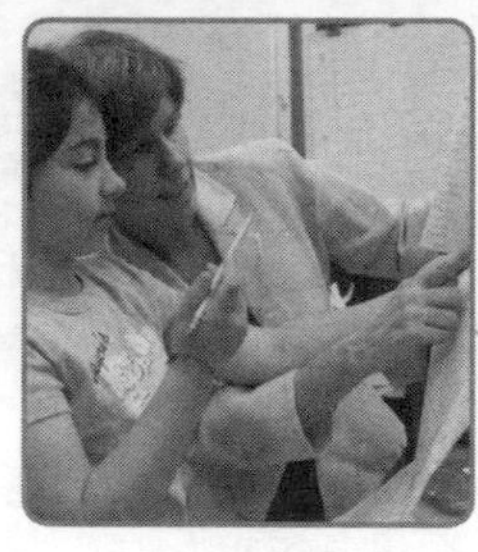

SHARE

Celebrating Comma Use

Ask children to share with their partners their most successful implementation of a comma from today's minilesson.

"Writers, please read though the writing work you did today, and show your partner the place where you think you used a comma very, very well. Talk with your partner about why you think that comma belongs there, and how it's using its full power! If you didn't use a comma today, you can talk with your partner about where you might be able to use one, or how you could rewrite so that you'd use one correctly. Partner 2s, you start, please."

This is a share that you can use after any minilesson: Simply ask those children who applied the strategy of the minilesson to their writing to share with their partner. Those who didn't have the writing context to try the strategy at this time can talk about their plans to try it.

Ask children to work with their partners to prepare for the upcoming celebration. Ask them to practice reading their writing until they are ready for the celebration. Rehearse as necessary.

"Now I know that tonight you are going to read over your pieces and make every last tiny little change you need to make them perfect. And tomorrow, we will have our celebration! Some very special people are going to be here tomorrow listening to your pieces. We need to practice a bit to make sure we read exactly the right parts aloud, and read them just the way we want to read them, with the voices and tones we want to use. So we're going to practice. Practice reading your writing aloud with your partner until you are ready. Then, we will rehearse the whole celebration, right here in our meeting area!"

Before you get to this portion of the share, you will need to read ahead to the next session's celebration. Once you can imagine your class having the celebration I describe in that next session, you'll be able to foresee exactly those moves your children need to rehearse. Of course, you might vary the celebration to suit your children's needs.

HOMEWORK ***Preparing for the Celebration*** Writers, can you believe our writing celebration is tomorrow? The first day we share our finished writing with the world is finally here! I'm so excited! I know exactly what you'll be doing tonight with your writing—you'll practice a bit more of the reading aloud that we practiced in our Share today, won't you? To make sure you can read that portion of your writing that you've chosen just how you want to read it, you'll need to read it aloud a few more times, making sure everything is perfect. You might want to call someone to read it to her, or you might want to read aloud in front of a mirror, so you can practice having an audience too. What a day tomorrow will be!

TAILORING YOUR TEACHING

If you think your students would benefit from more instruction and inquiry about using commas in their writing . . . you could try the same work that this minilesson presents using a passage from one of the mentor texts.

Consider, for example, this passage from *Fly Away Home*, by Eve Bunting.

> Once a little brown bird got into the main terminal and couldn't get out. It fluttered in the high, hollow spaces. It threw itself at the glass, fell panting on the floor, flew to a tall, metal girder, and perched there, exhausted.
>
> "Don't stop trying," I told it silently. "Don't! You can get out!"
>
> For days the bird flew around, dragging one wing. And then it found the instant when a sliding door was open and slipped through. I watched it rise. Its wings seemed OK.
>
> "Fly, bird," I whispered. "Fly away home!"
>
> Though I couldn't hear it, I knew it was singing. Nothing made me as happy as that bird.

You might first consider some of the word choices that Eve Bunting used, such as fluttered, the high, hollow spaces, glass, fell panting on the floor, tall, metal girder, perched, exhausted. Then analyze her phrasing and punctuation, even for the first paragraph. What are some ways you and your students might punctuate it to change its meaning and its sound? Which way best matches the intention of this scene?

If you notice that most of your children are writing without much variation in sentence structure . . . use your own or a mentor author's narrative to study sentence length and the use of connectives and conjunctions. For example, in *Salt Hands*, Jane Chelsea Aragon intersperses short sentences alongside longer ones, like this:

> My heart beat quickly as I sat as still as the grass, as still as the night. I didn't want him to run away.
>
> There was not a sound as he came near me. He came very close.
>
> As I looked up at him, I could see into his eyes. They were gentle, and I knew he was not afraid.

Ask your students to focus on the use of the connectives *as* and *and*, the effects these words have on the sound of the story. Then have students go back to their own writing to see if they have varied sentence lengths and to find places where they could use a connective to combine two small sentences.

MECHANICS

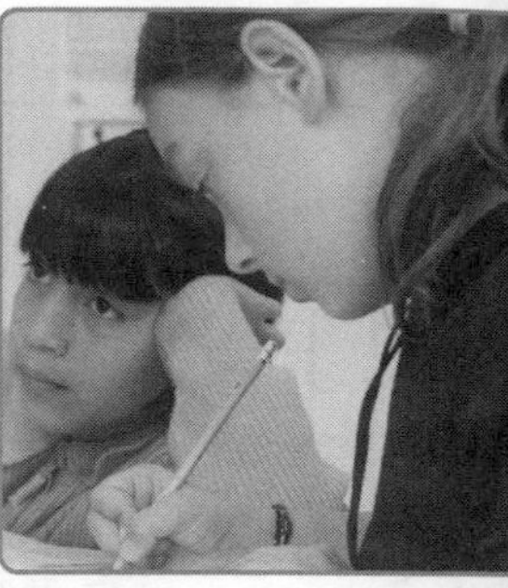

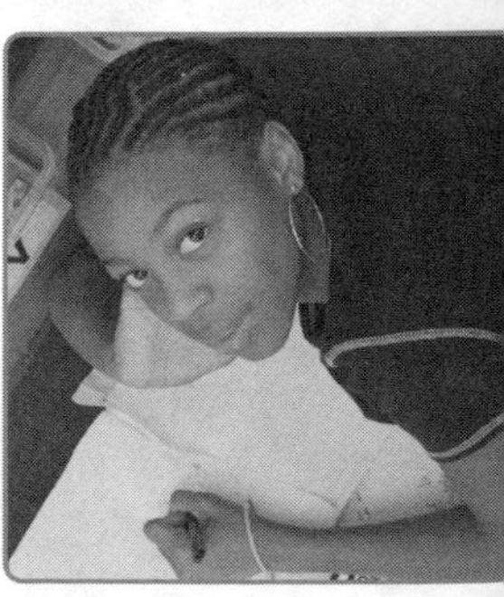

In this session, you've invited children to study mentor texts to discern the special powers that commas have to change meaning in various, subtle ways. You might take this minilesson's structure and use it to guide you in creating more minilessons about grammatical structures.

1. **Assess children's writing and goals as writers.**

To do this, you will want to first study children's writing to determine which kinds of mechanics instruction would be most likely to improve the quality of their writing. Are they writing with sentences of various lengths and structures? Are they comfortable using colons, semi-colons, parentheses and ellipses? Are they marking dialogue? As you ask yourself each of these questions, you might also ask yourself if students are using these structures and marks for a purpose that matches with their writing intentions. If you see an enthusiasm for colons for example, but you don't see students using them effectively, or if you see no colons in students' writing at all, colon use might well be a prime candidate for a minilesson's teaching point.

2. **Choose the teaching method, in this case, inquiry.**

Once you have chosen the teaching point, as always, you have several methods of teaching from which to choose: demonstration, explain and give an example, guided practice, and inquiry. (Of course, a combination of these is also possible.) You may well select the inquiry method in the manner of this session's minilesson about studying commas.

3. **Assemble the texts containing the grammatical structure or punctuation mark.**

Your next step is to assemble the material your students will study; in this case, you'd find a bunch of passages or short texts that hold colons. You could also leave the search for the materials, the search for texts that demonstrate colon use to the students. This would take a bit longer than assembling them alone, but it would help children form a wide-awakeness to the texts in their lives. For now, they'd be looking everywhere for colons, then they'd be looking everywhere for semi-colons until eventually they would acquire the habit of noting punctuation use in texts!

You'll want to make sure that the text to study are passages that contain the punctuation mark, in this case the colon, and are long enough to allow readers to feel the impact of the colon on the whole text, not just the isolated sentence. Punctuation marks' powers come not only from their specific effect on the sentences in which they are found, but also from the contrasts they present with other sentences and punctuation marks.

4. **Research examples to hypothesize about the particular effect on meaning the punctuation mark or grammatical structure has.**

Once the excerpts and short texts are assembled, whether that phase takes two minutes or two days, the next step is to study the examples of colon use and to make some generalizations about them. We generally do this in groups or partnerships and then compare notes, trying to make a coherent, comprehensive class chart of our findings. We'd then post that in a public place in the classroom as a reference.

5. **Take the newfound knowledge to writing and reading.**

Oftentimes, the charts start as long lists of very specific uses of the punctuation mark. Over time, we will edit the list down as a class, deleting incorrect assumptions, combining the observations that overlap, and making new rules that seem to apply nearly all the time. In the end, the class might hone a chart about colon use to two simple facts: colons are used to introduce and colons are found after independent clauses. At that point, the guidelines belong on an editing checklist.

To keep the study of colon use alive and well, you will want to celebrate and make public and open for discussion students' uses of colons in their writing. At first, that colon use is bound to be a bit incorrect and a bit overdone—that's to be expected! With practice and feedback, though, children's use of the newfound structure or newfound mark will settle into its proper place among the other language skills and bits of information they are learning. As that knowledge settles, you will want to hold students accountable to using colons earlier and earlier in their writing process, effecting that they've integrated knowledge of that mark's use.

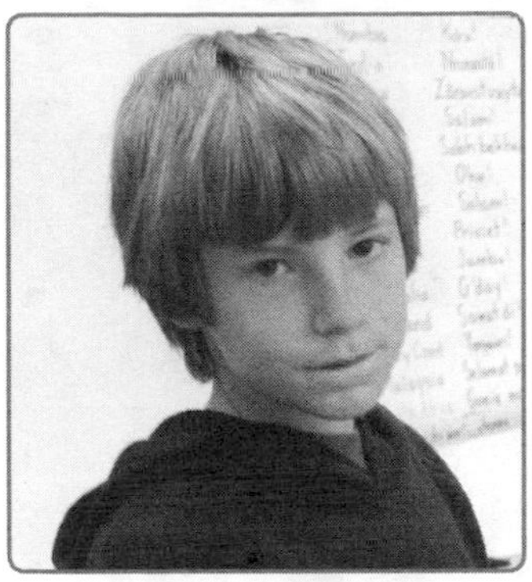

IN THIS SESSION, STUDENTS WILL HAVE AN OPPORTUNITY TO SHARE THEIR WRITING WITH AN AUDIENCE AS WRITERS STRIVE TO DO. CHILDREN WILL READ ALOUD THEIR PIECES, ADDING A CHORUS TO GIVE THE OCCASION APPROPRIATE CEREMONY.

GETTING READY

- Prepare four children to read their writing or an excerpt from their writing to the whole group
- Preassign each child to one of four groups
- Prepare rest of children to read their writing or an excerpt from their writing to their small group
- Set up room to allow for all present to hear first four children and then divide into four groups
- Children need to have memorized a few lines of a poem, one they've written or found, to chant as a chorus; write this on a chart
- Invite guests—parents, another class, teachers—as appropriate
- Prepare refreshments
- Baskets of note cards, enough for 3-4 per child, set up in prominent places around the room

See CD-ROM for resources

READING ALOUD OUR WRITING:

A CEREMONY OF CELEBRATION

***In this session, children will read their writing** to an audience of parents and each other. People will write letters in response to the writing.*

I want to encourage you to take Author Celebrations very seriously. Just as authors create alternate worlds through stories, so we, too, create alternative worlds through our teaching. When we teach, we create a counter-culture within our classrooms. If we've done our job well, just as surely as Lucy and Edmund and Peter and Susan in The Lion, the Witch and the Wardrobe *knew they were in another world, so, too, the children who enter our rooms can sense that we have created a Different Kind of Place. We teach by helping children know they are indispensable to a community of writers. We teach by helping children live in a place where words are cherished, where people lean in to listen deeply to each other's words, and read words as if they have magical powers. We teach helping our children to regard each other as authors, and by relishing the different tones and textures, passions and purposes in their stories.*

Of course, an Author Celebration is an extraordinary form of parent education too. These celebrations teach parents about what's happening at school and about qualities of good writing. Author Celebrations also give parents another chance to learn about their own sons and daughter. I will not forget last June, at the final Author Celebration of the year, when a young boy who'd come into the year writing only the shallowest of sports stories read a piece aloud in which he'd written with a wide-open heart and with exquisite sensitivity and talent. His father came up to me and to his teacher afterwards, with eyes brimming, and said quietly, "I never thought he had it in him."

It is incredibly important to create a sense of occasion around these celebrations, and to give children the extraordinary gift of knowing that their stories are reaching readers.

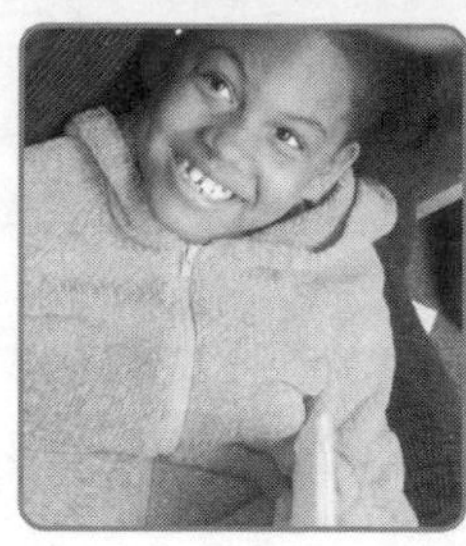

Celebration

Welcome children and their family members. Explain that when we read stories, authors bring us into other worlds. And today, the writers in the class will read aloud, bringing all of us into other worlds.

"Writers, many of us have read or watched C.S.Lewis' *The Lion, the Witch and the Wardrobe*. We've seen Lucy enter that wardrobe, pushing past the coats, and then suddenly something cold brushes against her arm. It is a tree branch, covered with snow. She looks down and sees she is standing in snow, and looks up and sees a lamppost, burning bright among the trees. From far away, she hears the distant jingle of sleigh bells, and soon the evil Snow Queen has approached.....and hold your hat! The plot thickens!"

You will notice that this celebration is a bit grander than the previous one; as you continue through the units, this trend continues. But your October celebration will only be a step or two fancier than the preceding one—if an Author Celebration is too splashy too soon, you'll find you are soon in over your head!

"In that story, as in every story that has ever been told, listeners are invited into a world. It is not just Lucy, but all of us who push past the furry coats into the back of the wardrobe, and all of us feel something cold, and find we are standing in snow. That is the magic of story. C. S. Lewis' story takes us into a land of Narnia, where four children are called upon to save the world."

"In this classroom, stories can also take us to other worlds: to the terrifying world in Terrance's apartment that day when someone smelled smoke, to the day in this class, when Sofiya conquered her fears and actually touched the skin of a snake. Stories can take us to stand with Joey, on the edge of the dock, looking into the murky water of the pond."

If we say to a child, "Your writing reminds me so much of Naomi Nye's writing," a decade later, that child will still remember those words, and for all these years, those words will have sustained her.

Explain the plan for today's Author Celebration. In this case, explain that after a few children read to the group, everyone will disperse to a corner to share writing in small groups.

"Today, we'll hear a few stories together as a community. And then we'll disperse to our story corners (the young writers know their corners and grown-ups, you can tag along). It is here where we can have a more intimate audience."

Tell writers that after each reading, listeners will respond not by clapping but by reading a poem chorally.

"All weekend, I thought and thought, trying to decide how we could best respond to each other's writing. And I came to the decision that this Author's Celebration needs to be treated like the big occasions in our lives: like a graduation, a wedding, an anniversary. When we people gather for those big celebrations, we often share poetry. The poet, Erica Jong, once said, 'People think they can do without poetry. And they can. At least until they fall in love, lose a child or a parent or lose their way in the dark woods of life.'" (*In Their Own Voices: A Century of Recorded Poetry*)

"So, after a writer reads, let's join in a choral reading of a poem. We've chosen a favorite that we can all read together.

"To start us off, will our four readers come and sit in the chairs here at the front of the room. I will read the poem, and then one reader will read. The room will be absolutely silent after Claudia reads (no clapping please), and then Claudia's mother, would you start us in the poem and we'll all join in. Then Zora? And Zora's mom or dad . . . ? Let's get started."

"Let's disperse into our corners. Writers you lead the way, parents follow. Begin right away with one child reading and remember to honor that reading with the choral reading."

If you are looking for a poem to use, I especially recommend "Things," by Eloise Greenfield, which is cited in a minilesson in Literary Essays. "Things" ends with a child who "went to the kitchen/made me a poem." When using this as the refrain in a celebration of stories, we alter the word accordingly.

This ritual may seem unnecessary, but on the last day of Teachers College's summer institute, people read their writing aloud to each other and oftentimes, listeners write notes in response. For decades now, I have seen teachers gather up those notes as if they were the love letters we'd desperately wanted. People have told me that, years later, they still keep those notes. I know what they mean because sometimes I, too, receive a note from a reader. After putting oneself on the line, as writers always do, it is a rather extraordinary thing for someone to write back and say, 'Your words mattered.'

Disperse the readers, providing everyone with snacks. Ask parents and children to circulate, writing notes to the readers. They can respond to writing they already heard and also read more children's writing during this interlude.

When everyone had read, I brought out the snacks and said, "For the next little while, every child will keep his or her narrative on hand. Could you get some food, and then would all of you—parents and children— circulate among each other, reading each other's stories. You'll see that I've left little note-cards in baskets around the room. Please take the time to write responses to the writing you heard earlier today, or to what you read now. Write responses that let writers know the parts that resonated for you, the way the writing made you feel. I've got a mail box up here, and as you write a response, could you bring it up here and I'll distribute them later."

As parents circulated among the kids, I kept an eye on the responses, and from time to time made a point of steering a particular parent towards a child whose work wasn't being read. In this fashion (and by adding my own notes), I checked that every child was receiving several writing 'valentines.'

Compliment the class as a whole, but also use this as an occasion to seek individual children out, to look the child in the eyes, and to tell the child what you have noticed that he or she can do uniquely well. Does one child have the knack for writing with rhythm, for prose that makes the reader read aloud so, so well? Tell the child that you see this. Does one child know how to speak the truth in words that are straight and true, words that go directly from the child's heart to the reader's heart? Tell the child this. I will never forget the Author Celebration when my son's teacher introduced Miles by saying, "Our next writer, Miles Skorpen, has a gift for seeing the world. He lives and writes with his eyes wide, taking in the details that others might never see. He loves telescopes, microscopes, magnifying lenses...and he uses language as all these." Now, fifteen years later, Miles' hobby is photography—and writing. And I wonder whether that teacher, long, long ago, created a pathway for him by seeing more in my son than he saw in himself.

Here is Takeshi's final personal narrative: *[Figs. XIV-1 and XIV-2]*

Alert Alert Typhoon Alert!
By Takeshi

I sat down on the seat. I was shivering, and getting sick from all the shaking because of the typhoon. I tried to sit down and relax. I took the remote and started to watch TV, but it felt more and more worse every second.

The airplane was still shaking. Would the plane crash right before I ever even get to be at Japan? It felt that we were inside the typhoon, twirling over and over again. Would we make it through? I wondered over and over again. I checked how close we were to reach Japan. It was just about 300 meters to reach Japan, but my mom couldn't hold it anymore. She asked to person who helps the pilot "Could I lay on the floor?" They said "Yes." I noticed that me and my brother were alone. "What should we do?" I asked my brother. My brother said, "Sleep and forget that this ever happened." I tried to sleep, but it felt like every time I was about to sleep the airplane started to shake. Did someone put a curse on me, I wondered as I looked around to see if anybody was there. 300 meters passed. I was relieved.

I was waiting for them to land, but it didn't land. After a while I heard the pilot say "Sorry, we are going to land to a different airport." My brother and I both said at the same time, "WHAT!" What did I do to deserve this, I thought.

Landing to the other airport took about an extra three hours. When we landed we waited an extra two more hours for our mom to come. I told my brother, "That took at least eighteen hours." He said, "You're right." When our mom finally came we got on a bus to go to our grandma and grandpa's house. After we got off the bus I told my mom "We finally made it." My mom said, "Yeah, you're right." We finally made it I thought again as I started to walk down the street to our grandma and grandpa's house.

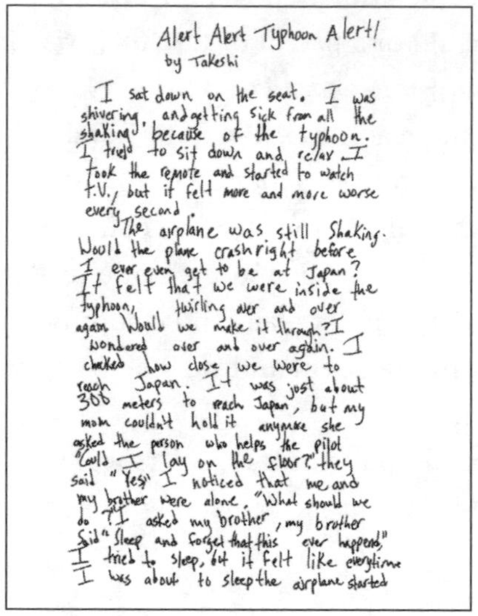
Alert Alert Typhoon Alert!
by Takeshi
I sat down on the seat. I was shivering, and getting sick from all the shaking because of the typhoon. I tried to sit down and relax. I took the remote and started to watch T.V., but it felt more and more worse every second.
The airplane was still shaking. Would the plane crash right before I ever even get to be at Japan? It felt that we were inside the typhoon, twirling over and over again. Would we make it through? I wondered over and over again. I checked how close we were to reach Japan. It was just about 300 meters to reach Japan, but my mom couldn't hold it anymore she asked the person who helps the pilot "Could I lay on the floor?" they said "Yes" I noticed that me and my brother were alone. "What should we do?" I asked my brother, my brother said "Sleep and forget that this ever happend." I tried to sleep, but it felt like everytime I was about to sleep the airplane started

Fig. XIV-1 Takeshi's final draft

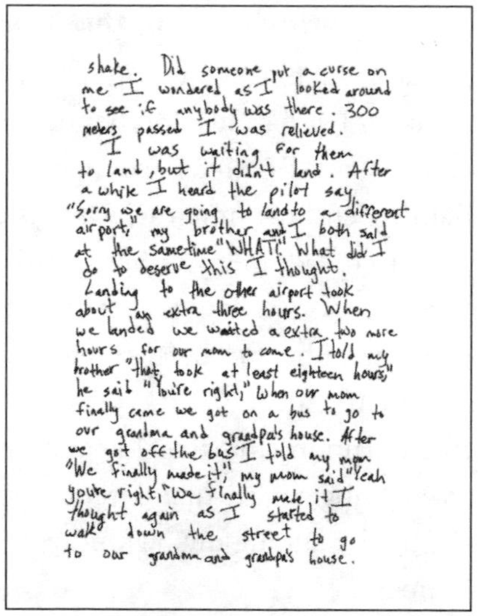
shake. Did someone put a curse on me I wondered as I looked around to see if anybody was there. 300 meters passed I was relieved.
I was waiting for them to land, but it didn't land. After a while I heard the pilot say "Sorry we are going to land to a different airport" my brother and I both said at the same time "WHAT!" What did I do to deserve this I thought.
Landing to the other airport took about an extra three hours. When we landed we waited a extra two more hours for our mom to come. I told my brother "that took at least eighteen hours" he said "You're right," When our mom finally came we got on a bus to go to our grandma and grandpa's house. After we got off the bus I told my mom "We finally made it," my mom said "Yeah you're right," We finally made it I thought again as I started to walk down the street to go to our grandma and grandpa's house.

Fig. XIV-2 Takeshi's draft page 2

This is Sophie's final draft: *[Fig. XIV-3]*

Excitement in My Heart
By Sophie

We walked in the Chuck E. Cheese. I held Claudia's hand tight. My palm was sweating. I was feeling really happy to be with Claudia.

"Hey, Claudia! What game do you want to play"?

"The bumble bee catching game."

That's my favorite. How did she know? I thought to myself. We were made to be friends!

"Okay." We both ran to the game. While we were playing, we were laughing and having a great time together. I don't want anything at all to ruin this day for me, I thought to myself.

"Claudia, I am having such a great time with you today!"

"Me too, Sophie!"

When we were done playing, I walked close to Claudia, waiting for the right moment to ask her. I was so nervous! I didn't know what she was going to say!

Okay. Sophie. Time to ask, I said to myself. I took a deep breath and said it!

"Claudia, I have something to ask you,"

"Yah, Sophie?"

"Well I wanted to know if you wanted to be my best friend and I'll be yours."

"Um, well..." Oh, no, is this a no? I thought to myself.

"Of course, Sophie!" I was so relieved I hugged her. She hugged me back. I still felt like I had butterflies in my stomach. I didn't understand why she stumbled on her answer but I was still happy.

"Claudia."

"Yes, Sophie?"

"You're the best!"

"Thanks, Sophie."

"Are you ready to go get our prize yet?"

"Ya, I'm ready. Let's go, Sophie!" We walked over to the register. When we got there, the wall was full of prizes.

"Hey, Sophie. What prize do you want?"

"I don't know yet. What do you want?"

"Well... the teddy bear," we said at the same time.

"Excuse me. Can we please have two teddy bears?" I asked.

'Coming right up," the lady behind the counter said. She handed us the two teddy bears.

"They're so cute," I said. We hugged our two matching teddy bears.

"Hey, Claudia."

"Ya, Sophie?"

"Now the teddy bears can mark our friendship forever."

"Forever," Claudia said.

When we went home we had our two new matching teddy bears marking our friendship on our laps.

"Claudia, you are the best friend anybody could have in the whole world."

Right then and there I knew we were going to be best friends forever.

Fig. XIV-3 Sophie's final draft

Here is Miles's final draft: *[Fig. XIV-4]*

Gifts That Count
By Miles

On Father's Day morning, I woke up in an Adirondacks campsite. I watched the beautiful red morning sun and thought about what I had planned for my Father's Day present: a piece of land that had been snatched from my heart.

I tip-toed over to my dad's tent and unzipped it, waking Dad. I said, "Dad, let me show you your Father's Day present."

"OK," he answered.

I shepherded hi between the two rows of trees, out into the sunlight, onto my point. The point was covered with soft meadow grass, sprinkled with tiny wild flowers. I watched Dad take in this precious bit of the world and knew I had given him the right gift. Then from its hiding place I drew forth a fishing rod and laid it triumphantly in Dad's hands. His eyes sparkled and I said, "You deserve the honor of being first."

Dad nodded and cast. The line sailed through the air.

We watched in silence. We all waited: Dad, Evan, and I. Dad held his breath, his fingers tense.

Suddenly the line jerked. A huge dark shape struggled under the water. Dad slowly brought it to the surface. We gasped. A huge bass . . . Suddenly, Snap! The string broke under tension and the monster fled to the bottom of the lake. So we christened the point, "Bass Point". On that day, Evan and I gave the love of fishing to Dad.

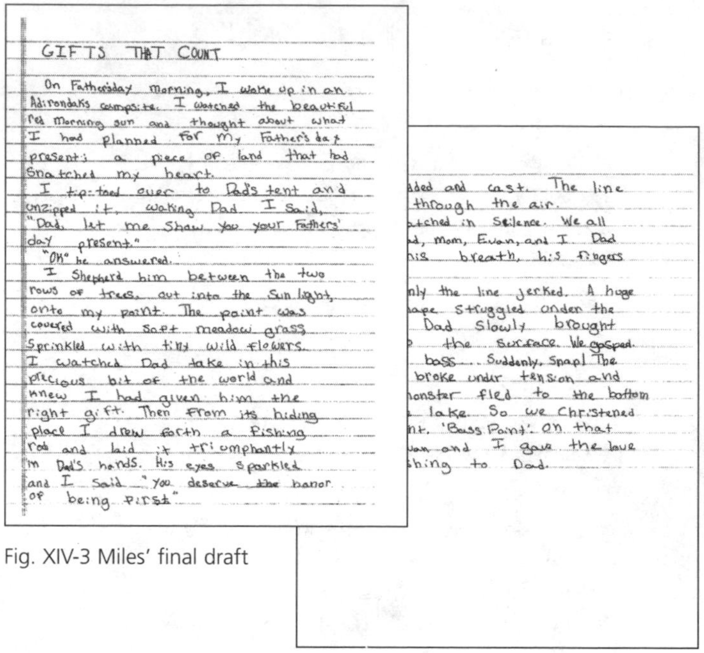

Fig. XIV-3 Miles' final draft

Here is Jasmine's final draft: *[Fig. XIV-5]*

Practicing for My First Communion
By Jasmine

I sat in a church pew, with all of the kids who will make their communion with me. Talbia my teacher walked down to us and pointed to me and five other kids. Talbia said, "You six kids are going to be reading from the gospel."

Right then I thought I was going to make a mistake when I was going to read. Me and the five other readers went up to the altar in a line and started to read.

After we finished we went home. When I got upstairs my mom was mopping the floor. I said, "Mom guess what?" "What?" my mom said. "I'm going to read something in the gospel."

My mom was so happy she had a smile on her face. She went to the phone and she called the whole family. My aunt drove to our house. My grandma took the bus, My uncle walked there. My cousin took the train.

Soon the whole family was in the kitchen working together making me a cake. I felt like it was my birthday.

For two months we rehearsed. I had a hard time reading two paragraphs from the gospel. There were words I didn't even know. My mom said, "every day we will practice at home." We pretended the table in the living room was the altar and the living room was the church. My mom said to me, "Practice makes perfect."

On the day of my communion I was so nervous. The whole family came to watch me. When I went up to read I thought I was going to make a mistake. But I looked at the paper and read the words one by one. When I was finished reading I was proud of myself.

Me and my mom were so tired that night we fell asleep on the couch together hugging each other.

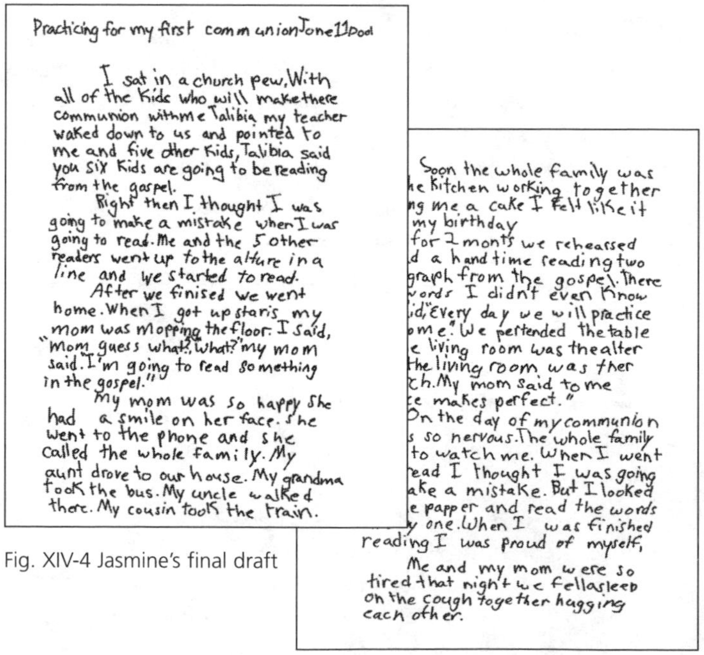

Fig. XIV-4 Jasmine's final draft